From the Inside Looking Out

Competing Ideas About Growing Old

Jeanette A. Auger and Diane Tedford-Litle

Fernwood Publishing • Halifax

Editing: Joanne Richardson
Cover photos: Health and Welfare Canada
Cover Design: Larissa Holman and Beverley Rach
Production: Beverley Rach
Printed and bound in Canada by: Hignell Printing Limited

A publication of: Fernwood Publishing
Box 9409, Station A
Halifax, Nova Scotia, B3K 5S3

Fernwood Publishing Company Limited gratefully acknowledges the financial support of the Department of Canadian Heritage, the Nova Scotia Department of Tourism and Culture and the Canada Council for the Arts for our publishing program.

Le Conseil des Arts | The Canada Council
du Canada | for the Arts

NOVA SCOTIA
Tourism and Culture

National Library of Canada Cataloguing in Publication Data

Auger, Jeanette A., 1945–
    From the inside looking out: competing ideas about growing old

Includes bibliographical references.
ISBN 1-55266-070-2

1. Aging—Canada. 2. Gerontology—Canada. I. Tedford-Litle, Diane II. Title.

HQ1064.C2A94 2002   305.26'0971   C2001-904140-3

Contents

Preface

When we decided to write this book we were very clear that we wanted to produce a different kind of gerontology text, one that would recognize that, when documenting the aging experience in Canadian society, the voices of older persons are as important and necessary as are those of gerontologists. Our collective experiences have shown us that gerontologists are seen as "experts" on aging in ways that older persons are not. When governments, policy makers, planners, educators, and the media seek information about older persons in Canada they do not contact older individuals but, rather, gerontologists—especially gerontologists who work in the academic and research sectors.

Our reason for writing this book is twofold: (1) we wanted to document, examine, and analyze the contradictions between the realities of aging as produced by gerontologists—whether they work within academia, research centres, the private sector, or governments—with the subjective experiences of older persons as they move through their everyday lives; and (2) we wanted to enable older persons to share their reactions to and awareness of the gerontological enterprise.

It is our contention that the gerontological literature creates an "us" and "them" dichotomy within which older persons are seen as research subjects and/or consumers of various social programs and services rather than as fully contributing members of a constantly changing society.

Much of the academic gerontological enterprise gazes from the outside, from a place of so-called objective, scientific inquiry, into the inner, subjective worlds of older persons. We wanted to shift this focus and gaze from the inner, subjective reality of older persons to the outside worlds within which they conduct their everyday life activities. In doing this, we hoped to open up visions, experiences, and behaviours for both groups.

We believe that gerontological theory, research, and practice can greatly assist governments, planners, and social policy analysts; the general public; and older persons and those important to them in understanding and improving upon the aging process. However, we also believe that gerontology needs to be more attentive to how older persons perceive their actual life experiences.

Old age is frequently constructed not only by gerontologists, but also by governments and social planners as a social "problem." It is primarily viewed in this way as a result of changing demographics that, in most countries of the world, show an enormous increase of individuals aged sixty-five and over as well as the high use of health and social services by the so-called "old-old"—those aged eighty-five and over. This "problem" is said to require scientific and policy solutions that do not necessarily involve either the contributions of older persons themselves or an awareness of how they define and conceptualize certain aspects of their lives as "problematic."

As the population of older persons aged sixty-five and over continues to expand in ways unheard of in earlier times and as life expectancy increases, so too does the notion of old age as some kind of social and scientific challenge to be overcome by the right kinds of research, genetic engineering, pharmaceutical miracles, and so on. We wanted to know how older persons themselves envision their increasing years and numbers. How do they make sense of the reality of aging and how do their perceptions differ from those found in scientific explanations?

Aging is a necessary part of life. Some people in the autumn of their lives face daily challenges as a result of declining health, income, and mobility; loneliness; and lack of access to goods and services that enhance daily living. The elders with whom we spoke address some of these issues and more.

We do not subscribe to the prevalent ideology, common within popular culture and also held by some gerontologists, that growing older represents a negative time of life—a time during which one becomes increasingly infirm, non-productive, dependent upon others, and age deficient.[1]

Rather, we celebrate aging as a necessary and challenging life transition throughout which everything and anything is possible, despite health or income limitations. We question limiting the notion of productivity to the ability to work for pay; instead, we regard it as a means through which older persons can provide non-monetary contributions to their families, friends, and the communities in which they live. We regard the concept of productivity as integral to the reciprocity between people of all ages, where relationships, goods, and actions that are provided to others—especially between parents and children, neighbours and friends, or grandparents and grandchildren—are repaid with something of roughly equivalent value.

NOTE

1. In youth we are said to be in our "prime," as we grow older we are seen to experience a variety of deficiencies in terms of physiological loss (e.g., hearing, vision, taste, smell, etc.) as well as personal loss (e.g., the death of partners, friends, associates, and the loss of paid work, status, and roles). In other words, we become what is termed age deficient.

Acknowledgments

Jeanette would like to thank all of the older persons who participated in the focus groups, those who responded on-line via various Web sites, and those who mailed in questionnaire responses. She especially thanks Sister Dorothy Moore, Director of Mi'kmaq Services, Nova Scotia Department of Education, for her introductions to the Mi'kmaw communities and for her support and boundless energy both in educating students about Aboriginal education and in showing us what it means to grow older with enthusiasm.

She also thanks her students in the sociology of aging courses as well as those enrolled in the other gerontology courses that she has taught over the years. Their enthusiasm and interest has been a great source of joy both to her and to the seniors with whom they have worked. Jeanette also thanks her children, Ceilidh Auger Day and Tove Morigan, for their unconditional love, support, and understanding.

Jeanette would like to especially thank Susan J. Riordan for bringing to her life a renewed sense of love, passion, and joy.

Diane would like to thank all the persons who so readily shared their stories with her during the many focus groups held in the Province of Nova Scotia. Geraldine Browning was especially helpful in introducing Diane to the Black communities in Bridgetown and East Preston. Diane would like to dedicate this book to the memory of her father, Clayton Tedford—who, with a mind that was sharp and witty to the end, so inspired her as he struggled for over twenty years with a body that didn't work—and to her mother, Ruby Tedford, who was his caregiver during that time. Not only was their example of courage, love, and humour inspiring to those who knew them, but it was also inspiring to Diane and her three sons (Sean, Steve, and Geoff), who learned so much from their grandparents about living one day at a time.

We are indebted to our editor, Joanne Richardson, for her thoughtful and helpful suggestions in making this book better than it was before her input. At Fernwood Publishing, we thank Beverley Rach and Brenda Conroy for their contributions to this book. And we thank our publisher, Errol Sharpe, for his continuing support and encouragement.

About the Authors

Jeanette A. Auger is an associate professor of sociology at Acadia University in Wolfville, Nova Scotia. She teaches courses in gerontology, and death and dying, as well as other introductory-level courses. She has been teaching for the past twenty-six years in both British Columbia and Nova Scotia. Jeanette has worked with and for older persons for the past thirty years as a researcher, community organizer and developer, social planner, and advocate. She chaired the Committee on Aging for the Social Planning and Research Council of British Columbia; she was a consultant/researcher for the CBC television show *The Best Years*; and, from 1999 to 2000, she was the president of the Gerontology Association of Nova Scotia.

In 1983 Jeanette conducted doctoral research comparing the role of gerontological knowledge and older persons' experiences of aging in the social construction of agedness. She is disappointed to note that, with regard to the involvement of older persons in the gerontological discourse, not much has changed over the past nineteen years.

Jeanette has been an active member on many committees and planning groups dealing with issues faced by older people. Currently, she is a researcher/consultant with the Annapolis Valley Branch of the Victorian Order of Nurses, who are attempting to build Nova Scotia's first freestanding hospice.

Jeanette's interest in, and commitment to, aging began when she was a child and was greatly influenced by her grandfather, a Lithuanian immigrant to England. His perseverance and strength in the face of adversity was an inspiration as well as a testament to the ability of the aged to make changes and to set examples for younger people. Throughout her life many older persons have inspired Jeanette with their tenacity and enthusiasm for living a life well chosen. She dedicates this book to them all.

Diane Tedford–Litle is a women's activist and palliative care volunteer with the Victorian Order of Nurses, Kings County, Nova Scotia. Diane has an undergraduate degree (major in religious studies, minor in psychology) from Mount St. Vincent University, Halifax. She has taken various women's studies and death and dying courses. She was active on advisory boards looking at elder abuse and has given several workshops on spirituality in conjunction with training volunteers both for the seniors network in Kings County and for the Victorian Order of Nurses.

4

Diane is also an active member of the Hospice Consultation Committee, which is attempting to open Nova Scotia's first freestanding hospice. She is currently (spring 2001) a member of the Minister's Task Force on Hospice Care in King's County, Nova Scotia.

Diane has facilitated workshops for the Gerontology Association of Nova Scotia, of which she was a board member. Diane was born and educated in Ottawa and moved with her family to Nova Scotia in 1975. She now lives on the beautiful shores of the Bay of Fundy in the fishing village of Halls Harbour.

Introduction

METHODOLOGY

In order to document the opinions of gerontologists and older persons regarding the aging experience, we utilized several methods of data collection. These are listed below.

Secondary Analysis of Existing Literature

We began our research with an extensive literature review, which covered both academic and popular books; articles in scholarly journals (especially those concerned with gerontology, sociology, psychology, health, social work, and anthropology); and government reports and periodicals aimed at an older audience (e.g., *Fifty Plus* [the monthly magazine of the Canadian Association of Retired Persons] and *Modern Maturity* [the publication of the American Association For Retired Persons]). We also read the newsletters of various seniors organizations, newspapers devoted to older readers, and the publications of various gerontology associations and centres of aging.

We consulted research literature databases such as *Sociological Abstracts*, *Psychological Abstracts*, and the *Social Services Index*, and we conducted on-line searches of the World Wide Web, where numerous sites dealing with gerontology and aging are available.

Focus Groups

Throughout Nova Scotia during the fall of 2000 and the spring of 2001, we held a series of focus groups with seniors, including those from the Black and Mi'kmaw communities.

We posted our questionnaire (see Appendix 1) on such Web sites as the Canadian Association of Retired Persons (via the *Fifty Plus* chat room) and One Voice (a national Canadian seniors network that is independent of government and works to ensure that older Canadians are full and active participants in society). One Voice also produces a regular newsletter and holds conferences and workshops across the country on issues relevant to older Canadians. The questionnaire was also sent to groups of seniors in British Columbia and was published in a variety of local (Nova Scotia) newsletters with a large audience of elders. An example of this type of publication is the *Nova Scotia Senior Citizens' Secretariat Newsletter*, which is published four times a year and distributed free of charge to seniors groups across the province. Other publications in which we sought people willing to complete questionnaires were *Aged to Perfection, Seniors Advocate,* and *One Voice.*

The majority of older persons with whom we spoke (i.e., those who were interviewed or who contacted us to respond to the questionnaire on-line) were female. It was not our intention to speak to more women than men; however, as there are more older women than older men and as they are more likely to participate in group activities than are men, it is not surprising that this turned out to be the case. The majority of older persons with whom we spoke lived independently in the community. Although we did speak with coordinators of nursing homes, we did not speak with residents.

In 1997 there were 159,040 persons aged sixty-five and over living in nursing homes across Canada. In Nova Scotia there were 5,513 people—approximately 8 percent of the population—aged sixty-five and over (Nova Scotia Senior Citizens Secretariat, personal communication, September 2, 2001). The majority of older persons living in nursing homes are aged eighty-four and over, and many live in such settings due to poor health, lack of mobility, lack of personal resources or family support, confusion, and other disabilities (interview with nursing home administrator in the Annapolis Valley region of Nova Scotia, September 3, 2001). We decided not to attempt to hold focus groups within such institutions for two reasons: (1) the ethical problems with gaining permission to speak with elders in such homes, where administrators would select who might be the most "appropriate" people to participate in the research; and (2) concern that the residents would not be able to relate to the topic or be able to communicate their responses to our questions. We both have experience with visiting nursing homes in Nova Scotia and elsewhere, and we concluded that data collected in such facilities would not necessarily reflect the opinions of enough of those who reside in them.

Overall we communicated with several hundred non-institutionalized older persons as well as with many who work with and for the older population.

We addressed eleven focus groups in all, and this is how they broke down in terms of location, number of people, gender, age range, race, and education.

1. Halifax (urban), seven women, sixty-one to eighty-seven, White, most university educated.
2. Seabright (semi-urban), South Shore, five women and two men, sixty-two to eighty-one, White, most university educated.

3. Wolfville (small university town), Annapolis Valley, five men and five women (couples), fifty-seven to seventy-eight, White, university educated/professional.
4. Wolfville (small university town), Annapolis Valley, five women and two men, seventy to ninety, White, university educated/professional.
5. Harbourville (fishing village), Kings County, ten women and two men, fifty-nine to eighty-nine, White, several university educated.
6. Halls Harbour (fishing village), Kings County, five women, sixty to eighty-four, White, high school.
7. Kentville (semi-rural small town), Kings County, bridge club consisting of four long-time women friends, seventy-five to eighty-five, White, high school (some higher).
8. East Preston (semi-urban), outside of Halifax/Dartmouth area, twelve women and two men, sixty to eighty, Black, high school.
9. Bridgewater (small town), Annapolis Valley, ten women members of a community club, ages sixty to eighty-four, Black, grades 3 to 11.
10. Eskasoni (rural), Mi'kmaw reserve in Cape Breton, eight women and one man, sixty-three to eighty-six, First Nations, high school.
11. Salt Spring Island (rural), small gulf island in British Columbia, life history writing group consisting of eleven women, sixty-five to eighty-four, high school (some university).

Within the text, the above groups will be referred to according to whether they are rural, semi-urban, and so on.

Summary of Questions

In all cases we provided a list of twenty-four questions aimed at discovering how older persons felt about gerontology and the aging experience. Our questionnaire was broken down into five main areas, and, in the summer of 2000, we pre-tested it with a group of seniors living in rural Nova Scotia.

The main topics covered by the questionnaire include: (1) definitions of old age; (2) knowledge and awareness of, and reaction to, gerontology and gerontological theories; (3) definitions, awareness, and experiences of "successful" aging; (4) involvement in seniors groups, organizations, or clubs; (5) suggestions regarding social solutions to the problems of aging; and (6) opinions on the involvement of older persons in decision making.

Using the Focus Group Data

Where relevant and necessary, we include the voices of older persons throughout the main body of the text. We also include two case studies of the experiences of Black Nova Scotia seniors and of seniors of Mi'kmaw heritage. We do this because it seems to us that these somewhat "closed" communities provide supportive environments within which one can grow older in ways for which mainstream culture does not necessarily provide. We made the decision to do this after conducting focus groups within these communities in early January and May of 2001. In all cases we were told how seldom the Aboriginal and Black peoples of Nova Scotia were involved in research on, or discussions of, aging within their communities. And it was apparent to us just how much there was to learn from these elders. There is a paucity of material dealing with the experiences of Black and Aboriginal elders within Nova Scotia (as, indeed, is the case for all Canadian provinces and territories).

We felt that, by conducting several focus groups within these two communities, we could supplement the meagre knowledge base concerning these important groups and, thus, make their experiences of aging visible.

In order to ensure confidentiality, when quoting informants directly, we use fictitious names. In all cases where individuals were members of a focus group, a release form was distributed and signed.

Inner Reflections on Aging:
Locating Ourselves within the Work

When I (Jeanette) was a graduate student in the mid-1980s at the University of British Columbia, a group of us were sitting around discussing our doctoral dissertation topics. Mine was on gerontology and the social construction of agedness (Auger 1983). As we talked about our work it occurred to me that we all study our own struggle. Having thought that, and then discussing it with some friends, it became clear to me that we did not select thesis topics in a vacuum, that, indeed, we did have subjective experiences, interests, and commitments that directed us towards some issues and away from others. Since then I have continued to reflect upon my interest in older persons and gerontology.

When I wrote *Social Perspectives on Death and Dying* (Auger 2000a) I included in it a section entitled "The Text Within." I wanted to include my own experiences within the book so as to share with the reader some of those elements of my life that led to my interest in the subject matter. Similarly, in this book, Diane and I wanted to locate our own aging narratives within the text. We decided to do this for at least two reasons.

First and foremost, as feminists we believe that we owe it to our informants and readers to own our experiences of aging. It would be unacceptable to ask others to share their thoughts with us without being willing to share our thoughts with them. Second, we believe that self-reflection is essential to further understanding and analyzing the social construction of old age both within our own lives and within society in general.

As educators, volunteers, researchers, and writers, we are as much a part of the worlds in which we live as are those about whom we write. We are not immune to the social pressures and stereotypes that surround what it means to be aging women in our culture.

In an excellent article published in the *Journal of Women and Aging*, Ruth E. Ray (1999:175) discusses what she terms "the power of the personal." She argues that, within feminist gerontology, the validation of personal knowledge and experience is crucial to a subjective research methodology. She suggests that conducting "self-reflection, self-critique and personal narratives" (179) pertaining to our own experiences enables us to become part of the more general cultural narratives of aging. She suggests further:

> Wouldn't it be wise for me—and others like me who wish to engage in conscious, critical research on older people's lives—to look inward and examine our own aging selves first? Shouldn't we become aware of the decline narratives we have internalised for ourselves before we conduct any kind of research—narrative or otherwise—on the subject of aging? (182)

Being in agreement with the principles Ray puts forth, we decided to take the plunge and to reflect upon our thoughts, feelings, beliefs, and experiences relating to growing older and to examine the roots of these realities.

Jeanette

I am fifty-six years old. When I first began to teach the sociology of aging and gerontology I was in my early thirties. I was active in a variety of community-based organizations, which worked with and for older persons, and I felt that I could use my energy and skills to make life better for some of the elders I knew.

I have always had very good relationships with older persons, and my grandfather was a very important person in my life. I grew up in the East End of London, England, and there were many older people among my relatives. Interestingly enough though, my own parents died when they were quite young: my birth mother at the age of twenty-eight, my father at the age of sixty-three, and my stepmother at the age of sixty-four. I suspect this is one of the reasons I was always interested in working with older persons: I never had the opportunity to provide assistance to my own parents.

I was born at the end of the Second World War, and the country had undergone vast losses, not just in terms of those who had died in the war, but also in terms of the economy and jobs. Within this context older people were looked upon as necessary resources. I grew up living next door to a pub, and every day a group of old women would sit in the "private bar" (the smallest of the many bars) drinking their barley wine (their drink of choice) and discussing the state of affairs in the nation. These old women were the cultural brokers of our neighbourhood: they knew who was married to whom, who had died in the war, who now had a job, how many children each neighbour had, and what they were doing with their lives. If anyone wanted to know what was happening on the local scene, then they went to these older women, who were always eager to trade gossip and stories.

Those who couldn't make it to the pub sat in their windows across the street from my house, and, when we would walk by, the predominantly older women would call out and inquire as to where we were going, what for, with whom, and so on. These bits of information would then be shared with the next passer-by, as long as they were neighbours. The daily market was another place where information was transmitted, and again older women were the ones most likely to be engaged in this work.

While younger men and women fought in the Second World War, their mothers, aunts, and grandmothers tended to the children and households. They also took care of the stalls and shops at the market and came up with interesting ways to make a few additional shillings or pence. When I was a child, my favourite stallholder was the old woman who sold grated horseradish. Every day except Sunday she would sit at the stall, always wearing black because her two sons had died in the war. She would grate horseradish onto pieces of newspaper and, if requested, would spill a few drops of beetroot juice on the radish to make it "red." Sometime she also sold live eels, which would be slithering on large chunks of ice in steel containers. When the eels of your choice had been selected, she would skilfully chop off their heads and wrap the bodies in newspaper. She knew everything there was to know about the market and the community, and when the market eventually closed I often wondered whatever happened to her.

The "beetroot" woman and my grandfather (who had immigrated to England after the Russians had invaded his home in Lithuania) were also the last of the artisans: individuals who had specific skills demanded by the public. My grandfather had been a tailor. I grew up in the "rag" trade, and all the men I knew wore tailor-made trousers. When machine-made clothes and installment plans (what the English called "hire purchase") came into being, men stopped having their trousers tailor-made and bought them "off the rack." Beetroot started to be sold in jars; eels came in plastic tubs and could be kept in a new machine called a refrigerator. So, when I became a teenager, the resourcefulness and value of older people in the community began to change.

I observed first-hand what happened to some older people when their skills were no longer needed within their communities. My grandfather had always insisted that he knew he would be "old" if the time ever came when he was no longer needed or if he could not manage for himself. One day, while in his seventies, he fell in the bathroom and could not get up. He refused assistance or a visit to the doctor, and spent the next two weeks in bed, where he died as he had wished.

As a young, working-class child, older people were to me a productive, crucial, and much loved group. Sadly, as technology and advanced industrialization changed the economy of the United Kingdom, it also changed the value we placed upon the elderly.

When I first taught courses in gerontology I always insisted that age was a state of mind, that we were as young as we felt, that there was no such thing as old age per se—just a series of age-related changes that we all experience in more or less similar stages. As I grow older and feel the arthritis in my knee causing some mobility challenges and recognize that my ability to thread a needle or to do other up-close work is diminishing due to decreasing vision, I seldom make these kinds of statements. I am starting to become one of the people about whom I teach.

Many of my friends are in a similar age range, and we often joke about our aging experiences. We laugh not so much because we think they are funny as because we all share some sense of surprise that we are actually having these kinds of discussions. We share our concerns about osteoporosis, menopause, cancer, having to live in an institution, having to go to bed earlier than we used to because we feel so tired, needing to reduce our beverage intake after 5:00 PM to reduce the chances of having to get up during the night to go to the bathroom, and other "typical" aspects of normal aging. We also share our joy at having good friends with whom we can discuss such topics.

I have two daughters who are both teenagers. When I first shared their lives with their biological mother, I was concerned that my grey hair caused me to look more like their grandmother than their "other" mother, so I coloured it. Now that they live elsewhere and I live alone, I colour my hair because I don't want to "look" old in case I meet someone new. Fortunately, while writing this book I did meet someone new—someone who appreciates and even celebrates grey hair and all that it signifies. Clearly I have internalized the values of my culture, which suggest that having grey hair equals oldness, which equals non-attractiveness, non-desirability, and asexuality. Intellectually I challenge this assumption, while in practice I buy into it. It is, indeed, a conundrum.

Recently my sixteen-year-old daughter was visiting and we decided that we would both colour our hair, she because she wanted a "different" look—something that represented her uniqueness, attractiveness, and sense of adventure—me because the grey was starting to come through. I thought how fascinating and telling it is that, in our culture, hair colour advertisements present at least two different messages to women and men on the basis of age. For younger women and men the message is about risk taking, about being glamorous, daring, adventurous, and mysterious; for older women and men the message is about looking younger. For older women, the voice-overs suggest that we "hide" the grey, "look the age we feel." There is implicit in some of these media-manufactured messages the notion that "no one need know" the truth about our hair colour. There is to these common advertisements a sense of disembodiment: older women are not who they appear to be. Having grey hair and needing to disguise it implies the need to lie about who we "really" are; that is, "old women." Being courageous, adventurous, and daring about one's looks seems to be something reserved for young women; old women are simply expected to try to look young.

In advertisements geared towards men, such as a recent campaign for a product called For Men Only, the television commercial shows a forty-something man who glances at his image in a mirror and declares that he "didn't realize [he] was going so grey." After he has purchased and used the advertised product, the next scene shows him with darker hair and a woman on his arm who tells him that he "always stays so handsome."

Even with grey hair disguised by cosmetics, men still get the women of their dreams. I have yet to see a television commercial, or printed advertisement, in which the older woman who uses hair colouring "gets" her man. Even more unlikely is the advertisement where a woman who uses hair colouring or other cosmetics gets the woman of her dreams, or a man the man of his dreams. Indeed, if we were to look to the advertising market, or the popular print media in general, for images of lesbians and gay men we would find them totally absent.

In a new twist to the issue of grey hair, a recent L'Oreal advertisement featured in the December 2000 issue of *Fifty Plus*, the magazine of the Canadian Association of Retired Persons, shows three women. Two of the women appear to be in their late forties, while one appears to be in her mid-fifties. The caption reads: "Celebrate Your Gray!" After describing the benefits of the hair-colouring product, women are encouraged to "Be exactly who [they] are."

I have an aunt who is in her seventies, and she maintains that women who don't colour their hair when it becomes grey are "letting themselves go." Somehow, in her opinion, such women are failing womankind. Most of the women in my family coloured their hair; in fact, I cannot remember an older female relative who had grey hair.

I have internalized many of my culture's assumptions about older people, particularly about women. On a daily basis popular culture reminds me that youth is equated with beauty, men with power, and women with subservience to that power. I read advertisements that portray old women as feeble; as suffering from some form of dementia or depression; as needing to use cosmetics to hide wrinkles, age spots, grey hair; as wearing clothes that are dull and drab, usually grey or black. I watch television programs devoid of older women, unless I watch re-runs of *The Golden Girls*.

I am unlikely to see movies in which beautiful older women have starring roles. Although there are an increasing number of good popular novels that feature old women as the main characters, in general these people are not present. I am inundated with cultural messages about what it means to be old, and, in general, the scripts for aging women are neither inspiring nor challenging.

In *Women and Aging: An Anthology by Women*, Sandra Healey (1986:62) articulates what aging means to her:

> What does it really mean to grow old? For me, first of all, to be old is to be myself. No matter how patriarchy may classify and categorize me as invisible and powerless, I exist. I am an ongoing person, a sexual being, a person who struggles, for whom there are important issues to explore, new things to learn, new challenges to meet, beginnings to make, risks to take, endings to ponder. Even though some of my options are diminished, there are new paths ahead.

Inspired by experiences such as the one just cited, I continue to walk my own path into old age. I am open to new experiences and challenges, and to teaching my students and others that growing older can be a rich journey.

Diane

I am sixty-two years old and have recently left a forty-year marriage. I have three adult sons: two married with children, one divorced. Since my fortieth birthday they have watched me as I sought to "know self." When I was fifty I went to university and, taking part in women's studies courses, very quickly identified myself as a "feminist." I discovered I had always been a feminist but simply had not placed a label on my worldview. To this day I have great difficulty wearing any sort of label.

For many years my father's parents were missionaries in India. My memory of them goes back to a time when they were on sabbatical and lived with us for six months. I remember my grandfather as a very strong, chauvinistic male, a great man with the ladies, while my grandmother I remember as staying quietly in the background. She was, however, a very angry woman, and I would sometimes experience the brunt of her anger about her lot in life. As I age myself, and as I reflect upon my own inner world, I can now see her situation with new eyes. She was the perfect example of a woman who was subordinate to husband and church. I remember my grandfather sitting in a rocking chair, reading the Bible and discussing issues of kindness, love, and the word of Jesus. I was to follow his example for a good part of my adult life.

My own mother is still living. She is eighty-six, and her life experience has consisted of "looking after other people." She no longer has anyone to look after and is now experiencing a great loneliness, a lack of meaning in her life. She, too, was a traditional wife who left her own gifts and needs behind in her attempt to please everyone. I speak of this now as I remember that, from an early age, I wished to be different. I did not want to follow these examples and so struck out on an adventure to find a self.

In doing this research I find myself asking such questions as, What meaning is there in my life? What is important to me? How do I see the world around me? How do I wish to grow older? Being connected to people is very important to me. My work with palliative care has introduced me to many older persons who are facing death, and I am intrigued by the different experiences these people undergo as they face their physical deaths. Believing that I am a spiritual being within a physical body, it has always been important for me to do what I came here to do. Initially, I belonged to the organized church, and, for many years, the people I met, the rituals I followed, were very meaningful and supportive to me as I travelled on my journey. However, as I asked more questions and searched my inner world more thoroughly, I could no longer accept the "man"-made dogma and doctrine presented to me. So the great Creator became both female and male for me, and I am experiencing a whole new way of being in the world as I journey forward.

I grew up with the image of a slim, female body as the norm. The women in my family placed great significance upon physical appearances. I have always struggled with a weight problem; however, as I grow older, what matters to me most is my health, not my physical appearance. Hallelujah!

As I get to know myself, I have more confidence in the life ahead of me. I no longer have to be beautiful in the worldly sense, as I feel beautiful inside. It is a great feeling. So very freeing. I see every living thing in this world as being connected to every other. When one hurts, we all hurt. So it goes with pain, happiness, and joy—any of the emotions we share as humans.

I am at a stage in my own life where I do not have to be totally responsible for anyone but myself. While I am my mother's care manager, I answer only to myself. In my research I have come upon many people who are growing older and are experiencing some of the new learnings, new attitudes, and new perspectives that I am currently experiencing. I find it exciting to be sixty-two, and I look forward to the new lessons and adventures ahead.

Age is no longer relevant to me. I am who I am, and I am thoroughly convinced, after listening to many inspiring older persons and reflecting upon my own journey, that we are not old unless our minds tell us we are. My hope is that we simply all grow older and wiser. (Here it may be noted the Diane and Jeanette don't necessarily agree about, or share the same experiences of, growing older. This reflects culture as well as life and educational experiences, thus displaying the diversity of the aging experience.)

FORMAT

Each of the chapters in this book includes both an academic component (i.e., the presentation of works by gerontologists and others writing in the fields of aging research and practice) and an experiential component (i.e., the presentation of the lived experiences of older persons). We shall weave together the opinions of academic scholars and the data gathered from focus groups. In all cases we are interested in comparing the two versions of a reality of growing older within (primarily) North American culture.

Chapter One

Scientific Constructions of Old Age
The Development and Scope of Gerontology

Over the past three decades, the phenomenon of old age has received increased attention from the social and medical sciences. In order to address issues of concern about growing older and aging, geriatrics and gerontology emerged as scientific disciplines that attempt to explain the health and status of older persons within global communities.

Gerontology is the scientific study of old age. Many agree with McPherson's (1998:221) definition: gerontology is an "interdisciplinary field that includes research drawn from the biological sciences, clinical medicine, and the behavioural and social sciences."

The biologist Elie Metchnikoff coined the term "gerontology" in 1903. At that time, he remarked: "I think it extremely probable that the scientific study of old age and of death, two branches of science that may be called gerontology and thanatology, will bring about great modifications in the course of the last period of life" (cited in Katz 1996:82).

Many have written on the history of gerontology as a discipline, most notably Birren (1959), Philibert (1965), Streib and Orbach (1967), Hendricks and Davis (1977), Green (1993), and Katz (1996). According to Novak (1997:12), the discipline in Canada progressed in the following manner: "In 1950 the government set up the first of a series of committees to study aging. This committee—the Joint Committee on Old Age Security of the Senate and House of Commons—studied the effects of aging on Canadian society and on individuals. It focused on income security, ... health, housing and welfare services." Novak goes on to remark that, in 1963, the Senate of Canada appointed a special committee to study the services, facilities, and preventative programs available to older citizens across the country. Throughout the 1970s and 1980s, government- and university-based research continued to increase. In 1971 Canadian researchers and scholars formed the Canadian Association on Gerontology. By 1980 Canadian gerontology had come of age. In that year Victor Marshall (1980) published the first collection of gerontology writings by Canadian scholars: *Aging in Canada* (Novak 1997:13).

In 1982 the Canadian Association on Gerontology first published the *Canadian Journal of Aging*. As Novak notes, in the year that this journal first appeared, "the program of the association's eleventh Annual Scientific and Education Meeting contained one-hundred and twenty-nine abstracts" (14). By the year 1995, over seven hundred researchers and practitioners presented papers at the annual meeting (15).

In 2000, Anne Martin-Matthews (2000:iv), then editor of the *Canadian Journal on Aging*, noted:

> The past two decades have seen significant change in the climate of gerontological research in Canada. The decade of unprecedented growth in the 1980's was followed by a decade characterized by many challenges and fewer opportunities. As research resources were reduced throughout the 1990's and as the public policy agenda changed to include more demands for accountability and relevance, researchers increasingly have had to turn to innovative solutions in order to address critical research questions .... The greatest change in gerontological research in Canada in the past decade has been the establishment earlier this year of the Canadian Institutes of Health Research .... The CIHR will redefine research on aging in Canada in several important ways. For one the CIHR will significantly enhance the funding resources available to researchers in gerontology and geriatrics in Canada. It will make available to researchers outside of what has traditionally been defined as "medical research" a range of personnel and health career awards previously only accessible by researchers in programs associated with medical schools.

As gerontology is both a theoretical and an applied field, some of its practitioners engage in academic work (e.g., theory building and testing, experimentation, and surveys), while others attempt to apply the knowledge obtained through academic pursuits to the actual lives of older persons (e.g., within government departments, nursing homes, and other care facilities as well as within the policy planning and program provision sector).

SUBFIELDS OF GERONTOLOGY

Geriatrics is the branch of medicine that deals with physiological and biological changes and diseases in older persons. Gerontology, as a multidisciplinary field, encompasses both the medical and social aspects of growing older. Since the formal inception of the discipline some thirty years ago, there are now several branches of study that attempt to discuss and to explain different factors of the aging experience. Some of these include geragogics, which is concerned primarily with what Zych (1992:5) calls "a pedagogy of aging and old age."

Discussion of geragogics is most frequently found in books and articles that deal with educational gerontology, where, as Glendenning (1992:5) notes, the goals are to provide "(1) education for older adults based on their perceptions and needs, (2) public education about aging, and (3) education for professionals and para-professionals in the field of aging." Further defining the field of geragogics, Glendenning suggests that the term refers to:

> Those issues and practices that are relevant to teaching and learning in relation to older people: memory, cognitive development, coping with transition and change in later life, teaching theory and method, learning theory, realization of full developmental potential and a philosophy which underpins the whole conceptualisation, as being controlled by the person concerned. (15)

Geragogics, then, sees adult learning as a self-perceived and perpetuated experience rather that as one in which instructors know best. Another of the goals of this particular subfield of gerontology is to recognize the diversity of the human experience in aging rather than to assume that older persons represent a homogeneous group. Again, according to Glendenning, "Older people have tended to be viewed as a social problem and as a disadvantaged group with special needs. Policy pares [sic] lump them all together with those who suffer from disability and members of black and ethnic minority communities. A paradigm shift away from this functionalist approach is necessary" (13).

In Canada, universities, colleges, and continuing education departments are increasingly focusing upon the need for adult learning. Programs such as Elderhostel and Creative Retirement in Manitoba aim to provide older adults with opportunities to learn new, or to enhance old, skills and interests. Geragogics, although it still has a primarily European focus, can be helpful to adult educators in other parts of the world as well.

Ethnogerontology is that subfield of gerontology concerned with cross-cultural issues of aging. Its framework is primarily anthropological, and it examines the relationship between ethnicity and aging and the role that cultural values, expectations, beliefs, and practices play during the course of individual aging. Torres (1999:33) notes that the primary concern of cross-cultural gerontology and ethnogerontology is the study of "how socio-cultural settings define and shape the experience of aging."

During the International Year of Older Persons (1999), many countries participated in making visible the contributions and concerns of their older citizens. Their situations were shared at international conferences, on the Internet, and in a variety of publications (such as that produced by Ageing International[1] and, of course, by the United Nations, which had declared the event in the first place). Many countries (Canada being one) produced fact sheets about the old, and this created a great deal of public awareness regarding the needs of older persons around the world. One of the goals of ethnogerontology is to continue this work at both academic and public levels.

The subfield of gerontology that focuses upon the psychological components of aging is known as psycho-geriatrics, and it explores several key issues. McPherson (1998:12) identifies some of these as "changes in personality, learning, memory, or creativity [that] occur across the life cycle .... Psychological aging involves the interaction of cognitive and behavioural changes within the individual, and environmental factors (a change in housing type or location) that affect our psychological state." As well as the aforementioned issues, psycho-geriatrics examines memory loss, intelligence, cognitive functioning, and coping strategies in the face of such stresses as retirement, ill health, widowhood, and so on.

As reading through any university or college calendar will show, many scientific and academic disciplines are involved in the study of aging. Some social science programs have recreation and leisure faculties, where the focus is on the administration, planning, and provision of appropriate fitness, exercise, and leisure activities in nursing homes, adult day centres, community centres, schools, and other facilities frequented by older persons. Most nursing homes require the skills of professional activity directors, and schools of recreational management provide an excellent training ground for those interested in attaining such expertise. Students who have taken such programs have planned fitness and exercise programs for a variety of special-needs elders; they have also worked with municipal planning departments to develop programs for older persons, both those with and those without disabilities.

Because faculty, students, and researchers in education programs and departments are interested in the special needs of adult learners, many university and college campuses hold summer programs for retired persons and provide them with free or subsidized tuition for regular, full-year programs. As well, across the educational spectrum, education specialists attempt to include issues of aging within already existing curricula. One of the issues seldom addressed through university-level courses is the need for more literacy programs that are specifically aimed at older persons and more English as a second language (ESL) courses aimed at elderly immigrants. We discuss each of these issues in Chapter 4.

Those engaged in the nutrition and health sciences are interested in dietary needs, adequate nutrition, and special food requirements for persons with specific illnesses as well as food education and awareness issues. Another component of this curriculum includes health prevention and promotion programs aimed at helping older people stay healthy and independent. Many involved in these related disciplines are, inter alia, employed in nursing homes, hospitals, residential care facilities, and homecare programs, where information about the dietary, eating, and lifestyle habits of older persons is crucial.

Persons involved in the fields of geography and urban geography are interested in whether to integrate older persons into the community by creating shelter arrangements, which are located within communities, or by providing age-based segregated housing units. The concept of "aging in place" refers to the process whereby older persons try to stay within the communities where they have lived for all or most of their lives. The goal of urban and rural planners is to create affordable, accessible living arrangements so as to ensure that older persons can remain in their communities for as long as possible.

In Canada there are many shelter options for the aged, ranging from living in one's own home to living in a "granny flat," or "garden suite," which is a property attached or near an already existing house. A garden suite enables an older person to live independently but in close proximity to her families or friends. There are also a variety of residential care options, ranging from nursing homes to independent but assisted-living situations.

Persons who work within the fields of Divinity, Theology, and Spiritual Care are interested in the religiosity and spiritual needs of older persons and their ability to practise them, especially when confined to a nursing home or other type of institutional care facility. According to Novak and Campbell (2001:115), "Some studies find that poor health and the lack of transportation lead to declines in formal religious activity, but studies also find that religious attitudes stay stable throughout old age."

The field of gerontology has many academic and professional layers. When speaking of the multidisciplinary nature of the field of gerontology, Lassey and Lassey (2001:21) note that "the range of applicable disciplines includes biology, sociology, psychology, social psychology, economics, health care policy, law, medicine, nursing, social work, housing, recreation and leisure, and other closely related fields." Many of these fields of inquiry and scientific/academic endeavour will be discussed in more detail later. Our intention here is merely to provide a flavour of some of the themes and topics that are covered by those engaged in the study of the aging process and its implications.

GERONTOLOGY AS AN IDEOLOGICAL CONSTRUCT

What gerontologists say and do involves their ideology, what they believe to be "facts" about life and growing old. What they say and do is also a function of their social background. This "knowledge at hand" (Schutz 1973)—the material written by other scientists on the topic, the papers written and read, the research conducted, the lectures heard, the films and video recordings seen, the Web sites visited, and the observations made—influences and reinforces their ideological stance. Because of his or her knowledge at hand the gerontologist is able to recognize everyday occurrences of oldness as data of gerontological interest and concern. It is through this process of connecting everyday events about old age into a whole—gerontology—that gerontologists are able to claim to be "experts" on matters relevant to the old. The lay public, as well as other professionals, take the topics that gerontologist's address to be those of major concern to the old and their care providers. In this sense, "facts" are what gerontologists say they are. Through social consensus they attempt to establish "scientific" truths about aging.

How is ideology manifested in the gerontological enterprise? We can address this question by looking at what gerontologists actually do as part of their work. We recognize that, at the outset, the gerontologist has a system of ideas that is somehow relevant to the topic of old age. This does not necessarily mean that all gerontologists are first and foremost interested in the behaviour of older persons per se. The network of researchers and practitioners who do gerontological work includes sociologists, biologists, psychologists, social planners, anthropologists, social workers, geographers, adult educators, and the like. Some of the major theories in gerontology are borrowed from other disciplines. An examination of any conference materials focused upon gerontological topics shows that most participants and presenters are listed as members of a variety of academic departments. In fact, gerontology is seldom listed as a separate department or other type of specific workplace. Within gerontology, already-existing theoretical models are applied to the study of older persons, who are considered as one particular segment of society. Older people are often chosen as objects of study in order to support or refute a particular theory rather than in order to further understand the process of aging or the particular life experiences that go with it.

When attempting to formulate and articulate a body of knowledge, one makes basic assumptions about values, ethics, attitudes, and beliefs. In addition, one discusses and exchanges ideas concerning what types of information and research will constitute such knowledge and who will have access to it. These decisions are sometimes made implicitly (as when we assume that statistics and other demographic information will provide an adequate "profile" of older persons), sometimes explicitly (as in the setting forth of goals and objectives of professional associations and in the planning of course curricula for special academic programs). In many cases the process of knowledge production is performed within social and professional settings, thus effectively excluding the presence, participation, and ideas of those who are being studied. In this case, the old are not usually granted access to the arena within which their lives and experiences become transferred into viable knowledge. When access is granted to the old, it usually has a different quality than does the access provided to the gerontologist, and it often takes the form of tokenism.

Gerontologists, in their role as social scientists and practitioners, have regarded older persons as a potential social problem that is in need of a solution. The old are viewed in this way because, as their numbers increase, they are seen to require additional health and social services—services that will be financed predominantly through public funds. The "problem" involves identifying potential needs, how services and programs will be funded, and who will administer them. The problem is a social one in that all wage earners, through taxes and resources, will be expected to contribute to the well-being of society's older members.

The issue of funding the programs and services that assist older persons is related to the concept of dependency ratio—the process by which employed people pay government taxes at all levels, thus assisting those who are dependent upon them (e.g., children, those who are unable to work for pay due to various disabilities, and some older persons). McPherson (1998:109) notes that the dependency ratio is "determined by dividing the number of people 65 and older by the number who are 18 to 64 years of age. At present, the old–age dependency ratio is about 18.6 in Canada (that is, 18.6 adults over 65 in Canada are supported by 100 younger people of labour force age)." This number is projected to increase to 24.9 by the year 2016 (Chui 1996).

Although many argue that the greatest challenge to countries with increasingly high numbers of older persons will involve how to provide them with the necessary services and programs, Lilley and Campbell (1999:12) think that "the challenge will be, not as often stated, in managing the cost of an aging population, but rather it will be in managing the gradual shift from spending on youth to spending on seniors."

Gee and Gutman (2000:12) refers to the concept of dependency ratio as "voodoo demography," arguing that it is an imperfect indicator of the costs of an increasing older population: "One of [its] shortcomings is the arbitrariness of defining everyone aged 65 and over (and under age 20) as dependent. Many teenagers work, as do some of the elderly population—recently released 1996 census data show that 372,415 persons aged 65 and over had employment income, with an average income of $20,446 (1995 dollars)."

As more older persons and some gerontologists speak out against viewing old age as a primarily negative experience, the discipline is beginning to shift its ideological focus away from producing knowledge that reinforces old age as what Atchley (1980:14) has called "the beginning of the end" to viewing it as a potentially positive experience. In 1978 the late Maggie Kuhn (1978b:423), founder of the US-based advocacy group the Gray Panthers, noted that those who practise gerontology hold particular ideological values about their work and about who older people are:

> Gerontology has certain unadmitted preconceptions about old people, which reflect the class interests and biases of middle class, educated professionals. These biases are reflected by the gerontological societies as they attempt to meet the needs of several thousand prolific professionals in search of publications, a grant, or professional identity.

Gerontologists note that their work is intended to help the aged. Generally, it is seen to help by providing a process that makes the old more visible (e.g., by creating more awareness of them and their lives through research, literature, public talks, meetings, etc.); specifically, it is seen to help by focusing on special issues said to affect the old (e.g., the need for adequate health care, housing, income, recreational opportunities, nutrition, etc.). Help is part of the ideological structure, the system of ideas, by which gerontology is socially produced and maintained. It is used as an organizing principle, an operational imperative by which much gerontological work is performed.

As the population of persons aged sixty-five and older grew, so too did the recognition and articulation of their unmet needs as perceived through the eyes of those sent to assist them. As the experiences of those within the helping professions merged with those of other gerontologists, it seems only natural that help, as a product of professional socialization and experiences, would be included as a relevant and appropriate function of the gerontological enterprise.

Observations of and discussions with older persons suggest that each person perceives help differently. Some perceive help as the provision of a service or facility, while others perceive it as an interactive process that enables them to learn how to do something and, in turn, to assist others to do the same thing. Still others view help as being left alone to help themselves. Several authors, among them Scott (1969), Kuhn (1978a), Estes (1979), and Novak (1980), have suggested that the helping professions are in the business of creating "helpees" where, perhaps, none exist. They further suggest that, if these professionals did their work effectively, then there would be no help or helpers needed. Professionals are seen as skilled and learned experts who apply their knowledge to the affairs, and in the service, of others:

> For generations, divinity, the law, medicine, even the military and now the newer professions in the fields of education, welfare, architecture, industrial management etc., have been acknowledged as being selflessly devoted to the good of the weaker and less knowledgeable members of society, thus enabling those who lack the capacity to fend for themselves to lead fuller, safer and healthier lives. However, the question must now be asked whether the professions in fact provide their services too altruistically, and whether we are really enriched or not just subordinated by their activities. (Illich 1977:22)

Supporting the view that the helping professions may be serving their own interests as well as those of others, Novak (1980:14) suggests that, in a specialized society, the individual becomes raw material for professional ministrations: "Often the professional is needed because the problems themselves have been generated by the clients' previous contact with other professionals .... Within this framework the elderly are not only a renewable, but almost infinitely fertile and exploitable field for professional work."

According to the above point of view, laypersons cannot be involved in research endeavours (other than as data providers) because they do not have a particular type of sense-making practice. Further, they do not have the "objectifying rights," the correct "perspective," that social scientists claim as their prerogative. Although gerontologists may claim that they are "helping," others see their efforts somewhat differently. According to Maggie Kuhn (1978a:72):

> Gerontology has assumed the deterioration of the aged and has attempted to describe it in terms which ignore the social, and economic factors which in large measure precipitate that deterioration. By reifying the attribute "old" gerontology reinforces societal attitudes which view older people as stuck in an inevitable chronological destiny of decay and deterioration .... When persons who are old, poor, and stigmatized by society become objects of Gerontological research, they are seen as problems by society, rather than as persons experiencing problems created by society.

Kuhn is suggesting that, far from helping the aged, gerontology actually hinders them in their attempts to deal with the social conditions of their lives.

More recently, Katz (1996:1) asks an interesting question regarding the formation of a discipline such as gerontology: "How is the development of gerontology linked to the disciplining of old age and the construction of specific subjects of power and knowledge: the elderly, the senior citizen, the pensioner, the dependent, the lifelong learner, the caregiver, the gray voter?" He recognizes that knowledge is power, that who knows gets; thus, he questions the practices through which some forms of knowledge come to be seen as legitimate (i.e., scientific ones) while others (i.e., subjective ones) may not.

The concept of self-determination, the ability to be in control of one's own life, is also part of the gerontological discourse. A concern with self-determination is currently becoming a trend in gerontological conferences, papers, and articles, not in terms of how the old actually participate in determining and shaping their lives but, rather, in terms of how professionals should help them do so. In July 1981, the International Federation on Ageing held a workshop entitled *Self Determination and the Elderly* (papers from this workshop were edited by Charlotte Nusberg [1981]). Those present were from a number of different countries that had implemented various programs for self-determination. Several of the participants made recommendations and offered suggestions as to how the old might be encouraged to determine their own affairs. For example, Robert Pringent, president of the International Federation on Ageing, said:

> It is imperative for everyone concerned with the problems of the elderly to support all possible forms of self determination .... This calls for intelligent surveys ... and the allocation of ample resources to support personalized techniques that differ from the usual sampling procedures so that individual and local situations can be better taken into account. (Nusberg 1981:8)

It seems that Pringent is suggesting not that the elderly help each other to take more control over their lives but, rather, that they help researchers (by providing them with more descriptive data). It would seem from this, and similar publications of conference proceedings, that self-determination for the elderly is something that requires professional expertise and competence rather than common sense knowledge. Unfortunately, this viewpoint is also becoming popular among laypersons.

When we use the term "common sense" we are referring to a subjective system of shared experiences that people invoke when speaking of their lived realities. We do not glorify common sense understandings as somehow superior to scientific explanations of growing older, but we do suggest that they are not inferior to them either. Clearly, common sense knowledge does not exist apart from age, gender, race, and cultural socialization; consequently it represents how one feels one "ought to" behave as an older actor in a society replete with age-oriented scripts. Nonetheless, we argue that these subjective experiences of growing older illustrate the realities of aging as much as do theoretical explanations.

THE ELDERLY AS A SOCIAL PROBLEM

As has been mentioned, one view of the old is that they constitute a social problem. This is because: (1) there are more of them, chronologically speaking, than there ever were before; (2) the old are expected to need more health care and other social services than are other age groups; and (3) the cost of these services will have to come from taxes collected from other citizens. The assumption, based on the work of financial analysts, economists, and actuaries, is that, as the general population expands and the working population steadies out, this dependency ratio will increase: "This implies a much higher burden on the working age population" (Powell and Martin 1978:25).

Thus, for many, the problem that faces society involves financial constraint and hardship. It is assumed that expenditures on the old, whom some see as "non-productive" members of the community, will be frowned upon by the members of those age groups who are eligible for employment but who are unable to acquire it. One of the side issues surrounding the notion of the aged as a social problem is the idea that society should be responsible for the plight of the old. As Baum (1974:1) writes, older persons have "been betrayed by society, by powerful interest groups and by the state." And, as de Beauvoir (1977:8) notes: "as far as old people are concerned this society is not only guilty but also downright criminal. Sheltering behind the myths of expansion and affluence, it treats the old as outcasts." Gladys Elder (1977:17), an old-age pensioner in Britain, supports this viewpoint: "This is society's treatment of the aged: it refuses them the necessary minimum, thus condemning them to extreme poverty, to slums, to ill health, loneliness and despair, asserting that they have neither the same needs, or the same rights as others in the community."

First, this notion of "society's" lack of responsibility to the aged suggests that they are not a part of the society in which they live, that they play no part in its social organization, and that they represent a homogeneous group with similar tastes, values, and opinions. Second, it implies that "society" is something easily recognizable as an agent of "blame," as something that is "out there" rather than within every one of us. If we continue to blame society, whoever or whatever that is, for the situation facing older people, then we need take no personal responsibility for the part we play in constructing and perpetuating so-called ageism.

Academics, professionals, government personnel, and laypersons alike frequently use the term "society" as a generalizable catch phrase, a box into which all institutions and social relationships can be placed. In general, we speak of society as the arena or stage upon which our daily interactions, policies, programs, and social rules are acted out. In this sense, the use of the term indicates the presence of a common life. The term "society" tends to be accepted as a given; that is, it is not fleshed out and examined in light of its various meanings within various situations. When gerontologists and the old use the term "society," it is assumed that they are referring to the immediate social environments within which older people and others circulate. These environments can include local community places, family, and friends as well as more global settings, which reach them through television, radio, films, and reading materials. Often, when individuals wish to excuse themselves for behaviour that they suspect may be unacceptable to others, they invoke the notion of "society." They argue that they are a "product" of their society and, therefore, somehow not responsible for their actions.

Over the past twenty years there has been some discontent within and around the discipline of gerontology. This discontent has focused upon the need for what Estes (1979), Philibert (1965, 1974, and 1977a),

Featherstone and Wernick (1995), Katz (1996), Green (1994), and Dychtwald (1999), among others, have termed "critical gerontology." Featherstone and Wernick (1995:23) regard a critical gerontology as one that would "recognize the social, political, cultural contexts in which older people live."

Growing older does not take place in a vacuum. Notions of how people should be defined on the basis of age, and how they should be expected to behave at certain ages, are embedded within a set of culturally and socially constructed values and assumptions. In order to understand and analyze the social construct of age, it is necessary to place it within the world of politics, finances, power, and decision making.

Through the gerontological enterprise, everyday life, as it is lived by older persons, is transformed and codified into data—the stuff of science—then re-created into official knowledge about old age. Through this process, as it is currently performed, it is possible, and, we will argue, likely, that the ideology implicit within the knowledge base of gerontology represents an elite viewpoint that is not necessarily shared by the old.

Other authors, including Estes (1979:4), believe that "what is important about ideologies is that they reflect the social position and socially determined values of their beholders and are only partial perspectives."

Much gerontological work has focused on how the individual adjusts to her or his own aging, especially with respect to changes in social status and role. This work has centred on what the individual has to do in order to cope with these life changes, which, Estes (1979:6) claims, are "externally generated." In this sense, some of the "problems" of the old—such as loss of work and income through retirement, along with all the factors so closely connected to one's ability to earn money and so be able to afford goods and services—are seen as "personal" problems.

If the paradigms of gerontology are correct in positing the old as being somehow responsible for their own misfortunes, then it is they, and not society, who must adapt and adjust. Disengagement theory, for example, views old age as a necessary "requirement or function of society" (Cumming and Henry 1961:32). It views growing old as an inevitable process that requires older persons to give up previously held roles so that younger persons may find work and buy homes. (See Chapter 2 for an in-depth discussion of disengagement theory.) It is in this way that some of the theoretical approaches aimed at describing and predicting "successful" old age place the old in opposition to the young and tend to depict them as victims.

If social life could be restructured so that the old could remain active or not, as they chose, then the ideological framework of gerontology would need to shift from viewing the old as being in a separate age unit based upon chronology to viewing them as complete and total participants within community structures.

Philibert (1974:317) has said that gerontologists base their ideological concerns about agedness on a priori assumptions that their work constitutes a "science" whose objective is to account for "facts." They assume that aging is a "tangible phenomenon" that can be described and analyzed—that it is the "nature" of the older person. Thus, they treat all old persons as the "objects" of inquiry, the "phenomena" under study. Older persons are treated as a homogenous group that can be studied as an entity unto itself. In his argument against the gerontological enterprise, which he sees as having ignored experiential data pertaining to aging, Philibert (1974:307) comments:

> They [gerontologists] have believed that from the juxtaposition of genetic, biochemical, physiological, psychological, demographic, sociological and economic studies, an interdisciplinary, synthetic, integrated knowledge of human aging would emerge. Today we are becoming aware of the naiveté of this projection—even of the fragility of the hopes and convictions of those who nourished it.

For Philibert, and others, an appropriate study of gerontology would include an investigation of the images of aging as reflected in popular literature, laws, the arts, life histories, religious doctrines, cultural rituals, and so on. In this way, the ideological viewpoints of a variety of people would be taken into account, enabling us to see the many ways in which individuals create notions of old age.

Estes (1978, 1979), Marshall and Tindale (1978-79), Novak (1980), and Philibert (1974, 1977a, 1977b), among others, have argued that some of what gerontologists do contains "structural or built-in interests" (Estes 1979:3). Illich (1977) has termed these interests "self-serving," while Kuhn (1978a:73) has termed them "contributory to a reinforcement of ageist attitudes." The "self-serving interests" argument seems to imply that at least some of what gerontologists do should be in the best interests of others, especially the old, rather than themselves. If, as Lerner (1939:72) has said, "ideas are weapons," and if ideologies are the accumulation of what Geertz (1973:230) calls "systems of interacting symbols ... patterns of interwoven meanings," then we must look at how ideologies function to set goals and objectives related to describing, explaining, and analyzing the world of the old. Because they both determine and reinforce how we think and act about old age, ideologies play an important part in the social production of the knowledge of gerontology. In other words, the gerontologist's belief that her or his work helps the aged is ideological; that is, it is socially determined. It is with this in mind that we treat what gerontologists say and do as somehow displaying "facts" about aging. (See Chapter 2 for a more detailed discussion of ideology.)

Estes (1979:49) has argued that gerontology has become an "aging enterprise" in which the "conglomeration of experts, institutions, and professions has arisen to care for the elderly, focusing on the individual to the exclusion of the social and political context." Similarly, Philibert (1977a) discusses "gerontologcracy"—a term he coined to explain how professionals in the fields of aging are attempting to "control" the lives of the aged population: "the gerontologists, have control and are on their way to increasing their power. If we do not take steps we will witness more control of the aged by the twenty-first century." Philibert (1965:4–5) has also argued that a critical gerontology should recognize that the basic problem is not the increased numbers of elders but, rather, "the fact that this increase is taking place in a society which accepts the downgrading of the elderly as a law of nature instead of seeing it as a feature of its own culture."

What Philibert is arguing here, and many would agree with him, is that examining, theorizing, discussing, and predicting issues about old age must be recognized as occurring within the context of ageism. Providing additional goods, programs, and services will, indeed, assist older persons to remain active within their communities; however, without educational and attitudinal resources aimed at fighting ageist stereotypes and assumptions, and creating cultural values that posit growing old as a positive experience, then no amount of research will improve the lives of the elderly.

AGING DEMOGRAPHICS

As we have already implied, the reason most frequently given for the emergent academic and government interest in and concern with older persons is that the absolute number of older persons in the total populations of most countries in the world has increased considerably over the past twenty years and will likely continue to do so. As Lassey and Lassey (2001:xi) note:

The proportion of the population age 65 and older in the economically advanced countries will grow from about 15 percent in the year 2000 to more than 25 percent by 2030, with considerable variation by country. The segment of national resources needed and the social organization required for service provision are thus likely to require major upward revisions. The implications are profound.

Not only are the numbers of individuals aged sixty-five and over increasing in the higher-income countries of the world, but they are also increasing in the middle- and lower-incomes countries as well. As Lassey and Lassey also note, the proportion may grow to "28 percent in less prosperous countries in Asia, Africa and Latin America" (4).

The worldwide increase of persons aged sixty-five and over is said to be the direct result of improved health care, improved water supply and sanitation, lower birth rates, lower infant mortality, and greater average life expectancy. In 1991 the United Nations predicted that, by the year 2000, those aged sixty-five and over would be the fastest growing age group anywhere in the world, with the largest increases being in Africa, South Asia, Latin America, and East Asia. Indeed these predictions were borne out by recent United States Census Bureau (2000) statistics.

Gerontology, as a discipline, has grown by leaps and bounds in many countries of the world. In the appendix to *Quality of Life for Older People: An International Perspective*, Lassey and Lassey (2001:466-67) note that there are now seventy-seven gerontology journals and other publications. Recognizing other materials which contribute to the topics of old age and related themes, Katz (1996:101), citing Hesslein, notes that "375 journals related to aging have recently materialized."

Interestingly, many of the texts devoted to the subject of gerontology do not define "old age," "aging," "the elderly," or "older people"; rather, it is assumed that the reader will know perfectly well what is meant by the term "older people." When I (Jeanette) ask students enrolled in my sociology of aging class to define the aged, they have no difficulty in saying that that they are people aged sixty-five and over. When I ask them why they offer this definition, they often remark that this is the age when people are eligible for retirement and old age pensions. Clearly, there is a popular notion that old age begins at sixty-five.

When gerontology texts or papers do offer definitions of old age, they generally do so in terms of an interesting schema of chronologically based ages. This fragmenting of older persons on the basis of the number of years they have lived produces what gerontologists call "age cohorts."

The breakdown is as follows: those aged sixty-five are termed the "young" or "nearly" old, those aged seventy-five to eighty-four are termed the "middle-old," and those eighty-five and over are referred to as the "oldest," the "really" old, or the "old" old. The latter group is frequently referred to as the "frail" elderly, as it is that group that is said to be most in need of health-related resources.[2]

In Canada, the census divides people aged sixty-five and over into six main categories, as set out in Table 2.1:

Table 2.1 Population by Age and Sex

65-69	70-74	75-79	80-84	85-89	90 and over
3.7%	3.2%	2.6%	1.6%	0.9%	0.4%

Source: Adapted from Statistics Canada, 2001: *Population by Sex and Age.* statscan.ca/English/Pgdb/People/Population/demo10a.htm

The total number of persons aged sixty-five and over in Canada in 1996 represented 12.9 percent of the overall population.

Other countries with high populations of persons aged sixty-five and over include those listed in Table 2.2:

Table 2.2 Aging Population by Selected Countries

United States	12.7%
Netherlands	13%
Japan	13.1%
France	14.5%
Italy	14.8%
Germany	15%
Switzerland	15%
United Kingdom	15.8%

Source: Statistics Canada, catalogue no. 91-213-XPB; and United Nations, 1993 *Demographic Year Book*, cited in Statistics Canada 1999b.

Demography plays a crucial role in the gerontological enterprise because the use of vital statistics pertaining to percentage of population, gender, geographic differences and so on can inform governments and other decision makers about what types of programs and services need be provided to support an increasing older population. Also fundamental to any discussion of the needs of older persons is an understanding of what, how and by whom these needs might be met.

When we asked older persons for their awareness of and reactions to gerontology they had a variety of opinions. Generally, participants in the focus groups had an idea about the subject of gerontology. We asked them such questions as: What do you think gerontology is? What do you know about gerontology? How do you know about gerontology and from where did you get your information?

For the most part people described the subject as having to do with "studying old age." Within the Caucasian focus groups, three-quarters of the participants had heard the word "gerontology," while in the Black and Mi'kmaw focus groups only one-third of the participants had heard the word. Some of the definitions we were given included this one from Rose, a seventy-six-year-old from a small Hants County town: "Gerontology is the study of the aspects of human aging including physical, social and emotional, and probably spiritual. I read about it and got some information on the Internet." In her response to our questionnaire, Marie, who is sixty-nine years old, married, and living in Ottawa, offered this definition:

> It is the scientific study of the aging process as well as a search for strategies to avoid or assist problems of aging. I probably heard about gerontology while in university, and it seems I have heard about this subject for as long as I can remember.

The knowledge expressed within these focus groups came from a variety of sources, including nursing school, university, the media, reading materials, and friends and acquaintances. Some mention was made of *Fifty Plus*, the magazine published by the Canadian Association of Retired Persons (CARP) and, more recently, of CARP's Web site. One participant exclaimed: "I have more fun chatting in the chat rooms. The day passes by so quickly when you are chatting away about memories, interests and just whatever."

Many participants were familiar with the *Senior Citizens' Secretariat Newsletter*, which is published out of Halifax. This newsletter is published four times a year and is an excellent resource, keeping people up to date with the latest workshops available, legislation updates, and various topics of interest to older persons. *The Seniors Advocate*, published out of Waverley, Nova Scotia, and *Aged to Perfection*, published out of Wolfville, were other publications mentioned in our discussions. Educational and television news programs were a source of information for many of the participants.

Other questions we presented to our focus groups included: Who studies gerontology? Why would anyone want to study aging? and Does gerontology have any impact on your life?

There was general agreement that nurses, doctors, psychologists, social workers, and caregivers would be the most obvious professionals to study the aging process. Interestingly, only one focus group mentioned product manufacturers. According to one community activist in this group:

> There are now many products manufactured with the "over fifty" in mind. Even vitamins, "Formula for Seniors, 29 Vitamins and Minerals for people over 50" are in drugstores everywhere. There are also special "arms" for getting items down from high shelves, special eating utensils for people who have had strokes, stools and grab bars for bathrooms, uplift toilet seats, you name it!

Pat, who is in her eighties and has been a widow for many years, sat looking out over the Bay of Fundy and sadly related the following story:

> I hope that the study of aging researchers will come up with a magic formula for dealing with "loss." This is the most pressing issue for me, and I sure would like to know any coping skills that have been discovered. I get so lonely. Even a daily phone call makes life easier for me. I try to keep busy but I have lost a husband and a child, and as I get older it gets more lonely. And now I am losing relatives and close friends. I feel very sad and lonely.

Others in this same group of rural women hoped that studying the process of aging might help to lessen its effects and somehow lead to people staying healthier longer. One jovial woman in her seventies commented, "Maybe they will find a happy pill we can all take. They sure give us enough other pills!"

Lyn invoked the prevention of illness: "So many people are living so much longer. When I was a girl people usually died in their sixties and seventies, but with all the new miracle drugs we are living so much longer. I guess they are studying how to keep us living forever!" She then went on to talk passionately about her experience in the local community club:

I don't know what I would do without the club. Everyone keeps each other going. We grew up together and supported each other in the good times and in the bad times. I remember a past president of the club, Deborah, who in later years was immobile with bad legs. She couldn't walk very far but she would keep in touch with the women in the club. She continued to bake for the bake sales we would have, she sent little notes of encouragement to us from time to time. She was no longer an active member in the club but she remained connected with us until she died. It's friendships and connections like this that can't be replaced. In my own life I couldn't carry on without these ties and close relationships. People in the professions need to know how important meaningful connections are to all of us.

While they support one another individually, there is no organized activity in this particular community that might help them look at their own journeys and what they are experiencing or feeling.[3] Anna, an eighty-four-year-old widow who lived in a rural community in the Annapolis Valley, discussed why she felt that aging is studied: "I guess it is studied because people are interested in studying aging. Actually it is a situation that all of us will be in, if we are lucky. I imagine many disciplines study aging: nursing, medicine, social services including law, psychology, physiology, pension plans, perhaps religions."

Another focus group in a small rural community in Nova Scotia suggested looking at the study of demographics and how it relates to issues of aging. Edna, an outspoken widow in her eighties, justified this as follows: "It seems to me they better know how many of us there are going to be around here and plan for the future. We are living longer and longer." Others suggested that studying aging would help to discover issues faced by older persons and, thus, make it easier to arrive at solutions to them. In one small fishing village it was noted that young people joining the various professions mentioned above not only needed to study aging, but that they also needed to come into contact with "the real thing." According to Edna:

Many of the younger people today live away from their families and are not in contact with older persons. We need to catch the young people wherever we find them and interact with them. It is up to us to encourage them in their endeavours and maybe, from time to time, squeeze in some of our own stories and experiences!

Most group members felt that practical experience should form part of the education of future caregivers. Indeed, many of the retired professionals in our groups spoke of the importance of fieldwork, believing that it is through "real experience" that one changes one's perspectives. Indeed, as we conducted this research, we were changed through hearing the stories of those older than ourselves.

Many participants hoped that the study of aging would take note of the sandwich generation—the generation "sandwiched" between those in their eighties/nineties and those in their thirties/forties. This generation, especially its women, are in their sixties or seventies and are trying to care for an aging parent or parents. Betty, who was from a small fishing village, told us her story. She was sixty and had looked after her aging mother, who was in her late eighties. Her mother had a geriatric assessment, and a team was set up to help her cope. As her mother's needs were addressed, it gave Betty the free time she needed to continue her care: "The whole concept of the studying of aging is important to identify the needs of not only the recipient of care but the caregiver as well. It is important that all helping professions have an understanding of the concept of aging and all its implications. When I got the help I needed I got some of my life back!"

Betty's case had a positive outcome, but a good number of the women who were the sole caregivers for a parent or parents suffered badly from burnout. For example, Ethel, a seventy-year-old woman in the same focus group as Betty, stated: "I was glad to do it, but I could never do it again. I would not want my daughter to have to go through what I went through!"

During our research we encountered a variety of experiences. Where people knew how to gain access to services and were insistent upon having their needs met, there was some relief available, especially for the sandwiched women. However, it was evident that, if individuals did not have the "drive" or the "know how" to gain access to the system, then people fell through the cracks. In many cases there simply weren't enough homecare workers to give the requisite relief. When you can only get two hours of homecare every two weeks, or two hours of house-cleaning per day (as is currently the situation with Home Care Nova Scotia), what happens during the remaining hours and days?

We noticed that participants aged eighty and over tended to lean on families for support and encouragement, while younger aging persons tended to be more open to non-traditional methods of service. Younger group members recognized that it was not always possible for families to help out. Many of their adult children had moved out of the area to find employment and were not available for their long-term care. As Beth, a seventy-year-old from a rural small town mentioned:

> I have all the help I need from Homecare with respect to my personal care, cooking and helping me with grocery lists and the taking of my "meds." However, what I really need is someone to do my gardening and outside maintenance. That is what stresses me the most. I love my garden!

In other words, the focus group participants think that what governments and social agencies are doing with regard to learning more about the needs of the aging population is fine but that more work needs be done with regard to individual needs. Government policies seem to be very general, and people are lumped together as though they all need the same care. However, as participants noted, individual problems need to be recognized. For example, the issue of gardening and outside maintenance came up fairly often. People seemed to derive spiritual solace from their gardens, and losing the ability to garden was a major concern for many.

Many of the participants in our focus groups hoped that the studying of aging would lead to its demystification. Jennie, a seventy-seven-year-old retired nurse from a small town took an extension course at George Brown College of Nursing in the late 1980s. During this course she was given a handout prepared by the Ontario Psycho-geriatric Association entitled "The Gerontological Principles." She explained:

> The principles suggested that the elderly are a heterogeneous group with a variety of lifestyles and needs. They differ from one another more than they do from the young and even more than the young do from each other; the great majority of older people are relatively healthy and are living at home. Most of them are not disabled, dependent or depressed; older people have the desire and the potential to be productive, contributing members of society. Remember Maslow's theories of hierarchy? Well, the needs of those growing older are the same: (1) physiological, (2) safety, (3) belonging, (4) self-esteem, and (5) self-actualization. We still have these same needs, and our potential is really not related to chronological age but more to income, occupation and education. We have different needs for health and social services than the young-old, those from say sixty-five to eighty, and the old-old. But it's never too late to start good

health habits, and older people, myself included, want to be independent for as long as possible.

Jennie, getting caught up in remembering her studies and courses, went on to say: "I believe family support, housing and socio-economic factors are more important than health services in keeping us independent. I think I see my condition as better than those around me think it is. It goes without saying we all want to make our own decisions!"

In the June 2000 issue of *Canadian Living* there is an article by Julie Ovenell-Cart (2000). It is entitled "Older and Wiser," and in it she asks the question, "What is old, really?" and attempts to dispel several common myths about aging. In her preamble she states that aging is not a "disease and that it is perfectly normal to be a thinking, alert 90-year-old." She reminds us that the Canada Coordinating Committee for the International Year of Older Persons had stated: "Aging is inevitable and irreversible but does not automatically lead to ill health."

The first myth Ovenell-Cart looks at is: "Living to be 100 is unnatural and centenarians are exceptional" (73). She suggests that scientists are now calculating a maximum age span of about 120 years. She states that the average life expectancy in Canada is currently about 78.6 and that Statistics Canada predicts that, by 2041, 23 percent of Canadians will be over sixty-five.

Another myth Ovenell-Cart mentions is: "After a certain age it is hard to learn anything new" (73). She discusses research that indicates that brain cells can actually learn new roles, which could explain why stroke victims are often able to regain many of their normal functions. We only have to look at the number of seniors going back to university, writing books, taking on politicians, and learning how to operate computers to know that this particular myth is completely untrue. However, it is difficult to dispel. Society in general needs to realize that older persons may learn differently from, and take a little longer than, others; but this does not mean that they cannot learn new things. We, as researchers in the early stages of aging, expect to be learning new things until we take our last breaths. The majority of older persons we interviewed were of the same mind.

With regard to the popular myth "seniors are an economic drain on society," Overnell-Carter states, "according to Statistics Canada, fewer than one in five seniors currently live in a low-income situation. Most have retirement savings and are financially independent" (74).

In *The Best Is Yet to Be*, Sybil Shack (1984) also challenges myths about aging, one of which is that older people create a financial drain on the rest of the population. In this essay she suggests just the opposite—that older people create jobs. Not only the sciences of geriatrics and gerontology, but also a whole new industry of manufacturers has been created to help take care of older persons. Shack discusses the fact that older persons paid into pension plans, annuities, stock markets, and the like. All these monies are being used as investments for big corporations: "We create jobs because of our age .... A whole industry has developed around the care and handling of us ... to educate us .... Reporters, researchers, programmers, social workers, clergy, counsellors, nurses, aids, administrators, cooks, teachers, and cleaners—many of them would be out of jobs if it were not for us" (35).

While we will not go into all the myths surrounding the aging process, suffice it to note that today, in 2001, we are still trying to dispel the myths that were written about in the 1980s. Why is this? The seniors we interviewed wondered this same thing. Here, again, we see the power of ageism. Marie, our questionnaire respondent from Ottawa, summed it up this way: "Gerontology has changed the political climate in terms of people being more aware about the increases in an aging population, the impact on health care costs and the need for preventative strategies." We would tend to agree with Marie. Certainly the aging process has a much higher public profile now than it did during most of the twentieth century. Senior citizens are speaking out; they seem healthier and more active than they have in past generations, and they are taking preventative health measures rather than "cures" for old age.

CARP is one example of how seniors are participating in tending to their own needs. Seniors write articles on subjects such as money management, travel ideas, prevention of illnesses to name just a few. CARP's Web site, http://www.50plus.com/carp/about/main.cfm, supplies information on health, money, family, leisure, home, community, learning, and travel. There are chat rooms, jokes of the day, fun and games, discussion forums, and crossword puzzles, to name but a few options available for the active older person. Older persons who are still active in their professions submit many of the articles written and advice given.

Gerontology, the study of aging, has indeed raised the public profile of the older person; but this work has only just begun. As our participants have told us, we need to strike a balance between the academic study of a particular group and the voices of the members of that group.

Many focus group participants felt that it was crucial for older persons to be more involved in the homecare arena. To them, the fact that we were asking for their input was an eye-opener. We received a very positive response to the fact that we were listening to what they had to say. When we asked how gerontologists and older persons could work together, many responded with comments such as: "[By] doing what you are doing! Coming here and talking with us, asking us questions and being genuinely interested in what we have to say." It was important for them to be heard. Some participants invoked the notion that certain features of growing older (such as reduced eyesight, loss of hearing, slower response times, arthritic joints, and so on) are a natural part of aging and that such losses could be seen as challenges rather than as personal problems. For example, Sally, a seventy-seven-year old former nurse living in a small rural community said: "As I have gotten older I have slowed down and need to give myself extra time to get things done. But this is a normal part of the aging experience."

NOTES

1. Ageing International is an international group of gerontological researchers and practitioners who publish a journal of the same name, hold conferences and workshops around the world, and sometimes conduct research surveys.

2. For further discussion of the classification of older people, see Warner Schnie (1999) or just about any other gerontology text.

3. Many seniors groups have a variety of organized programs, such as bingo, card games, exercise programs, lunches, quilting bees, yard sales, community advocacy, and so on. Often these activities, which are structured around a specific theme, also encourage and provide the opportunity to share thoughts, feelings, and experiences, thereby providing participants with a chance to socialize and to extend their awareness and perceptions beyond their own lives. As well, some women in rural communities are busy with food catering and other fund-raising events that help to keep buildings and programs in operation.

Chapter Two

Theories of Aging and Their Practical Application

THEORY AND IDEOLOGY

One of the activities in which scientists engage in order to distinguish their discipline or profession from others is the construction of theories. The work of a theory is, given certain stated conditions, to describe, explain, and sometimes predict the behaviour of specific phenomena. As well, theories are constructed in order to be able to show the connections between variables such as age and retirement, age and gender, age and ethnicity, and so on. Cause and effect relationships are also often examined through the use of theory. In general, theories are expected to have universal applications; that is, it should be possible to test them in a variety of global settings.

One of the key variables that most theories of aging and gerontology utilize is that of "successful aging." The questions under consideration include: What factors enable one to age successfully? Why do some older persons age more successfully than others? Does one age more successfully if one remains active within the community? Or does one age more successfully if one disengages from some activities and engages in others? As individuals grow older, how do they interact with the broader social structures of their culture? What roles do older individuals play within society? These types of questions are what gerontologists and other social scientists attempt to answer through the construction and testing of theories.

Since the inception of gerontology, there has been a great deal of debate about the effectiveness and practical applicability of theory. Marshall (1996:12) has stated that one of the theoretical dilemma's within the field of aging stems from the fact that "the state of theory in aging and the social sciences is made more complex by the fact that most work in the field ... does not deal with aging at all, but rather with age-related issues." In another vein, Katz (1996) has argued strongly that gerontology is essentially unreflective when it comes to examining the theories produced by some of its practitioners. In a review of his own work, David Ekerdt (1998:44) notes: "To this day, gerontology rehashes disengagement and activity theory, not for its students, not because the theories are current, but because they are OURS" (emphasis in the original).

Another criticism directed at gerontological theory is that it too frequently utilizes a positivistic approach to understanding the aging process—an approach that is both empirical and reductionist (Moody 1994:xv). Those who take this stand recognize that there is not enough qualitative and normative data to adequately support theories of aging. As well, the role of lay or common sense theorizing within the lives of older persons is absent from most gerontological theory, as is the attempt to account for the aging experience through the use of narrative.

It should be noted that most of the theories that address issues of aging were formulated at the beginning of the development of gerontology; that is, they were formulated in the United States during the late 1950s and early 1960s. It is also important to stress that academic development in gerontology cannot be disconnected from practical, historical issues. During the post-Second World War period, as Katz (1996:120) has noted:

> The aging population was rapidly growing and altering longstanding demographic patterns. At the same time, mandatory retirement policies were becoming increasingly pervasive and the joint concern of government, labor unions, corporations, academics and the popular media. Intense assessment studies of retirement produced a discourse on aging that redefined the relation between work and age in ways that delimited nonretirement options.

As a result of the experiences cited by Katz, governments at all levels in Canada, as well as educational funding bodies such as the Social Sciences and Humanities Research Council and the National Sciences Research Council, also made funds available to academic researchers to produce data concerning the situations faced by older Canadians. In the late 1970s the federal government created the National Advisory Council on Aging as well as funding projects initiated by and for older persons, such as the New Horizons Program and the Seniors Independence Program (neither of which, ironically, exists today). Most recently, in 2000, the federal government created the National Framework on Aging, whose goal is to "promote the well-being and contributions of older people in all aspects of life" (http://www.hc-sc.gc.ca/seniors-aines/nfa-cnv/en/index/htm).

Theory is not just a scientific exercise: ordinary people constantly theorize about how the world works as they try to make sense of their own actions and the actions of others. These everyday realities are seldom folded into scientific accounts of growing older.

Those academics and practitioners concerned with the advocacy role of gerontology argue that a more useful theoretical approach to creating knowledge about old age would involve constructing a critical gerontology that would be radical in its terms of reference and that would include a political component. This would mean that, where the data suggest the need for action, gerontologists would advocate on behalf of older persons. Cole, Andrew, Achenbaum, Jakobi, and Kastenbaum (1993) stress these ideas in *Voices and Visions of Aging: Toward a Critical Gerontology*. So while there are many theories of aging, there is also a great deal of dispute regarding their effectiveness and their practical ability to address issues of concern to older persons and those with whom they interact.

There are a large number of theories in gerontology that attempt to explain how and why it is that people grow older in the ways that they do. Social theories are interested in explaining how various societal institutions function to accommodate aging individuals. A theory, then, is a sense-making device that helps us to understand what happens to individuals and social structures as they proceed through the life course.

Bengston and Schaie (1999:5) argue that the principal role of theory is "to provide a set of lenses through which we can view and make sense of what we observe in research. The principal use of theory is *to build knowledge and understanding*" (emphasis in original). According to these authors, theory has four functions: (1) the integration of knowledge ("a good theory summarizes the many discrete findings from empirical studies and incorporates them into a brief statement that describes linkages among the crucial observations, variables, or theoretical constructs"); (2) the explanation of knowledge ("a useful theory provides not only description of the ways empirically observed phenomena are related [this is what 'models' reflect] but also *how* and especially *why* they are related, in a logically sound account incorporating antecedents and consequences of empirical results"); (3) predictions about what is not yet known or observed ("research based on theory can lead to subsequent discoveries based on principles proposed by earlier theory"); and (4) interventions to improve human conditions ("theory is valuable when we attempt to apply and advance existing knowledge in order to solve problems or alleviate undesirable conditions") (all parenthetical quotes taken from page 7, emphasis in original). For Bengston and Schaie, theory building is a crucial step in formulating knowledge and understanding about old age and aging, and it involves collecting data in a systematic and cumulative way in order to support or refute the theoretical propositions being put forth.

Theory production is one of the ways in which gerontology claims to be a knowledge broker in the business of creating academic and public information about the lives of older citizens. As Tulle-Winton (1999:284) notes: "Gerontology is the principal 'discipline' which codifies power/knowledge with respect to later life." Gerontologists are seen to be the primary agents involved in discourse on old age and aging, whether they do this within academic settings or as consultants and social policy planners working for governments or the private sector. Katz (1996:44) has recognized that, in the production of knowledge about old age—and in theory construction—gerontologists have become recognized as the owners of "power/knowledge relations which prevail in the wider society."

In Chapter 1, it was proposed that gerontologists help construct ideological notions of agedness. These ideological notions are related to the process of theory construction in that the variables being tested are based upon certain assumptions about how the world works—assumptions that are, in turn, based upon ideas. Here, we want to discuss the topic of ideology with respect to its role as an analytic tool within the social production of knowledge. An ideology is a system of shared ideas that motivates persons to move towards mutually agreed upon goals. It also represents the social consensus of a specific group, in this case gerontologists, concerning the nature of concepts held to be universally true for a given group of individuals. Ideology becomes, in the words of Dorothy Smith (1975:2), "a kind of practice in thinking about society. To think ideologically is therefore to think in a distinctive and describable way. Ideas, concepts, as such are not ideological. They are ideological by virtue of being used in ideological ways." When one group of persons uses ideas to manipulate another they are frequently spoken of as serving a vested interest. According to Berger (1963:111), "We speak of an ideology when a certain idea serves a vested interest in society. Very frequently, though not always, ideological systems distort social reality in order to come out where it is functional for them to do so."

Clifford Geertz (1973:196) views the concept of ideology in a somewhat different way from Berger. For him, ideology is not an "entity in itself—an ordered system, of cultural symbols" but, rather, something that is to be examined within its "social and psychological" context. Arguing that the social sciences have chosen to view ideology in an evaluative, mostly pejorative, way, Geertz suggests that, before conclusions are reached as to how ideologies might be used, scientists should reconstruct data gathered from everyday life events and reconstruct them in ways different from those in which they were originally presented. In particular, he raises an awareness of how ideologies help to structure situations through the use of cultural patterns and symbols. Obviously, ideology is a diversely defined concept.

As we argued in Chapter 1, part of the ideological perspective from within which gerontology operates still holds that aging is a "social problem." As recently as 2001, Cox (2001:22) reiterates the oft-quoted mantra: "at age 65 older Americans are often confronted with a series of developmental and adjustment problems." Clearly, this negative view of old age is still prevalent in the minds of some gerontologists.

Another tenet of the ideological base of gerontological work is that it "helps the aged." Basic texts on gerontology raise the issue of helping the old, citing it as a useful and important thing to do. Such materials often include chapters or sections on caring for aged parents, protective services for seniors, and caring for the old in the community. In the minds of many, the terms "help" and "caring" seem to be synonymous with gerontology. Within the body of ideas that make up what many recognize as gerontology is the ideological stance that helping and caring for the old is one of the discipline's major functions. The notion of "help" thus becomes part of the rationale for becoming involved in gerontology. It also does the work of presenting the self as a caring and kind individual committed to the needs of others. It is difficult to account for such an individual as primarily "self-serving" because the notion of "helping" implies that she/he is in the service of others.

A distinction should be made here between the ideology of individuals and the ideology of a group. An individual may hold a variety of different opinions on many subjects. She or he will normally attempt to share and articulate, perhaps even argue, these opinions with others. In the case of gerontology, we are interested in the ideas of the group even though those ideas may be presented to us by individuals. An illustration of the process of turning individual thoughts into group ideology will perhaps be useful here.

In the 1970s, as a member of the Committee on Aging set up by the Social Planning and Review Council of British Columbia, I (Jeanette) was involved in policy discussion and the formulation and subsequent implementation of the Long Term Care Program, which came into effect in the province in 1978. As a member of this planning group, I was required, along with my colleagues, to articulate and clarify my basic ideas about a policy that, with support services, would enable unwell people to stay within their homes for as long as possible. In order to produce plans for such a program, our individual ideas concerning equality for all persons in the health care field, a shared commitment to care for the unwell, and the need to restructure and reallocate health care delivery systems and costs became what we as a group decided to call our "ideology" of long-term care. When we met with provincial government officials, we used the term "ideology" to describe all the basic ideas that, as a group, we had agreed upon as important and relevant to our task; namely, formulation of policy.

We are suggesting that gerontologists, as a group, are involved in a similar process—a process through which individual thoughts, feelings, and experiences become part of what can be recognized and supported as a collective ideology about their work and those they study (i.e., the old). The vehicles that maintain, reinforce, and make visible ideological concerns about elderly people can be found in the theoretical paradigms of gerontological work. Theories, in part, are the mirrors that reflect how social scientists (and others) view old age.

METHODS

Within the social sciences in general, theory-testing involves at least two methods of data collection: the quantitative and the qualitative. In the former, the emphasis is on the quantity of data that is collected. Quantitative methods include surveys and mass interviews, the goal being to acquire as much data as possible in the least expensive and most efficient manner. When using such methods of data collection a great deal of general information can be obtained from vast numbers of people in any given sample. One example of a quantitative method is the Canada census; other examples include Gallop polls and telephone surveys about consumer buying habits. Qualitative methods, unlike quantitative methods, generally involve an intense intersubjective relationship with the person or persons being studied. Examples of qualitative methods include case studies, face-to-face interviews, focus group discussions and oral histories.

SOCIAL THEORIES OF AGING

In order for knowledge to be visible, it has to be thought about, written down, spoken of, taught, learned, and compared with other knowledge. As well, it needs to be operationalized within such contexts as the formulation of policy; the provision of goods, services, and programs; government decisions; and so on. In our society, knowledge, in its most correct and pristine form, is believed to be found within educational settings. Given this, the knowledge of the gerontologist (i.e., the scientist/academic) differs from the knowledge of the old person (i.e., the non-academic/layperson). Whereas scientific/academic knowledge is based upon the observed and documented experiences of many older persons and is obtained from a variety of social settings and activities, the everyday knowledge of the old is equally important to an understanding of the total aging process. Living, as we do, within an interactive, social community, even though our experiences may be unique to us as individuals, we nonetheless share a world in common with those around us. Whereas scientific knowledge is accumulated through the systematic collection of data, everyday knowledge is accumulated through the continuous exploration and observation of routine, everyday events.

In order to utilize the personal knowledge of the old within the gerontological enterprise as it is currently constructed in North America, the aspects of aging as a lived experience are codified, translated, and tabulated; they are transformed into material that is recognizable as data that fits into the scientific body of knowledge known as gerontology. Ideologies play an important role in this process of reinterpreting people's lives to fit some other ordering. Bailey (1975:32) reminds us that ideologies are "an organized set of convictions ... which enforce inevitable value judgments." When choosing to look at one aspect of aging and not another, gerontologists are utilizing a value judgment; that is, they are making an ideological commitment to one avenue of inquiry over another.

A review of gerontology textbooks produced during the last twenty-plus years shows that nearly all of them include a chapter on theories of aging. Many also note that these theories can be discussed in terms of two levels—the micro and the macro. Micro-level theories focus upon the older individual and her/his social interactions with others. Such theories examine the relationships between older persons and their social networks, their reactions to ageism, their experiences of living with aging bodies, and so on. So, for example, to examine the life of an older person through a microscope, with your range of vision limited to that human organism and how it reacts to various stimuli, is to engage in micro-level theory.

Macro-level theories examine how the aging individual and the social structures and organizations within which she or he lives interact with, and react to, one another. So, for example, to examine the governmental polices and societal values that require older persons to retire at age sixty-five, or to ask why it is that more older women than older men live below the government-designated low-income cut-off line, is to engage in macro-level theorizing.

Within the standard texts, theories of gerontology and aging are generally presented in terms of three main perspectives: the functionalist, the conflict, and the symbolic interactionist. Some texts, especially those written by women, also offer a feminist perspective. According to Novak and Campbell (2001:19), the functionalist perspective treats "society as a system that consists of social institutions like the family, the military, and educational institutions. These systems keep society in a dynamic equilibrium." What is key to the functionalist perspective is "equilibrium," or "balance." In order to explain how it is that a society deals with growing older, functionalists posit that various social structures—such as retirement policies, government health and income services, and community-based programs such as adult day care—are all society's ways of dealing with the changes to the social system that result as the number of persons aged sixty-five and over increases. As Novak and Campbell further note, "Structural functionalism sometimes draws the analogy between society and a living organism. Just as our bodies will adjust to an increase in our blood sugar, so will society adjust to an increase in its internal condition" (19). Theorists who use the functionalist perspective are interested in explaining how the social system adapts to changing demographics and how it can be used to predict how society will "attempt to create an orderly transition to a new, stable state" (19).

The conflict perspective relies heavily on the work of Karl Marx (1918), who asserted, among other things, that capitalist society is a site of struggle and inequality that generates conflict and change. Following from this, growing older is seen to create disharmony and conflict between older persons and others in the population, especially with regard to such issues as retirement, ageism, discrimination on the basis of age, and, more recently, the role that new technologies play in the lives of older workers. Other issues conducive to the conflict perspective include those related to modernization, globalization, and development. Political economists often employ the conflict perspective in order to explain the state of redundant labour—a state caused by enforced retirement programs, which result in older persons becoming dependent upon governments.

Novak and Campbell (2001:21) argue that the conflict perspective traces the "struggle between social classes and the resulting dominance of some groups and the subordination of others." The conflict perspective also allows us to examine the uneasy alliance between older persons and the discipline of gerontology. It enables us to see who has the power to influence policy (i.e., the experts) and who does not (i.e., old people).

Related to the conflict perspective is the political economy perspective, which examines the plight of older persons with limited financial resources within the context of the political and economic structures of capitalist societies. It also looks at "how social programs and policies for older people serve the interests of middle aged, middle-class professionals" (Novak and Campbell 2001:21). The political economy perspective enables one to examine how it is that governments decide which services and programs are appropriate for the older population. It also enables us to examine how global issues affect less well developed countries as they strive to become more like capitalist ones, and how industrialization and improved technology forces older people out of the workforce so that they can be replaced with younger, supposedly better educated ones. This perspective can also be useful in documenting intergenerational conflict over existing resources in terms of the allocation of funds on the basis of age.

Both the conflict perspective and the political economy perspective can utilize either a micro or a macro approach, although, because they are concerned with the interaction between older persons and the social structures within which they live, they normally employ the latter. On the other hand, the interpretive approach to the study of aging usually relies on a micro-level approach because it is primarily concerned with the ways in which older persons define, maintain, and socially construct the aging experience. The interpretive perspective allows older persons to be the creators of knowledge and information about their own lives; they are both the objects and subjects of study.

The symbolic interactionist perspective assumes that aging is a product of the everyday interactions of individuals as they move through their lives. It also examines the social and physical environments within which older persons engage in daily activities, the assumption being that these facilities are created in order to enable certain types of interaction. For example, do nursing homes, adult day centres, programs for seniors, and so on encourage independence? Or do they encourage learned helplessness?

The feminist perspective is a relatively recent addition to gerontological theories and is generally subsumed within the perspectives just discussed. Browne (1998) has noted that, in the past, feminist scholarship concerned itself with issues such as motherhood, women and the workforce, sexuality, reproduction, and so on. She argues that "many of the problems faced by older women are a direct result of a lifetime of multiple oppressions" (xix). Some of these oppressions include sexism (which pervades all cultures); discrimination on the basis of age, race, sexual preference, and gender; inequalities in the workforce, within family life, and in society in general; the double standard of aging, which posits older men, but not older women, as "mature, interesting and attractive"; and a variety of other socially prescribed attitudes that provide an "interlocking of sexism and ageism" (xxiii). Feminist gerontology also addresses the ironic situation faced by older lesbians, who, unlike their heterosexual sisters, are seen primarily in sexual terms (Auger 1992).

By now it should be clear that gerontological theories are more than mere explanatory, predictive devices; they are also particular ways of looking at, and reflecting upon, visions of old age. The role that theories play in the social production of knowledge functions to legitimize certain attitudes and beliefs about aging by positing them as more valid than those derived from "non-scientific" information. In addition, by selecting certain variables as dominant, theories also help to create "givens." In other words, by encouraging the researcher to focus only upon those phenomena that fall within its framework, theories often act as blinders, thus seriously limiting what they can tell us.

As was mentioned at the beginning of this chapter, all major social theories of aging attempt to describe, explain, and predict peoples' ability to adapt to old age; that is, their ability to engage in what is known as "successful" aging. What should now be clear is that theorists make certain assumptions about the notion of successful aging and then seek to discover which particular personal or social characteristics can best account for it. It is now time to discuss certain gerontological theories in some detail.

Disengagement Theory

Disengagement theory, which was devised by Elaine Cumming and William Henry in 1961, is one of the most predominant in gerontology. It attempts to explain the social organization of old age using a functionalist perspective (which was originally borrowed from the biological sciences). It asserts that the behaviour of all individuals is the direct result of the social structure's need for equilibrium. Within this perspective, individuals are seen as parts of the social structure that must maintain order through performing various functional requirements. So, for example, seen through a functionalist lens, growing older and retiring at a specific chronological age serves the social function of redistributing society's resources through making room in the paid workforce for younger people.

When disengagement theory is specifically applied to aging, the latter is seen as an essential "function" of life in that it enables the young to replace the elderly with regard to the performance of various social roles. This replacement is seen to be a functional prerequisite for maintaining constant balance within the social system. According to Cumming and Henry (1961:13): "In our theory, aging is an inevitable mutual withdrawal or disengagement; resulting in decreased interaction between the aging person and others in the social system he belongs to."

The authors see disengagement as inevitable because death is inevitable. Death, as a function of the social structure, must be incorporated into it without causing any disruption or risking the equilibrium of the system. According to disengagement theory, mandatory retirement as well as loss of income and social prestige can be seen as necessary and inevitable functions of society. This theory normalizes what might otherwise be seen as disruptive, problematic, or dysfunctional. The notion of inevitability is one of the theory's major universal propositions. However, there is a great deal of information about the aging process in other cultures, where people do not and cannot retire at a certain age, where, unlike in North America, they do not lose respect and prestige.

Recent publications by Sokolovsky (1997) and Lassey and Lassey (2001), as well as the Newsletter of the Anthropology and Aging Society (Washington, DC), provide excellent overviews of the global status of older persons, showing that, in countries such as India, China, and Japan, there is in fact a great deal of respect for elders. This theme is echoed in the (albeit scarce) material on the status of Aboriginal elders in Canada. For example, see the works of Gold (1980), Frideres (1994), and Moore (1995).

Because disengagement theory uses a functionalist perspective, it cannot explain why and how some individuals do not withdraw, or disengage, from society as they grow older. Implicit within the functionalist view is the assumption that society is normatively structured to operate smoothly. This being the case, it is essential that everyone behave in the same way at certain times in their lives; therefore, disengagement theory is incapable of dealing with deviations from expected behaviour.

Disengagement theory attempts to explain why it is necessary to produce a system in which older people must be encouraged to withdraw. Because it is concerned with explaining aging in functionalist terms, it does not address how the older person perceives his or her aging process (especially with regard to enforced or involuntary disengagement). This theory sees successful aging as involving the individual accepting and, indeed, planning in advance for her/his withdrawal from certain social roles. It sees such withdrawal as natural, intrinsic, and typical. The tacit consequences of disengagement theory are that older people expect to alter their way of life after age sixty-five. Further, it provides a functionalist rationale for why older persons should be excluded from mainstream activities within their communities. It follows that, if, as the theory claims, mutual withdrawal benefits the old, then inactivity is to be encouraged in the elderly. Social services for the elderly would then be directed not towards helping them to attain self-determination but, rather, towards helping them to live lives of diminished activity.

The vision of old age that disengagement theory posits would see the elderly segregated from the rest of society by virtue of chronological age, the assumed behaviours that are concomitant with reaching a certain age, and social practices such as retirement.

But what about situations, especially for those older persons with deteriorating mental health (e.g., those afflicted with Alzheimer's disease), where disengagement is a consequence of a disorder rather than of a conscious choice? What of situations in which disengagement may come about due to widowhood or the loss of a partner, lack of adequate transportation or health services, low incomes, and so on? In these situations disengagement is neither natural nor intrinsic to the aging process; rather, it is the consequence of a lack of government and/or private-sector services.

We found that many of the people in our focus groups were familiar with disengagement theory and took exception to some of its fundamental assertions. Participants in the Halifax focus group reacted to it in a loud and assertive manner. Nellie, a sixty-six-year-old former tour guide, jumped off her chair, stood in the middle of the room with her hands on her hips, looked Diane straight in the eye, and said:

> Disengagement theory! That is pure military talk and I don't like it. Why do they [scientists] have to use military language anyway? Disengaging the enemy, is that what they think we are doing? I haven't disengaged from anything! I chose to retire from paid employment. Disengagement sounds like I am running away. I didn't disengage from living or doing what I want to do. I only changed what I am doing. I didn't even disengage from the workplace altogether. The volunteer work I do involves businesspeople, private people and the like. I totally disagree with this language!

Annie, who was in her sixties and was a former nurse in the same focus group, put it this way:

> We haven't disengaged, we have changed. We are using our experiences in different vocations. We may have less obligations but we are still very much engaged with life. I volunteer on hospital boards, health boards and, from time to time, with other community organization where my expertise in the health profession can be helpful. I now have the time to do what I find life-giving. I love to help others and now I can do it on my own time and in my own way. Whoever came up with that idea anyway? Or, more importantly, the language? I don't like to be labelled as disengaging from anything. I have simply changed what I do.

In a group consisting of women from several small towns in the Annapolis Valley, Anne, a seventy-five-year-old member of the local small town bridge club and a retired teacher, commented:

> I made the decision to leave teaching. The word "disengage" doesn't fit how I see my actions. I guess you could say I disengaged from the classroom but I find that word too final or negative in some way. I like to say that I left teaching and am now on the next part of my journey in this life. I have a passion for gardening, for community activity and my social life is booming! I don't call that disengaging!

Lil, a seventy-seven-year-old former nurse in the same group, put it this way:

> I don't think women ever retire, we simply change jobs some-times. However, what I have noticed is that many men seem lost when they first retire from long time professions. It usually takes about a year for some of them to recover and find new interests. Women who retire simply go with the flow, doing the house and finding new activities to interest them—sometimes ones they always wanted to do and never had the time. I always wanted to paint—now I do.

The members of a group from a small fishing village on the Bay of Fundy did not have any previous knowledge about the theories of aging.

They were very active in their community and did not see themselves as disengaging from much. The two men in the group seemed to go along with whatever their wives suggested, happily chopping wood, playing cards, and driving their partners to shopping activities, meetings, and doctors appointments. Several of the women had worked outside the home and were now engaging in the hobbies they loved. Doris described her passion for rug hooking and braiding:

> The floors of my house are covered with my creations. I just started one day and I haven't stopped yet. I hook rugs for everyone in my family, my friends and for sale. I am now braiding around the creations I have hooked. I can be as creative as I want to. I am having a ball! I didn't disengage. I simply followed my passion to create new things!

Marie, our Ottawa respondent, pointed out that perhaps people who are eighty or over might "participate less in social, cultural and recreational activities, perhaps because of financial or health constraints, but that isn't really disengagement."

Ann, a seventy-year-old grandmother living in a small fishing village on the Bay of Fundy, was uncomfortable with the term "disengagement"; however, she did note that she had had a very difficult time leaving her place of work and finding new activities:

> It was hard for me to leave work. I wasn't in the best of health and I found myself cut off from my friends at work. For a while I didn't even feel like getting up in the morning. It took me awhile to get adjusted. Probably a year or so. Now I am really busy with club work, the church and knitting mittens for all my children and grandchildren. They love my mitts and it keeps me busy because their hands grow and they are forever losing their mittens. I don't know about the word "disengagement," but I know the feeling when a part of your life just "ends." It takes awhile.

The late Maggie Kuhn (as cited in Seskin 1980) described involvement and aging as follows:

> You don't retire from life. You just recycle and redirect your goals. (126)

My generation was programmed to keep quiet, to accept things the way they were, to comply. We're trying to challenge that thinking .... I think older people should do with their lives whatever they wish. If they want to retire and do nothing, that's their own business. (130)

Kuhn goes on to offer her critique of disengagement theory:

The doctrine I've been preaching is one of interdependence and cooperation. That's a whole different value system from disengagement. The people who live in the fancy condominiums in Florida feel no identification with, or responsibility for, the people stealing dog food for their dinner. They're really disengaged, whether out of powerlessness or a feeling of preserving the status quo. (131)

Kuhn describes old age as a time of freedom, a time to make a difference, a time to speak out about social and health care policies that do not adequately meet the needs of older people. She believes that "young and old can and should work together for social change. Their needs and concerns are not mutually exclusive" (133).

Participants in one of the focus groups from Wolfville saw disengagement as more economic than social. As one participant put it, "we don't disengage from life!" Many agreed they had changed vocations and that they had more time to do what they really wanted to do. Don, a retired Anglican clergyman, explained: "I retired three times and three times I came back! At eighty-three I am still standing in for other clergy. I am still helping others when I can. I really don't like the word 'disengagement.'"

Needless to say, the people in the group who were involved with the peace movement didn't like the military language inherent within disengagement theory. Indeed, focus group participants in general had problems with its language, even though they could identify with some of its principles. In general, they thought that it presented a rigid and confining explanation of the aging process.

Activity Theory

In contrast to disengagement theory, activity theory asserts that withdrawal is not intrinsic, natural, or typical and that, when it does occur, it is usually against the desires and needs of normal aging persons. Havighurst and Albrecht (1953) first suggested the main ideas for activity theory in a book entitled *Older People*, which discusses their study of how people adjust to old age. A group of persons aged sixty-five and over, who lived in a Midwestern town in the United States known as "Prairie City," were interviewed about such issues as attitudes, activities, personal characteristics, and types of family structure. Their responses provided the data from which activity theory arose. In general, Havighurst and Albrecht concluded that "a person with an active, achieving, and outward-directed way of life will be best satisfied to continue this life into old age, with only slight diminution. Other people with a passive, dependent, home-centered way of life will be best satisfied with disengagement" (170). Although the researchers were interested in tracing successful aging within a developmental framework, their ideas were later formulated into theory by, among others, Lemon, Bengston, and Peterson (1972); Barron (1959); and Rose and Peterson (1965).

Utilizing activity theory, Lemon, Bengston, and Peterson (1972) hypothesized that there is a positive relationship between activity and life satisfaction. Activity is seen as a period during which the individual holds a variety of social roles, and their hypothesis asserts that the greater the loss of roles, the lower the life satisfaction: "Activity provides various role supports necessary for reaffirming one's self-concept. The more intimate and the more frequent the activity, the more specific will be the role support" (515). When Lemon, Bengston, and Peterson talk about "role supports," they are talking about the process whereby an individual chooses a role or set of roles and how that choice is supported by an audience. The notion of role support is concerned with interactionally rewarded credibility. Lemon, Bengston, and Peterson posit "life satisfaction as the degree to which one is presently content or pleased with his general life situation" (513). They define activity as "any regularized or patterned action or pursuit of personal maintenance" (ibid.).

Activity theory, unlike disengagement theory, suggests that persons are more likely to achieve successful aging if they do not disengage from society. Activity theory also holds that:

> Except for the inevitable changes in biology and health, older people are the same as middle-aged people, with essentially the same psychological and social needs .... The older person who ages optimally is the person who stays active and who manages to resist the shrinkage of his social world. He maintains the activities of middle age as long as possible and then finds substitutes for those activities he is forced to relinquish; substitutes for work when he is forced to retire; substitutes for friends and loved ones whom he loses by death. (161)

One of the problems with activity theory lies in the notion that individuals can merely exchange one set of roles or activities for another. For many, it is very difficult to replace the worker role. Most individuals are not free to shape and re-shape their social roles, and, for many, enforced retirement reduces the number of activities they can afford.

Gerontologists speak of role loss as one of the main disengagement issues that must be faced by older people. These people are seen to have lost opportunities to behave in certain ways: as employed persons (due to enforced retirement); as relative, partner, spouse, or friend (due to death, ill health, or lack of income); as parent and provider to young children (due to family members leaving home).

Because activity theory relies upon a developmental framework (i.e., because it attempts to describe behaviour from birth to death as a series of pre-thought-out steps), it cannot deal with a person's unplanned reactions to events such as retirement, loss, and ill health. Although developmentalists may claim that people are constantly preparing for the next stage of their development, that they are, in a sense, always "learning to cope" with the next stage of life, very little research has been conducted to show just how (or if) individuals actually do this. Contrary to what developmentalists say about life planning, many older persons assert that there is a lot more "fate" involved in life than psychology would suggest.

Activity theory, which assumes that the more active a person is in later life, the more successfully he or she will deal with aging, offers an idealistic vision of growing older. This is especially so for the scientist who studies it and believes that it can be used to adequately predict behaviour. However, for those who believe that mere activity is not the only key to growing and changing with every passing year, this theory is somewhat unrealistic. Interestingly, activity theory, which was felt to be very similar to continuity theory (see below), was the most popular among our focus group participants, who pointed out that the biggest obstacles to being able to be "active" were poor health and immobility.

In one small fishing village the women stressed the need to stay active. Most of them had continued doing what they had always done; they had simply adapted their activities to fit the needs of their physical bodies. Dot, an eighty-year-old who had been a widow for over twenty years, described her life in this way:

> I don't know too much about all those theories, but what I do know is this. I really need to keep busy to cope with the loneliness. I love to go to my meetings, laugh with my friends,

and for a few hours I forget the loneliness. I also love to drive my car. Sometimes I will simply jump in the car and take off. I don't go anywhere in particular. I just drive. It seems to dispel the doldrums. When I come back, I feel better. I try to bake as much as I can and do all the things I always have. I visit my son in Quebec twice a year so that makes me feel better. The days pass more quickly when I am busy. When I do something for someone else, whether it's baking or talking on the phone, it takes my mind off my "stuff" when I can listen to others. I believe it is important to think of others. That way we don't end up just thinking about ourselves.

Marie, cited earlier, agreed with activity theory because it reflected her own experiences of aging: "I keep busy as much as I can. We travel a lot, the same as we used to. Now that we are retired from paid work, there is more time to travel and do what we want to do. We keep busy. We were always busy people anyway. Now we can just pick and choose more freely what we want to do."

Betty, who is from the Halifax group and is a self-described doctor's wife, homemaker, and seventy-something grandmother, described her active life this way: "I live a more gentle life now. I am still busy. I still do most of the committee work I have always done but now I put aside special time just for me. It is important for me to keep up my contacts and interests but I also need time to re-charge my battery, so to speak." Betty was soft-spoken, and her gentle manner in describing her life stood in stark contrast to the manner of some of the other women in this focus group.

Nellie, the retired tour guide cited earlier, got up and danced around the room, exclaiming:

> See, I am active! I move around a lot these days but on my own terms. No schedules to meet, no absolute commitments. I am free to do what I want to do. Yes I have to stay active. I am happier that way. But I can dance around the apartment now if I want to. I don't care what others think! I can sing more often too!

Eve, an eighty-five-year-old widow who belongs to a bridge club in a rural small town, bemoaned the fact she could no longer drive:

> I am not accepting my situation very well. I have always been active and now I have to re-adjust again. I will get there but it

will take some time. I love people and I am just going to have to get out of my apartment and visit people in the building. I will have to find a way to stay active because it makes me feel better. If I get out or do something different I forget about my problems and I can even laugh and be silly. Some kind of activity is very important for me. My mind starts to wander if I don't get out and see other people. I try to arrange card games and things like that.

Don, who is eighty-three and from a small university town, summed up his reaction to activity theory as follows:

We can decide what makes us content. We can have a meaningless or meaningful life. Activity doesn't necessarily mean physical involvement. As my eyesight gets worse, I have to work at removing obstacles so that I can continue to function and do what I want to do. However, more of my activity takes place in my thought process, in my inner world. It is not only a physical thing.

For many participants in the focus groups, this activity theory resonated with their own experiences. For them, being active is what keeps them involved in their communities and helps them to age successfully.

Continuity Theory

Continuity theory is similar to activity theory. It was proposed by Atchley (1982:183), who argued that "old age is a continuation of a person's past, rather than a different set of activities and behaviours related to growing older." He points out that, "according to our informants ... as people grow older they adapt to changes in their lifestyles, and to new situations, by relying on coping strategies used in the past" (183). In 2000, when Atchley again wrote about continuity theory (cited in Gubrium and Holstein 2000:47), he noted that the central premise of this theoretical framework is the notion that, as we age, we make "adaptive choices, middle-aged and older adults attempt to preserve and maintain existing internal and external structures and ... they prefer to accomplish this objective by using continuity, i.e. [by] applying familiar strategies in familiar arenas of life."

According to Atchley, continuity has both an "inner" and an "external" structure. The inner structure involves "the persistence of a psychic structure of ideas, temperament, affect, experiences, preferences, dispositions and skills" (184). The inner components of continuity theory, then, are concerned with an individual's intrinsic nature and personality, whereas the external components are concerned with "past perform-ances related to continued skills, activities, interests, environments and roles" (ibid).

As with disengagement theory and activity theory, so with continu-ity theory: persons with decreasing mental and physical health will not necessarily be able to draw upon these "inner" and "external" resources. Indeed, their memory of them, if it causes distress and feelings of incompetence, could result in less successful aging.

Although, for some elders, continuity theory seems an appropriate description of the aging process, for others it seems less reliable. Many of the changes to which older individuals must adjust are not comparable to those experienced in their younger days. Having to move into a nursing home when one wants to remain in one's own home; living within a body that no longer functions as it used to, thus hindering activities; facing the reality of one's own death: these have no equivalents in earlier life. Thus it is possible that coping strategies that worked well for other life changes will not work for these. Estes (1978:44) criticizes continuity theory for its "solipsistic basis—there are as many paths to happiness in later life as there are people."

Even though we have reservations about both activity theory and continuity theory, the participants in the focus groups preferred them over all others because they seemed to provide an adequate fit to their own experiences. Gubrium (1990) has noted that there is often a connection between the theorizing of academics and that of older persons:

> Not just professional social gerontologists theorize age: we all do to the extent that we set about the task of attempting to understand the whys and wherefores of growing old. It is argued that when the proprietary bounds of Gerontological theorizing are set aside, striking parallels can be found between the every-day theorizing of ordinary men and women concerned with ageing and their more celebrated Gerontological peers.

As noted earlier, most in the focus groups felt that there was a great deal of overlap between activity theory and continuity theory. Although they preferred the former, they recognized that the longer they could retain continuity with familiar events and activities, the more likely it would be that they would remain active.

Socio-environmental Theory

The socio-environmental theory of aging, which was proposed by Daniel J. Gubrium (1973) in *The Myth Of The Golden Years,* was the result of research conducted in Detroit. It uses a symbolic interactionist perspective in analyzing the inter-relationships between the individual and her/his surrounding society. Gubrium's study explored the utility of combining environmental and individual concepts when analyzing the morale and life satisfaction of the aged. His theory asserts that successful aging is the result of the inter-relationship between an individual's social and environmental, or physical, worlds. In other words, an individual's life satisfaction is not only dependent upon success in social activities and interactions with others, but also upon physical space, the settings within which he or she lives. Gubrium suggests that morale is heightened in an environment that is: (1) socially homogenous; (2) close to shops, friends, relatives, church, community centres; and (3) locally protected from crime (26). He also suggests that social scientists ought to produce measurement scales for life satisfaction and morale that include the older person's perceptions of his or her physical environment. Socio-environmental theory asserts that "in order for persons to successfully cope with adjustment to old age they must live in supportive environments in which their individual resources allow them to manipulate unfavorable situations at their own speed" (27).

Unlike the other theorists so far discussed, Gubrium is critical of measurement scales, even though he uses them. He advocates the type of research that attempts to observe the social conditions of everyday life and to describe their effects upon the behaviours and perceptions of aging persons. It is difficult to be critical of socio-environmental theory because it makes a great deal of sense. Sociologists, particularly ethnographers, interactionists, communications theorists, ecologists, and ethnomethodologists, are acutely aware of the impact of physical space upon social interaction. Similarly, small groups researchers note how people orient their behaviour towards the physical environment. Because many older persons find themselves in institutionalized spaces, Gubrium's theory seems clearly relevant. His *Living and Dying in Murray Manor* (Gubrium 1975) provides an excellent account of life in an institution for the aged. It also explores his theory in more detail. Gubrium recognizes the crucial importance of focusing upon social interactions, cultural values, and meanings when dealing with old age; he also recognizes the importance of determining how different perceptions and definitions of aging can affect different individuals.

Gubrium is interested in the perspectives older persons take towards their physical, social, emotional, and physical environments, and he recognizes that what come to be constituted as "facts" about aging in gerontological theorizing need to be located within the actual embodied experiences of people who are growing old. He also suggests that older people have different agendas and realities, and that there are many kinds of aging experiences:

> It might be said that elderly people do not think the same way as those who theorize about them. They have attitudes and exhibit activities. Their concerns are practical, having to do with real life, its conditions, changes and possibilities. Theorists in contrast, have theoretical and scientific interests. They hypothetically link attitudes and activities in order to investigate whether, in fact, they are empirically connected. Experience is the testing ground for the world of theorizing, not the other way around. (133)

From the perspective of socio-environmental theory, where an older person lives, whether or not it is appropriate and accessible to older persons and their needs, has much to say about whether or not an individual can age successfully. This theory has implications for the design and availability of accommodation for older persons, the types of services and programs available to them, the manner in which they are involved in decisions that affect their lives and so on.

Many focus group participants saw socio-environmental theory as being social constructionist in nature (which, indeed, it is) and suggested that it really referred to the notion that "life is what you make it." However, it must be pointed out that the equation of social constructionism (which, being premised upon the notion of intersubjectivity, is extraordinarily sensitive to the inter-relations upon which human existence is dependent) with the quip "life is what you make it" is not only simplistic, it is misleading. The former recognizes the complexity of human relationships, while the latter lends itself to a crude form of individualism, which, in turn, can lead to blaming the victim for circumstances not of her/his making. Bertie, a social activist in her nineties from a small university town, points this out:

> Some people have no control over their lives. They live from generation to generation on welfare and never escape! Poverty is a great crippler of the human spirit sometimes. If people do not have role models how do they change? Economic barriers and

loss of human rights can greatly influence how one lives one's life. It is fine for us to say anybody can do anything they put their mind to but that isn't always the case.

Similarly, Marie, the respondent from Ottawa, pointed out that social and historical forces also affect an individual's ability to control her/his life circumstances: "Many people are constrained by family circumstances, poor health, lack of opportunity, even geographic location and can't achieve as much in life as people who start out in a more fortunate environment." Many of the participants who lived in a small fishing village on the Bay of Fundy talked about attitude and how it affects the way we live. Holly, a fifty-six-year-old artist, commented:

> Our attitudes are so important in this life. How we view ourselves, as we get older, how we have always lived our lives, how we have solved our problems or faced our challenges depicts what kind of lives we live. If one worries all the time about things that might or might not happen, that person's life won't be very peaceful! On the other hand, I know a lady down the road that has lived thirty-six years by herself. She doesn't worry about what might happen to her. She lives every day as a blessed event. She is in control of how she sees her life.

Others saw personal connections as important pieces in the puzzle of living. Dot, an eighty-one-year-old grandmother from a small rural town, put it this way:

> I have always cared for my family and my neighbours. It is this connection that gives me hope, and I live a hopeful life. I try to live day to day. I am blessed with fair health. I can still hear the birds sing and see the deer skipping across my backyard in the springtime. I don't think too much about the future. I really enjoy today.

The consensus amongst those in the focus groups seemed to be that attitudes are very important with regard to how we structure our lives. And there was a recognition that those who face difficult political or economic situations have less control over their lives than do those who do not. It was generally agreed that where and how one lives has a great impact on the aging experience (specifically, in terms of having access to adequate resources and social networks). Group members also recognized that they were fortunate to have adequate resources, and they realized that others, including those in institutions, were not so privileged.

The Aged as a Subculture

In looking at the aged as a subculture, Rose and Peterson (1965) address the aging experience from an interactionist perspective. They begin by exploring the interactions between older individuals and other age groups in society. According to them, a subculture emerges when members of one category of persons interacts more among themselves than with members of other categories:

> This occurs under two sets of circumstances: (1) The members have a positive affinity for each other, e.g., gains to be had from each other, long-standing friendships, common backgrounds and interests, common problems and concerns. (2) The members are excluded from interaction with other groups in the population to some significant extent. (3)

Rose claims that demographic, ecological, and social organizational trends in North America are creating an environment that forces the aged into a subculture. He says that, due to the increase of elderly in the population, and due to preventative medicine and advances in health care technology, more persons are actively able to enter this subculture.

Other conditions leading to the aged being identified as a subculture include segregated housing arrangements, retirement policies, development of social services that bring older people together, and the increased use of recreational facilities designed solely for the aged. According to Rose, these factors and others explain how it is that the aged have come to constitute a subculture. Through adopting the interactionist perspective, one can claim that older people are forced to interact with each other more frequently than they are with other age groups.

One of the problems with the subculture theory is that there is no evidence that all old people socially interact solely with their age cohort. In other words, this theory is quantitative in that it provides a universal statement about old age but does not allow for personal (i.e., qualitative) stories. It has been our experience that older people interact across generational lines; in fact, many state that they prefer the company of younger people to the company of older people (a comment that, itself, displays a form of ageism). The subculture theory implies that older people identify themselves primarily as "old" and that it is this visible characteristic that brings them together.

Our experiences have shown that older people think of themselves, first and foremost, as individuals. A conversation that Jeanette had with a seniors advocate in Vancouver in 2001 attests to this: "I don't think of myself as old, just older. When I do think about myself as something, I think of me as a retired health care worker. Being retired is a clue to my age, but I don't have any feelings about this one way or another. I'm still me and that is ageless to a great degree." The membership categorization device "old" is unable to express how she feels and behaves as an individual. In her attempt to assert the more socially acceptable category that displays not age but individualism—the "me" in her statement—she claims that her image of self is "ageless." In other words, she exhibits a reluctance to accept the label "old."

The late Chuck Bayley, a seniors advocate and former author of a column for the elderly in a Vancouver newspaper, also viewed the aged as a subculture. He did so for at least three reasons:

(1) Age—they are all sixty-five years or more.
(2) Ritual—pensions, seeing themselves and others as old and acting the way they think they should act.
(3) Common experiences—historical experiences like the two world wars, no radio or TV, only newspapers then, depressions, and changes in technology. Then there were cultural styles they shared—dress, music, religion, what we now call "lifestyles." All of these things put the aged into a subculture. (Lecture to Sociology 450, University of British Columbia, November 13, 1981).

Many of Chuck's peers agree with his evaluation.

The theory that the old constitute a subculture has been useful when examining the lives of older persons living within shelter options. In this case, as Hochschild (1978) notes, they do indeed form an "unexpected community." In her work, and, notably, that of Matthews (1979), Gubrium (1975), Jacobs (1974), and Rabinowitz and Nielsen (1971), how older persons self-identify as a minority, or subculture, is explored within nursing homes, single-resident occupancy situations, and retirement villages.

Few of the focus group participants agreed with the subculture theory, although some thought it might have some merit. Again, it appeared that how one saw "self" affected how one assessed this theory.

Without having a clear idea of self and one's relationship to the world, it would be easy to place oneself within a subculture—a position that, in all too many cases, is one of powerlessness. Those participants who had a clear idea of who they were, or who were still very active, didn't see themselves as being part of a subculture.

Marie responded to our questionnaire as follows:

> I disagree that older people place themselves in a subculture. I think there are as many differences in interests and abilities in older people as in any other age group; and an older person is more likely to socialize with people of like interests, regardless of age, than with people just because they are older. Of course, younger people may place all seniors in a subculture unless they actually know them and realize there is a lot of variety in older persons.

There was agreement that society in general, and younger people in particular, may see older persons as part of a subculture. However, most seniors do not place themselves within such a category; rather, they see themselves as integrated into society as a whole. As a retired eighty-three-year-old clergyman from a small university town put it: "I don't consider myself to be part of a subculture. I feel quite integrated. However, again, I feel 'others' may put us in that category. I hope that is changing!" Even though many who participated in the focus groups did not self-identify as members of a subculture, they did agree that there was a public perception that older persons are somehow "different" from younger ones. In this sense they acknowledged that they could be seen as members of a subculture.

The Aged as a Minority Group

In so far as it, too, relies on an interactionist perspective, the theory that the aged constitute a minority group bears some similarity to the theory that they constitute a subculture. Put forward by Barron (1959:477), this theory describes the minority group characteristics of the aged as follows: "1) They're viewed by some as a menace and a group to fear; 2) they experience prejudice and stereotyping in employment; they possess feelings of self-consciousness and defensiveness; 3) they benefit from anti-discrimination legislation paralleling that for ethnic minorities." Palmore and Maddox (1977:38) agrees with Barron's theory and adds: "There is more prejudice, segregation and discrimination directed towards the aged than towards other oppressed persons such as women, children and ethnics."

Streib (1965) suggests that the aged are discriminated against on the basis of a shared biological characteristic. According to this theory, discrimination against the old, like other forms of discrimination, depends upon the visibility of personal characteristics. If older people do not "look their age," then supposedly they are not discriminated against. Streib argues that, because the aged are underprivileged, and because this is exacerbated as they continue to age, they are a deprived group. Furthermore, "The more modern the society, the more true this is" (315).

The problem with both the aged as a subculture theory and the aged as a minority group theory has to do with definitions and with who labels whom. If we think of the aged as belonging to a specialized group rather than as older members of the mainstream, does this affect interactions with them? Do the aged identify themselves as members of a particular group? And, if they do, then what presentation of self must they make in order to be accounted for as "such and such" a group member? The labelling process is a problem for most of us throughout our lives. And it is especially frustrating for older people because of the negative stereotyping that goes along with it. As Lenore, an eighty-year-old member of a local seniors network, told us in a recent focus group:

> It is very bad, you know. We are too old for some things, nearly old enough for others, and too young, if we don't carry our bus pass, for others. When I was in my fifties, after my husband died, I couldn't get the OAS [old age security] because I was too young. When his pension ran out and I was in my sixties, I couldn't get the welfare because I was too old. I never seem to get in at the right age! Some folk think that we get too much at our age; others think we don't get enough. It's those darned labels; you know—how old do you think I am ... and what has it got to do with how I feel?

We interpret this person as saying that, if we label people as members of a group—whether we do it on the basis of ethnicity, religion, gender, sexual orientation, or age—then we do a disservice to them as unique individuals. The notion of belonging to a "minority" group signifies being stigmatized or somehow rendered powerless. We tend not to speak of politicians, executives, and professionals, as members of minority groups. Older persons do indeed seem to be the victims of discrimination on the basis of age. In this sense, they can be seen to be members of a minority group in much the same way as are lesbian and gay persons, different racial groups, disabled persons, and others who are often the brunt of negative stereotyping and ridicule.

In a recent edition of *Fifty Plus* (October 2001), the editors discuss a a paper that the Canadian Association of Retired Persons (2001) presented to the 17th World Congress of the International Association of Gerontology in Vancouver in July 2001. The paper is entitled "Declaring War on Ageism," and in it the authors note that age discrimination is a "huge societal issue" (42). They go on to say that "ageism exists, it's wrong and we must start taking action against it" (ibid). CARP notes that ageism is the "worst" kind of discrimination because it denies older people the respect they deserve and, "in its more blatant form, it infringes on their basic human rights" (42). The panel within which the aforementioned paper was presented listed "countless examples of direct and indirect ageist practices in our legal, social and occupational health systems worldwide" (43). According to the authors: "Only when we start addressing this issue through improved education and awareness can older people begin to get a fair share in society at large" (ibid). This message from CARP echoes the cry of many marginalized and stereotyped groups who feel singled out and discriminated against. In light of this, it is clear that the old can be viewed as a minority group. (See Chapter 3 for an in-depth discussion of ageism.)

Those in our focus groups did not necessarily feel that they belonged to a minority group as such, although some did recognize that they could be viewed as members of a subculture. Participants did not raise the issue of personal experiences of ageism or minority status, and we did not initiate such discussion.

Exchange Theory

Exchange theory was proposed by James Dowd (1975, 1980). It assumes that, as people grow older, their interactions with younger people decrease because they have fewer resources, especially economic ones, to bring to the relationship. The theory also argues that all interactions rest upon an exchange of rewards and costs that is expected to maintain a "profit": "The basic assumption underlying much of the research collectively known as exchange theory is that interaction between individuals or collectives can be characterized as attempts to maximize rewards, both material and nonmaterial" (Dowd 1980: 599).

As Dowd (1980:592) goes on to note: "In effect, all behavior entails costs even if the cost involved is only the probability of rewards that are associated with the activity other than the activity being presently pursued." When applying this theory to old age and the notion of successful aging, Dowd claims that decreased social interaction is the eventual result of a series of exchange relationships in which "the relative power of the aged vis-à-vis their social environment is gradually diminished until all that remains of their power resources is the humble capacity to comply" (594). For Dowd, the aged represent a decreasing power source; therefore, their ability to exchange goods, services, experiences, and resources for profit is lessened: "Where once the now-retired worker was able to exchange expertise for needed wages, the final exchange required of most older workers would be their compliance, in the form of acquiescence to mandatory retirement, as exchange for sustenance" (104).

In summarizing his theoretical assumptions regarding the exchange rates of older persons, Dowd concludes that the old have very little to exchange that is of any instrumental value. If persons are viewed as worthy in terms of money, material possessions, and political power, then it is possible that the elderly's potential for exchange is not so great as is that of other age groups. However, depending on the type of interaction taking place, the rewards and costs may be differently defined. An ex-businessperson's experience may be very beneficial to someone currently involved in this field but less rewarding elsewhere. Some skills do not become "outmoded," and, indeed, "retired" workers are often invited back into the workforce.

Dowd adopts some notions from development and learning theories that imply that there is a time when learning ceases. However, studies in adult socialization suggest otherwise, as do the results of our focus group discussions. We constantly heard stories of eighty-one-year-olds learning to make and sell weaving, pottery, and sculpture; of "retired" professors who now teach subjects that they did not teach when they were "paid" for their work. And one conductor of music took Jeanette to task when she suggested that she was "too old" to train her ear so that she could play an instrument ("I was sixty-two when I took up music. Now at sixty-eight I conduct the Victoria Bach orchestra and choir. So don't ever say that you are too old.").

Exchange theory, which relies heavily upon an economic perspective, does have some utility with regard to examining the roles many women play as primary caregivers to older relatives and friends. Were it not for their free provision of services, the costs to government would be huge. In Jeanette's research on women's roles as caregivers (Auger 2000b), many of her informants invoked the notion of "familial piety"—a notion common amongst many Asian peoples. The assumption is that, as one informant noted: "Well, Mum took care of me, my siblings, Dad, and other relatives all of her life, it only makes sense that I would now take care of her. I owe it to her to do this" (17).

Throughout Jeanette's research, the idea of exchange between caregivers and care receivers was invoked not in terms of monetary value but, rather, in terms of a mutual sense of love, gratitude, and caring (in spite of the great stress and hardship often endured by care providers).

Suzanne Atkinson (1997) found that, when family members provide care to one another, exchange theory could be utilized to explain how caregiver stress is obviated by the notion of exchange. Throughout this research, family caregivers of patients with Alzheimer's disease invoked the notion of exchange to talk about how they "owed," or were "obligated," or had "no choice" other than to provide care to their relatives.

As can be seen, the notion of exchange can be invoked not only in terms of finance, but also in terms of duty, reciprocity, obligation, and so on. This being the case, exchange theory seems to have a certain amount of utility. However, exchange theory incensed many in our focus groups. When Diane described this theory, there were audible "gasps" from many of the participants, who felt that it added "insult to injury." Even those who were normally soft-spoken and reflective exhibited a strong reaction. In a focus group held in Wolfville, Don, an eighty-three-year-old retired priest, had this to say:

> Our society is a very materialistic one. Value or exchange is seen in a monetary manner. Success is viewed in terms of financial security, exchanges, and worth. It is therefore understandable that the explanation of this theory is described in such a man-ner—the less value of older persons. If our society viewed the world in a more humanistic manner, one in where all peoples were connected and the individual rights and freedom of all were paramount, such a theory would not be prescribed. That is the trouble in this world. All is geared toward profit and gain in monetary terms. The sacredness or importance of a person is downgraded.

Don had spent time reflecting on this matter and was deeply troubled by society as a whole. He could see the larger picture: "This whole business coming up in Quebec City is a grand example of free trade gone amok! The protesters and alternative summit will be held back and out of sight of the larger summit, held behind chain link fences! Where are the human rights in that!" His whole countenance took on a very troubled look. Many in this focus group were actively involved in human rights issues, the peace movement, and environmental issues. It was generally agreed that society's worldview was skewed. The focus should be on people, their well-being, security, and happiness; it should not be on economic profit only. Most of the participants in this group are financially comfortable; their concerns were for the less fortunate and more at risk. Don went on to say:

> This whole idea of an "economic person" is dehumanizing ... this whole process has been going on for over 200 years, since the Industrial Revolution. Everyone must produce, and once you no longer "produce," or retire, you are seen as an economic burden. We have to change the model! We can't be put into slots! We need to see history as the "stream of life." It is bigger than any individual life, but when we look at our lives as part of that history, they become more meaningful. We can begin to see that attitudes are changing. Many people are interested in peace, a more human society, and a safe environment. There was a time we weren't even talking about these things! So we must continue to talk and raise the consciousness of members of our society. We can do that as we get older and gain more life experience and wisdom. This current health debate is a good example! We need to remind the politicians that along with trade agreements, human rights and the formation of trade unions must work hand in hand.

Alice, who was seventy-eight, married, and a member of both the peace movement and an environmental group in her hometown, agreed:

> It is important for us to have a larger worldview of the reality around us. As a group we can make a difference, we can influence governments. I have been a member of the peace movement, protested the Vietnam War, worked with Project Ploughshares for several years, worked on various health boards and have always been political and an activist for social change. I won't change now. I love my children and my grandchildren, and I am determined to make a difference. I want the world to be a different place for my grandchildren. I will never give up hope! And so I must remain active and vocal.

Again, this group reiterated that the older and younger generations can exchange experiences, time, money, and wisdom. One ninety-year-old writer, Tess, put it this way:

> As long as we are alive we are exchanging. However, one has to be conscious of that fact. We are always learning from one another. Every minute counts, every day counts. I love to talk to younger people and share my ideas. I am looking to get my book published about stories of the Mi'kmaw children. I have many ideas to share.

Other older persons strongly disagreed with exchange theory but did suggest that advertising depicts the young generation as more valuable than the old. Lise, a seventy-eight-year-old grandmother from a small town, put it this way: "Beautiful young women and virile young men can sell more cars! They are sexier!" Marie, the Ottawa respondent, had a mixed response to exchange theory:

> There is a measure of truth in this in a modern industrial society because the experience of elders is less relevant to daily activities and paid work than in a traditional society. However, many grandmothers take over child care so their daughters can work, and other older parents give financial help when needed, and many volunteer organizations couldn't function without seniors—so there are a lot of exchanges going on.

Florence Goldman (cited in Seskin, 1980:192), sixty-seven and a director of a seniors centre, explained her point of view: "The old can offer the young experience, knowledge, and a certain kind of wisdom from having lived through their lives and, I think, compassion. The young can offer the old hope, ambition, spirit and a certain amount of excitement." Rose Gale, also cited in Seskin (1980: 249-50), explained it like this:

> There's one last thing I'd like to say about growing older. You tell them that age doesn't necessarily make someone wise or necessarily mellow. It can, and if it does it's lovely. I think for young people to know old people is a very wonderful thing. It gives them a sense of continuity. If they're willing to listen while they're growing up, it's a way of knowing that there was something before them and there will be something after them. This to me is the value of being in the company of older people.

Another woman quoted in Seskin (1980:205) is seventy-six-year-old Helen Borchard: "The young can give the old kindness and understanding. They don't have to make them feel as if they're old fuddy-duddies. I think the majority of young people today are absolutely fabulous. The ones I know add hope, affection and gaiety to my life."

Age-stratification Theory

Age-stratification theory was formalized by Riley, Johnson, and Foner (1972) and is similar to the subculture perspective in that it suggests that old people represent a particular stratum of society. It utilizes age-cohort analysis, which assumes that, because old people were born during approximately the same time period, they share similar ideas, attitudes, and values:

> Because of age grading, birth cohorts—people born during the same interval in history—tend to develop a subculture of their own. They tend to become cohort-centric, they tend to select friends and marriages from among age mates and collectively to interpret the various stages of life from the standpoint of the historical era in which they experienced it. (22)

Age-stratification theory is primarily interested in the processes by which different age-strata are produced and in the types of interactions that take place between generations. It attempts to determine the relationship between age and social structure, and the role of older persons in a status hierarchy that values youth over age.

Most of the age-cohort research on attitudes towards such subjects as religion, politics, and marriage shows that there is a great disparity from group to group. Age-stratification theory asserts that all old people share certain social and personal characteristics, despite some individual variance; that is, it holds that social roles and regulations are invariant. It attempts to determine the relationship between various socio-structural elements and to assess their effect on the aging process. In this sense, age-stratification theory is similar to socio-environmental theory.

Many in our focus groups agreed that they might fit within particular strata of society, although some felt that such normative hierarchies did not adequately define an individual's place within the social system. Nellie, a participant in the focus group from Halifax, was quite vocal about this:

> I don't see society stratified that way. I see a difference in people

who go with the flow and people who don't. Some older persons refuse to change and can be seen to be at the lower end of the scale. When people continue to be active in society and integrate with all age groups, the stratification is at the least, not as visible. I know while advertising on TV, in the magazines and newspapers tends to show young people, some editors of the magazines are now aware of the power of older persons and advertising is geared to that age group. I see forced retirement as one of the problems. There has to be a better way to assess people's willingness and ability to continue working. That separates people more than age.

Some rural women thought age-stratification theory was credible. They felt uncomfortable with the moral attitudes of the younger generation and tended to stay within their own age group. Dot, an eighty-something widow from a small rural community, described how she felt: "I go to the malls and I feel surrounded! Groups of young people in all forms of dress and all different hair colours, loudly talking and swearing. I feel frightened and insecure. I would rather stay at home or go to a smaller store." Mary, a seventy-year-old widow who is actively involved with her grandchildren, didn't see it that way: "I just love my grandchildren. I have one grandson who is especially kind to me. He takes me out to dinner, talks to me, asks me questions and we have fun together. As for the hair colours, oh, well, that will all change as they get older. Didn't we do crazy things too in our teens? Some of us did anyway!" Mary wouldn't tell us what they did; she just laughed and said, "Never you mind, I'm not telling now!"

Other participants believed stratification occurred in many elements of society and was not necessarily age-related. Marie, the Ottawa respondent, commented: "In capitalist societies class and wealth determine the stratification systems and there can be old people at the top. In traditional societies there is often less stratification and often elders are at the top, e.g., China and tribal Africa."

Modernization Theory

Modernization theory, which is also known as modernity theory, was put forward by Cowgill and Holmes (1972) and relates to the ways in which developmental issues affect the lives of older people within a global context. Quadagno (1999:32) notes that one of the fundamental premises of this theory is that "the aged were revered in the past and that modernization has caused the status of the aged to decline." Furthermore, as countries develop technologies that lead to changes in the workforce, older people lose valued social roles, especially those involving the high status associated with being managers, educators, doctors, lawyers, and so on. Retirement and nursing homes are increasing because older people are often no longer cared for at home.

Brenda Robb Jenike (1995) has studied the status of the aged in Japanese culture, especially with regard to the roles women play as primary caregivers. She notes that, as a direct result of industrialization, many women are giving up their traditional roles as caregivers and seeking employment outside of the home. As a result of this and of various government programs aimed at encouraging families to share the cost of caring for the elderly, more older persons are living in institutions. Obviously, the productive roles of the elderly within the Japanese family are diminishing, and Japan has moved from a family-based care model to a state-orchestrated, or community, care model.

Kaiser and Chowla (1994:44) note that, prior to modernization and globalization, the elderly in Chile, Thailand, Sri Lanka, and the Dominican Republic,

> besides contributing to economically productive activities such as gardening, tending animals and food preparation, carried out other key cultural activities. These included socializing and entertaining children, teaching of vocational skills, leading religious discussions and having a special role in joint family activities such as ritual.

Many anthropological studies (e.g., Sokolovsky [1997] and Lassey and Lassey [2001]) of the aged in non-Western countries show that, as modernization takes over traditional cultures, customs and beliefs about the roles of older persons change drastically.

When we spoke to those in the focus groups about modernization theory, many saw it in terms of the technological changes that they had experienced over the past fifty years, and most were very enthusiastic about it. However, they showed little enthusiasm for the "banking system." To begin with, most did not like having to press so many buttons on the phone before getting a "real human being" at the bank.

Very few people liked having to call a number, say in Moncton, New Brunswick, in order to talk to their bank in Nova Scotia. The lack of human connection was a concern. As Annie, a newly widowed seventy-something woman living in a small fishing village, put it:

> I just hate phoning that number! I can never remember or hear properly the number I am supposed to punch. When I finally do get someone, my call has to be transferred to my branch and then I usually get voice mail and have to leave a message anyway. Whatever happened to just picking up the phone and calling the person at the bank that knows all about you and your investments? I am totally frustrated with this system.

However, computers were another story. Most of the people with whom we spoke were enthusiastic about learning computers. Many of them were already familiar with them, and these "machines" were a part of their lives. Others were planning to take computer courses and were looking forward to doing so. Jill, an eighty-year-old homemaker from a small university town, enthusiastically described her adventure with this "new gadget":

> At first I didn't want to have anything to do with it. I would stand in front of the thing and wonder how to turn it on! However, when I saw my five-year-old grandson playing games on it I figured it was about time I got to know the thing! I took a seniors course at the university and I am having a wonderful time e-mailing my friends across the country. Surfing is fun too!

For the most part, our participants agreed that many of the modern "helpers" were, in fact, making life easier for everyone. In a research project (entitled Everyday Technology and Older Adults) being conducted at Mount Saint Vincent University in Halifax, Nova Scotia, older persons were interviewed, or participated in focus groups across the province, to discuss how technology was changing their lives. Many were very concerned with the trend away from human-based services to machine-operated ones. Of most concern to rural elders were the closing of bank and credit union branches, the increase in numbers of automatic banking machines, and the difficulties that those with hearing problems encounter when trying to gain access to government information over the telephone. Also mentioned were problems experienced by arthritis sufferers when trying to conduct banking business over the phone and often pressing the wrong numbers. In their newsletter, *Everyday Technology and Older Persons: Friends or Foes?*, Jeannine Jessome and Clare Parks (2000:4) note that a prevalent theme emerging from their research involves older persons' basic mistrust of automated technology:

> Older adults expressed mistrust of industry's intentions underlying the use of Automation, as well as mistrust of the efficiency and/or reliability of technology itself. Again and again, older adults stated that they believed automated technologies increased profits, not customer service and convenience. Participants recounted "horror" stories of botched transactions, "eaten cards," and endless phone loops. Some participants asked if anyone knew where the envelope actually went after being deposited in the banking machine. Does it just fall to the floor?

For the participants in this particular study, modernization leaves a lot to be desired, and their comments clearly display a need to be educated about the use of computerized technology.

Feminist Theory

There is, of course, no one feminist theory; rather, there are several feminist theories, including, among many others, socialist, postmodern, Marxist, liberal, radical, lesbian, and cultural (Browne 1998; hooks 1984; Donovan 1996; Jagger and Rothberg 1984). When one addresses aging issues from a feminist perspective (i.e., a perspective that acknowledges the gendered nature of society), the role of older women is seen as being largely invisible within mainstream public life and academic discourse. As Garner (1999:3) states:

> We have systematically denigrated older women, kept them out of the mainstream of productive life, judged them primarily in terms of failing capacities and functions and found them pitiful. We have put older women in nursing homes with absolutely no intellectual stimulation, isolated from human warmth and nurturing contact, then condemned them for their senility.

These are harsh, but true, comments, and they are shared by many scholars and practitioners (feminist and non-feminist alike) in the field of aging who argue that basic structural inequalities founded upon gender are at the root of discrimination against all women, particularly older women. Such explanations for why and how older women are faced with what Sontag (1973) refers to as the "double standard of aging" address the high poverty rates of older women in most counties of the world; the fact that more older women than men are institutionalized; the fact that there are more widows than widowers; the number of television and print advertisements that portray older women in less positive ways than they portray older men; the number of jokes and cartoons that depict older women in negative ways; and so on. Feminist theories argue that all of these socially accepted and maintained realities exist because of the basic sexism that pervades all societies and that devalues the roles that women play within the home, within political life, and within the economy.

Dianne Garner (1999:6) suggests that there is a natural affinity between gerontology and feminism in that they have such common goals as:

> development of social consciousness about inequities, utilization of theories and methods that accurately depict life experiences, and promotion of change in conditions that negatively impact older people or women. Feminism recognizes the intrinsic value of women, their right to equal treatment, and their right to be viewed as individuals. Gerontology recognizes the intrinsic value of older people, their right to equal treatment, and their right to be viewed as individuals.

Noting the paucity of work in feminist gerontology in the past, Garner suggests that, as gerontologists themselves grow older, their interest in their own lives come to the foreground. This self-awareness of their own aging enhances feminist concerns with the aging process.

These opinions were also expressed by Shulamit Reinharz (1986:223), who argues that what gerontology and feminism have in common is "an attempt to create social consciousness, social theory and social policy which will improve the life chances of a specific group." Further, she argues that, regardless of the type of feminist theory, they all agree that aging occurs within an institutional context of "sexism, racism, anti-Semitism, heterosexism, capitalism, elitism, beautyism etc." (225). She suggests that, as gerontology is fundamentally about anti-ageism and that feminism is fundamentally about anti-sexual discrimination, the two are likely allies in the fight against attitudes that denigrate women.

A standard criticism of mainstream gerontology (and, indeed, of all social and natural sciences) is that most studies dealing with the "aging individual" have relied exclusively upon the experiences of male informants. As Quadagno (1999:39) notes, "Such research often treats women as if they were men, measuring women against the masculine model."

Not only do feminist scholars point out that male-dominated studies of aging have not included female participants, but they also point out that no one addresses the basic inequalities between aging women and men in terms of access to social welfare programs, basic economic inequality, and a social system that empowers men and disempowers women.

Most of the participants in the focus groups were women; although we did not ask them if they were feminists, some said that they were. Most felt that many of the issues covered in the feminist approach to aging were accurate, and they hoped that more emphasis would be placed on the needs of older women.

General Comments on Social Theories of Aging
The theories just discussed are utilized by gerontologists in order to explore old age, especially the notion of "successful aging." Can people age "unsuccessfully?" and, if so, how would we recognize this? Is the gerontologist's fascination with successful aging an attempt to produce a predictive model of "good" old people? Or is it, as some have suggested, a means of acquiring power over the old? In producing and maintaining theories and "facts" about aging, gerontologists are creating social realities that ultimately extend beyond their academic workplaces: "Our knowledge is having *real* effects on *real* people … and we must come to terms with the recognition that 'facts' ultimately reside in the producers of knowledge and that such knowledge has social and political consequences" (Estes 1978:49, emphasis ours).

Gerontological theories tend to view old age as a social problem, either for the old personally (with regard to their ability to cope with aging) or for society (with regard to its ability to cope with an increasing aged population). By so doing, they help to create myths and labels that are discriminatory in nature. Ironically, these theories, and the ideological perspectives inherent within them, also function to label gerontologists in equally negative ways. As journalist Sharon Curtin (1972:178) puts it:

> There is a prestigious Senate Committee on Aging which holds frequent hearings into the special problems of the old. But I wonder what all this activity really amounts to? I wonder what real difference it makes that seventeen specialists in the field of gerontology appeared before a senate committee and said …. They just keep saying over and over "Ain't it awful." I see nothing new coming from the eminent gerontologist-sociologist-psychologists who all suffer from the same blindness and poverty of imagination.

Some analysts claim that theories function as "restraining myths" (Hamilton 1975) that, although unsubstantiated by empirical data, are treated as "true" because a "scientific" community has deemed them to be worthy of investigation. The implication is that, if professionals believe in the merits of disengagement theory or activity theory, then less scientifically oriented people will believe in them too. What Hamilton says of theories in general is also true of gerontological theories. Even though other scholars, on both empirical and methodological grounds, have frequently disputed each theory of aging, they still appear in every new textbook on aging and are always included in courses on gerontology. Although we, too, question their usefulness as universal statements about growing old, they nonetheless provide a historical overview of key themes in the development of the culture and discipline of gerontology. They introduce students to theoretical perspectives within such disciplines as sociology and psychology, and they present for analysis some of the major methodological concepts in gerontological research (such as life-satisfaction, morale, quality of life, and successful aging). They also display part of the ideological base upon which gerontology is founded. Marshall and Tindale (1978-79:164) point out that, through gerontological ideology, the aging individual's

> moral or life satisfaction, adjustment to the social system or interaction with it provide the key themes in social gerontology .... The overwhelming thrust of gerontology in practice, and Gerontological theory, concerns the adaptation or adjustment of aging individuals to the prevailing social reality.

Gerontology's current theoretical paradigms present a "reality" that is basically "good" and within which the old are expected to adjust, to "fit." In other words, the social rules and practices are not questioned: what is questioned is how the old fit within them.

Gerontologists are able to deduce logical inferences from one social form—oldness—to other social forms (e.g., gerontology). The demographic profile of a given community, the health status of particular individuals, the housing needs of others: these realities, thoughts, or ideas become recognized and constituted as the stuff of gerontology. Inherent within these ideas are methods for generating facts and information about a given issue. It is in this sense that Smith (1975:9) speaks of ideology as a methodology, as a particular way of ordering the social world so that "what ought to be explained is treated as fact or assumption." For example, instead of beginning, as does disengagement theory, with the assumption that old age and the social practices associated with it are a necessary function of society, one could begin by asking, "What work does old age do in our society?" If we do this, if we look at how old age is accomplished by assorted actors in everyday life, then old age becomes whatever people say and do in the process of constructing it.

In order to put into action a system of ideas about old age, gerontologists, like all professionals/scientists, use a special language to communicate with one another and with non-gerontologists. This special language, be it spoken or written, is what Smith (1975) refers to as a "currency of exchange"—a particular way of speaking about observed everyday events that functions to display one as a specialist. We use the gerontological currency when we wish to present ourselves as people familiar with, and expert with regard to, a particular task; namely, producing knowledge about old age. Language, as a manifestation of thoughts and ideas, of knowing the "currency of exchange," is one way in which ideology is made visible. For the gerontologist, an everyday event, such as attending a community centre, might be translated into "age-cohort activity," or "the use of leisure time," or "acting with an age role."

When this type language, or jargon (as it is commonly termed), comes in the form of written material, it does the work of providing an example of "gerontology." What gerontologists speak, write, and do—whether in the form of conducting research, publishing articles, addressing conferences, or organizing programs and services—functions as a display of gerontology. It is part of the social organization of knowledge, of how gerontological knowledge and ideologies get produced. It is in this sense that what people say reflects what they do. And what people say and do reflect what (and how) they think.

The ideology inherent within gerontological theories has political consequences because the data it generates are held to constitute "factual" and scientific "truths" about aging. They help to bring about action and to shape policy decisions because one group of "experts" (e.g., bureaucrats and planners) tends to accept the knowledge of another group of "experts" (e.g., social scientists and professionals in the field of aging). Just as theories play an important role in the production of knowledge, so they play an important role in positioning the expert; that is, they do the work of admitting one into a particular group or segment of society. As Znaniecki (1975:9) puts it: "A person who is 'instructed' or 'learned' in certain theories is admitted to the performance of certain roles and to the membership of certain groups in which the 'ignorant' are not allowed to share."

Most of our focus group members/questionnaire respondents thought that people in the health care system, government, financial institutions, gerontology, sociology, religious studies, psychology, and pastoral care would use these theories, but few thought that they had any impact on their individual lives. They were more interested in discussing the notion of "successful aging" and sharing their ideas about how to cope with various obstacles (particularly declining health) to living what they perceived to be a meaningful life.

Indeed, theories of aging do present a very narrow picture of the lives of older people, and, because many scientists do not accept them as empirically or methodologically valid, they do not even work as predictive instruments. Nonetheless, they do function as descriptive accounts of what gerontologists do, and they tell us something about the issues that they deem to be appropriate to the study of old age.

THEORY TESTING

The construction and testing of theories is part of what constitutes gerontological knowledge. Theories are tested through various measurement scales (e.g., pertaining to life-satisfaction, quality of life, morale, etc.) whose purpose is to determine how people adjust to old age. These scales, usually in the forms of questionnaires, are administered in an interview-type format. For example, some of the questions asked by Cumming and Henry (1961: 258) led to answers that were said to support the postulates of disengagement theory: "Measures of morale: 1) How much do you regret the chances you missed during your life to do a better job of living? 3) How much unhappiness would you say that you find in life today? 7) Nowadays a person has to live pretty much for today and let tomorrow take care of itself?" The responses to these and other questions of a similar nature were then coded to determine whether a person had high morale, the idea being that people with a high morale would cope with old age more successfully than would people with a low morale. These seemingly non-age-specific questions, which are essentially philosophical in nature, were part of the ideological basis upon which disengagement theory was said to be supported by the data. The sample used by Cumming and Henry was made up of 279 people, each of whom was interviewed five times. According to the authors, the various interviews were given for the following reasons:

> Interview one was designed to get a general idea and necessarily superficial picture of the respondent and to secure his co-operation

for future interviewing .... Interview two begins with a general query about the respondent's welfare and asks him to describe the best and worst things that have happened since he was last seen .... Interview three is composed almost entirely of preceded short questions designed to discover the respondent's perception of his present interaction rate compared with the past .... Interview four was designed primarily to collect psychological material and secondarily to test some hypotheses developed from the first three interviews .... Interview five repeats questions from earlier interviews about rounds of activity, the morale index is repeated, and material regarding various "crisis points" in the respondent's life is gathered. (30–31)

The use of measurement scales in the testing of theories and in the production of gerontological knowledge was the subject of much debate within gerontological circles when these theories were first proposed. It is interesting to look at some of the issues raised then and to see how and if they apply to modern notions of successful aging.

Frances Carp (1969) is the most famous critic of measurement scales as an indicator of successful aging. In an article entitled "Senility or Garden Variety Maladjustment?" she reports on a study undertaken to test the assumptions inherent within the Chicago Senility Index. This index has "widespread influence because it serves as a criterion measure in classic studies on aging. The issue here is clarification of the nature of a set of behaviors which many investigators assume to be associated with growing old" (203). Burgess, Cavan, Havighurst, and Goldhammer (1949) used this index to formulate and test activity theory because it was seen as a "useful list of fifteen statements purporting to show the mental and personality changes that come with old age .... The index emphasizes mental and attitudinal changes."

Carp, in order to support her view that the Chicago Senility Index was neither an adequate nor an old-age-specific measuring device, administered the test to two groups of subjects. One group consisted of ninety-five persons aged between fifty-two and eighty, all of whom lived independently in an urban community; the other group consisted of ninety-five persons aged between seventeen and twenty-five, most of whom were high school or university students. Carp (1969:205) found that "the younger group had a higher proportion of 'senile' signs. This total was significantly higher." The results of her study, which, in essence, found younger people to be more "senile" than older people, led Carp to conclude that "the consistency of findings in these tests of the specificity of 'senility signs' to old age suggests strongly that the signs are not unique to the later years" (207).

The construction of reality produced by gerontologists who continue to use these measurement devices seems to be neither old-age-specific nor adequate to describe how older people cope with their life process. And it should be pointed out that, when using the word "cope," gerontologists are making a value judgment about the life of the aged; they are viewing it as hard, as something to be put up with. Older people, on the other hand, may not feel this way about their lives. A retired, sixty-eight-year-old, female Asian psychology professor spoke of the ongoing process of life:

> I dislike very much the notion of "coping" with life because it implies that we are not active participants within it. I know that the term is a jargonistic piece of psychology and social work, I probably even used it myself—but not without regret. We do not cope with life, we enjoy it and relish it and see it as a challenge. To speak of coping is to speak of needing help, not from friends or family but from some expert who will help us to cope, to survive as it were this terrible thing called old age—or so they seem to believe it to be. (Interview conducted by Jeanette in Wolfville, 1995, while researching women and retirement)

In another article, Carp (1977:15) offers some suggestions to those who wish to continue using measurement scales in their research on old age:

> Gerontologists concerned with the "morale" of old people, whether in practice or research, should sit down and answer, in regard to themselves, all the questions in the grab bag, "take" all the tests, do all the observer ratings and compute their own scores; and then cogitate upon this "inner experience" for an hour or two.

In other words, if gerontologists used their own lives as "testing grounds" for their research, then perhaps the enterprise within which they participate might take on a different flavour.

If gerontologists intend to continue to base their expertise and knowledge upon measurement scales that isolate specific life situations as somehow particularly meaningful and relevant to old age, then, according to Rosow (1977), they will continue to "short change older people."

Rosow suggests that gerontologists have devoted an "unconscionable" amount of attention to the morale of older people and that they have done so for the following reasons:

> In gerontology, the practitioner's perspective has inundated and eroded that of the social scientist .... But social scientists are not practitioners. Their concentration on morale may arise from humanitarian motives and implicitly as an advocacy stance. But it also exacts significant costs, fostering a parochial view that cuts them off from the resources of their disciplines .... Our obsessive concern with morale has largely restricted gerontology to a substantive area rather than a vigorous, integral part of the social sciences .... We are abrogating our special expertise and, in the process, exacting a price from the elderly whom we want so much to help. (45)

Rosow suggests that, whereas the measurement of morale, life satisfaction, and the ability to cope with old age may well have relevance to gerontological practitioners such as health care workers, service planners and providers, and community facility operators, it is "restrictive" when it is used by gerontologists working within the social sciences.

Measurement scales are considered important to gerontological work because they highlight specific issues of concern and inform the theories upon which gerontological knowledge hangs. This being the case, some consider it important that researchers reflect upon why they use such data-gathering devices. Bloom (1977:23), for example, suggests that researchers try to find some alternatives to measurement scales, perhaps using "naturalistic data," where "people do not respond to the researcher's imposed categories, but they themselves clarify the meaning of material that they have spontaneously presented. They carry their own 'true' criterion with them, so to speak." This interactive process would enable both the researcher and the respondent to mutually negotiate the meaning of any questions being asked. As Bloom goes on to say, the process could induce a certain amount of reflexivity in the mind of the researcher:

> Imagine yourself having a pleasant conversation with an elderly friend or relative. Can you conceive of yourself asking "As you look back over your life, would you call it happy, moderately happy, average happy, or unhappy?" Then specifying that your conversational partner could only respond by agreeing, disagreeing or answering "not sure"? (25)

Suggesting that gerontologists prefer to obtain data through the use of measurement scales because they are easier, less threatening, and more "efficient" than are some other forms of data collection, Bloom notes:

> I think that it is obvious that we researchers ask questions that are convenient for us in the same fashion that hospital beds stand waist high from the floor for the convenience of the staff, not for the convenience of the patient getting in and out of bed …. I suggest that we need motorized morale-type scale items to let the subjects adjust them to fit themselves, rather than the procrustean scales we now employ. (25)

Constructing and testing theories by measuring morale, life-satisfaction, and so on seems to confuse rather than to clarify the concepts being studied. The nature of such phenomena as happiness, satisfaction, and quality of life are complicated for all individuals, not just the aged. As Weisskopf (1977) points out, following scientific procedures is not the only way to learn about our universe. In fact, he says, "scientific results … may even be counter productive." He goes on:

> A Beethoven sonata is a natural phenomenon that can be analyzed physically by studying the vibrations in the air; it can also be analyzed chemically, physiologically, and psychologically by studying the processes at work in the brain of the listener. However, even if these are completely understood in scientific terms, this kind of analysis does not touch what we consider relevant and essential in a Beethoven sonata—the immediate and direct impression of the music. In the same way, we can understand a sunset or the stars in the night sky in a scientific way, but there is something about experiencing these phenomena that lies outside science …. There cannot be a scientific definition of concepts like … the quality of life or happiness … there remains an important part of the experience that is not touched by scientific analysis. (272)

Weisskopf is not saying that we cannot capture feelings of happiness or describe the features that make up the quality of life; rather, he is saying that there is something within the scientific paradigm that suggests we ought not to.

Successful Aging: According to Whom?

At the beginning of this chapter we indicated that the theories of gerontology were formulated in the late 1950s and early 1960s, mainly by American researchers and scholars who used predominantly White male subjects. We also suggested that theories of aging function as ideological frames of reference and that one of their main objectives is to predict what might lead to "successful aging." The concept of successful aging still abounds in American and British gerontological studies, and authors still grapple with establishing an adequate definition. Bowling (1993:450), for example, suggests that the main components of successful aging are: "Good physical and mental health; Adequate income; Social support; Autonomy; Sense of control over one's destiny; Satisfying social relationships; An active lifestyle and Quality of home and environmental setting."

Quadagno (1999:123) notes that successful aging has three primary components: the biological, the psychological, and the social. The biological component refers to the human organism's ability to "wear well" into old age; the psychological component refers to the ways in which individuals are able to adjust to changing circumstances as they grow older; and the social component refers to the roles and expectations cultures place on older individuals. Because various cultures have different expectations and values, it is difficult to define what might be a universally accurate notion of successful aging.

Ken Dychtwald (1999) notes that a major national poll conducted in the United States asked older persons to rank the criteria by which they would define successful aging. The researchers were surprised to report that "power, wealth and influence" were placed at the bottom of the list, whereas "being true to myself, not selling out, and achieving inner satisfaction" were placed at the top (89). These results led Dychtwald to conclude that, "in contrast to earlier generations who tended to define success from the outside in—title, status, power and so on—middlescent boomers seem to be redefining success from the inside out, with a heightened emphasis on self-esteem, the quality of personal relationships and personal freedom" (ibid.). Thus, notions of successful aging are situated within specific cultural and historical contexts. When older persons are asked to define this concept, they do so using different criteria than are used by academic researchers.

In a very interesting article that examines the notion of a "good age" in seven different communities around the world, Fry, Dickerson-Putnam, Draper, et al. (1997) attempt to ascertain the ways in which individuals invoke the notion of successful aging. They conclude that, amongst their respondents, who lived in countries as diverse as Africa, the United States, Hong Kong, and Ireland, there was consensus that a "good age" consisted of: "Physical Health and Functioning; 2) Material Security; 3) Family; and 4) Sociality" (102). Even though there were differences between the ways in which individuals within different groups of respondents discussed these issues, and although there were cultural variations, the authors conclude:

> In our cross-cultural study, we heard from respondents in each community that there are strengths and positive aspects for all residents. For all sites, health and functionality are the singular factor promoting successful aging. Health problems and disabilities detract from a good old age and can have profound consequences for the quality of life. (121)

Thus, according to the elderly informants in the above-mentioned study, good health and the ability to function independently in the community are crucial components of successful aging.

The late American poet May Sarton (1978:85) wrote the following poem, which beautifully captures the joy of growing older, on her sixtieth birthday:

> How rich and long the hours become,
> How brief the years,
> In this house of gathering,
> This life about to enter its seventh decade,
> I live like a baby,
> Who bursts into laughter
> At a sunbeam on the wall
> Or like a very old woman
> Entranced by the prick of stars
> Through the leaves.

Participants in the focus groups were very interested in discussing the concept of successful aging, and they had many definitions of it. Some of those discussions follow. Both in our focus groups and in the literature we read it was often mentioned that successful aging is the result of attitudes, self-image, and relationships with friends and family. Without exception, a positive attitude was pronounced as the most important feature of successful aging. Participants described this attitude in many ways. Mary, who was widowed in her seventies and living in a small fishing village, commented:

I love life. I mingle with my children and grandchildren. I take every day as it comes. I have a new male friend. We enjoy the same things and it is great companionship. I made up my mind a long time ago that I would be cheerful and think "young"— whatever that means! What's the good of complaining all the time. No one wants to hear that all the time. When someone asks me how I am I say, "Great, thanks," and let it go at that. I know they don't want a list of my ailments!

For Mary, "thinking young" was an attitudinal directive that enabled her to age more successfully than would be the case if she "complain[ed] all the time." Interestingly enough, in saying this, she unconsciously invokes a series of stereotypes about both younger people (i.e., that they do not complain) and about older people (i.e., that they do nothing but).

Anne, a seventy-four-year-old former schoolteacher from a small town suggested:

> Our attitude is so important. Acceptance and forgiveness are the most advantageous qualities we can have. Acceptance of our situations, whatever they are, and forgiving others and ourselves for past mistakes. When we can do that, contentment comes. I know from experience that we have to let go of the past and come face to face with our reality as we get older. We will change, physically, mentally and emotionally. Accepting that fact goes a long way to ... aging with grace.

She went on to say, "We must talk about our feelings. Get it all out there and then we can move on."

Carolyn Heilbrun (1997) discusses old age and why some people are happy and others are not. She mentions Doris Grumbach's journal *Coming into the End Zone* (1991), in which Grumbach bemoans the fact she has turned seventy, that her body is aging and her life nearly over. In contrast, Heilbrun notes that she herself was quiet and subdued until her sixties and seventies, at which time she burst forth with new energy, insight, and a sense of freedom. She mentions May Sarton's (1984:7) remarks in her journal, *At Seventy: A Journal*, when she asks the question, "Why is it good to be old?":

> I answered spontaneously and a little on the defensive, for I sensed incredulity in the questioner, "because I am more myself than I have ever been. There is less conflict. I am happier, more

balanced, and (I heard myself say rather aggressively) "more powerful." I felt it was rather an odd word, "powerful" but I think it is true. I might have been more accurate to say "I am better able to use my powers." I am surer of what my life is about, have less self-doubt to conquer. (7)

Heilbrun suggests that it is too easy to do what one has always done, and she suggests attempting a new project or endeavour. Upon her resignation from Columbia University (where she was a teacher), Heilbrun found a new state of freedom—no more deadlines, no more need to pretend civility around her male counterparts. It appears her sixties gave her the opportunity to reassess her life and everyone in it. She purchased a home of her own when she was sixty-eight and gathered around her a number of friends who had not necessarily known her in the academic world. When the desire to quit teaching hit her, she was ready.

Seeing this time in her life as an opportunity and an adventure gave Heilbrun the purpose she needed to enter the next stage of living. She accepts and relishes her situation: "I find it powerfully reassuring now to think of life as 'borrowed time.' Each day one can say to oneself; I can always die; do I choose death or life? I daily choose life the more earnestly because it is a choice" (10). For Heilbrun, to age successfully is to find a new purpose in life, a new way of being.

Many members of the focus groups stressed the need to feel good about themselves. They noted that, if one is confident, outgoing, and active during one's lifetime, then this usually continues in old age. Several of the older women who had difficulty accepting their situations mentioned that they were nervous about speaking out and that they suffered from low self-esteem. One eighty-six-year-old widow living in a small rural town put it this way: "I have always been trying to please other people. I could never live up to expectations so I just tried to look after everybody and 'fix everything.' Now I have nobody to fix, so what do I do now?" This woman's feelings were shared by some others, mainly those aged eighty-five and over. These women had been socialized as caregivers throughout their lives, and now, with no one to "look after," they were having difficulty.

Shevy Healey (1986:62) described successful aging as follows:

Successful aging is to be myself. To deal with what is different, special, unique about being older—to learn to live with loss and death, to prepare for my own death ... to attend to the current business of living with vigor and involvement while at the same time attending to the unfinished business of my life, putting old rancors in perspective, letting go of pettiness, acknowledging love.

Ruth Thorne (1992) shares many of the ideas put forward by Healey as well as by some participants in the focus groups. Speaking of her own successful aging process, she comments:

> To grow up, to discover ourselves—to be someone we like and want to be before we are really old. If we are searching and discovering adults we will survive the aging process and continue to be a unique person. Continuing more of same to discover, to ask questions, to recreate and consolidate our inside and outside .... The truth of neoteny and not a sentimental denial of aging offers a challenge and opportunity to rediscover the qualities of our childlike selves, a way to stay open to life and all its possibilities right up to our last breath.(45)

Dot, a gregarious, seventy-seven-year-old retired teacher from a small town, spoke in the same manner: "I guess getting older is when we really grow up! I don't know how grown up I am, but I am at least thinking about it now."

The topic of self-image kept resurfacing throughout our group discussions. Thorne (1992) recites a wellness list produced by two of her friends. These two people were gifted group leaders, and they made this list in order to remind themselves how to live life to the fullest. This list contains sixteen items, including: good nutrition, exercise, meditation time, building a solid support group, knowing what you really love, re-creation instead of wreck-creation, and openness to change and new experiences. Thorne goes on to describe the advantages of group therapy and peer therapy, and she sums up her notion of overall wellness as follows: "As aging and old women, we can gain power in our lives by recognizing where we are engaging in self-defeating behavior. We can claim responsibility for our well-being by reflection—clear, practical, gentle—where we find energy and wisdom for our lives" (110).

What Thorne, and many others, suggest is that some process of self-reflection is required in order to age successfully. Of course, there is a difference between acting in the world and thinking about acting in the world. The former requires everyday actions geared to "getting on with it," the latter requires a process of critically working through values, beliefs, images of self, and one's actions in the world. Ben Weinenger and

Eva Menkin (1978) discuss the whole process of aging in the form of a dialogue between the two of them. Menkin asks the questions, Weinenger responds. In the foreword to their book, Eric Fromm wrote: "To learn how to age must begin in one's youth. If one wants to learn it at a later age, it is probably too late because one has failed to develop in oneself the kind of personality which can experience aging without fear and with equanimity" (5). In his introduction, Weinenger sums up an ideal relationship to self as we age:

> To let go of the past,
> Yet retain a friendly relation to it.
> To let go of one's teachers,
> Yet remain in good relations with them.
> To let go of one's children without regret.
> To let go of one's life and see that whatever life we had we touched the Eternal. (11)

Eva Menkin, in her introduction, argues that "if there is joy in life, there is joy in aging" (12). When Menkin asks, "With younger people busy and perhaps separate from the old, where does that leave the old?" Weininger replies:

> Old people tend to find it very difficult to accept that they are perceived by society as being old and useless .... Older people must learn to accept that the things they see around them are true ... they are indeed seen as old and useless. But they can go from there to build their own support systems. All the aged really need, aside from medical attention and decent housing, are a few friends around, a sanctuary to be a part of .... When an older person is in contact with others, he doesn't feel as if he is dying. (28)

Weininger encourages people to accept their reality and then to get on with it. However, it is very difficult to accept the notion that one is "old and useless." We do agree that, in some sense, "life is what you make it" and that social networks are a crucial and necessary component of successful aging. Sadly, we also recognize that making new contacts and maintaining old ones is difficult for some older persons.

Throughout our research we found a common belief in a creator and a life after death. This was implicit in the fact that about two-thirds of the focus group participants discussed membership in church groups and activities, and often said that their faith kept them going. Lynn, a seventy-something woman from a small fishing village, was surprised that no one mentioned the topic of faith as, for her, it was a foundation. Several people responded with comments like, "Well, I guess we just take it for granted. We don't mention it because it is so much a part of our lives we don't even think about it."

For many, a belief in a life after death provides them with hope that they may end up in a better place. One eighty-year-old widow from a small fishing village commented: "If I didn't think there was life after death I would be scared to death here on Earth!" The hope that pain and suffering would be no more and that they would meet up with loved ones in the hereafter kept many participants going. While different views were discussed, the overall hope was the same.

John Jerome (2000:115) speaks of successful aging as "learning the importance of the simple." According to him, "The misanthropy of aging comes in large part from looking about and seeing what all those other idiots still think is important." For Jerome, simplifying life and taking time to reflect and to figure out what is important enabled him to get rid of the "stressors" in his life and simply "live." He encourages people (men in particular) to keep social contacts, to maintain support groups for mental stimulation and help in times of need. He goes on to explain that most males who lack an "external link" (i.e., work, sports, social networks, etc.) find each other boring. They can't seem to get to the meat of such concerns as sexuality, power, fear, and emotions. He believes that men find discussing these topics somewhat "shameful," while women do not. He hopes that, as he gets older, his gender will begin to slip away (with regard to his take on the world, not with regard to his sexuality) (243).

While acknowledging that successful aging is different for everyone, it can be generally stated that the ability to accommodate change, the ability to accept one's situation, and the ability to remain creative and positive are helpful. At an Acadia University Alumni meeting a hundred-year-old former student was asked, "What is your secret for successful aging?" She replied: "I don't have to worry about peer pressure!"

Chapter Three

Old Age
By Whose Definition?

SOCIAL CONSTRUCTIONS OF OLD AGE

Chronology

There are many ways to talk about the concept, definitions, and reality of old age. We can discuss the notion of chronology—the number of years a person has lived. In Canada and elsewhere in North America and Europe, the age of sixty-five has been arbitrarily selected as the time when individuals begin to receive Old Age Security and other income and health benefits. Therefore, many see sixty-five as the beginning of old age. Chronological age, however, actually tells us very little about the individual other than the year she or he was born. Because people aged sixty-five and over vary greatly in terms of life experiences, cultural values, health status, activity levels, and so on, using such a measure merely serves to stereotype older persons as somehow being all the same.

Chronology is related to life expectancy—the number of years an individual can expect to live. Currently, in Canada, women aged sixty-five and over can expect to live to be eighty-one years of age, whereas men in the same age group can expect to live until they are seventy-five.[1] This does not mean, of course, that individuals cannot far exceed their life expectancy (or, in some cases, not meet them).

Unfortunately, these life expectancies do not include those of the Aboriginal peoples of Canada, who, due to high mortality rates related to circulatory diseases, cancer, and respiratory diseases (not to mention mortality rates associated with acute poverty, alcoholism, and domestic violence), have much lower life expectancies than do other Canadians. According to Statistics Canada (2000b), "The high death rate from lung cancer and respiratory diseases is likely linked to the rate of smoking among adults in the Aboriginal population, which was double the rate for Canada as a whole in 1997."

Mortality Rates

Mortality rates refer to the incidences of death in a population during a given period of time. Canadians living in 1920 could expect to live until the age of fifty-nine if they were males, sixty-one if they were females. These are relatively young ages by today's standards. Because of advances in medical technology, improved health care and lifestyle decisions, Canadians are living much longer, healthier lives. In 1992, the ten major causes of death amongst all Canadians, regardless of age, were as follows:

a.	Circulatory system diseases	76,211 people
b.	Cancer	55,648 people
c.	Respiratory system diseases	16,663 people
d.	Digestive system failures	7,224 people
e.	Suicides due to a variety of causes	3,709 people
f.	Mental Disorders	3,593 people
g.	Motor Vehicle Collisions	3,437 people
h.	Substance Abuse	3,161 people
i.	Suicide (non-firearm)	2,659 people
j.	Accidental Falls	2,138 people

(Ministry of Industry, Science and Technology 1994).

Life expectancy has increased dramatically over the past one hundred years, and, with increasing lifestyle changes that promote health (e.g., exercise, nutrition awareness, improved social interaction and community involvement), will probably continue to do so.

Demographics

Demographics provide vital statistics for any given population (e.g., the number of people living in any given place at any given time, along with their ages and their occupations). Using these quantitative measures can help us to plan what programs and services will be necessary for future generations of elders, and it can also enable us to assess the adequacy of those services presently being provided. Demographics are often used to discuss what is known as population aging, which refers to the process by which the population of individuals in any given country or region of the world grows older. As Lilley and Campbell (1999:4) point out, population aging should not be confused with the aging of the population: "Individual aging is the process of development over the life span, involving biological, social and psychological changes. Every individual experiences aging differently. Population aging, on the other hand, is experienced by society as a whole." Using the preceding definition, Lilley and Campbell go on to explain that "a population is said to be aging if there is an increase in the *proportion* of older to younger age groups over time, rather than a simple increase in the number of older adults" (ibid., emphasis in the original).

In recognition of the significance of the demographic increase of older persons in the global community, the United Nations General Assembly declared 1999 the International Year of Older Persons. The increase in the numbers of older persons in different parts of the world has important ramifications for the provision of services and programs for each region. These include the costs of services and programs to assist older persons to function independently in the community and the provision of adequate facilities and social supports for those unable to stay in their own homes (or in the homes of family or friends). One must also consider increased spending on health care, transportation for people with special needs, community based programs, and so on.

Not only are the numbers of individuals aged sixty-five and over increasing in the higher-income parts of the world, but they are also increasing in the middle- and lower-income countries. As Lassey and Lassey (2001:4) note, the proportion may grow to "28 percent in less prosperous countries in Asia, Africa and Latin America." Although Canada, the United States, and Europe see tremendous challenges in providing services and programs to an increasing number of older persons, developing countries face even greater challenges. For example, countries with little or no employment have very low tax bases from which to subsidize care for the aged. Also, lacking education and literacy skills, younger people in these countries are unable to find employment in order to create a tax base in the first place. Poverty, malnutrition, poor health (especially in African countries with high rates of AIDS, where grandparents care for their children and, when they die, for their grandchildren), the unequal status of women (who are the predominant caregivers of the old as well as for everyone else), and political and financial instability all create challenges that are not so prevalent in the higher-income parts of the world.

In Canada, as elsewhere, not only are there more citizens aged sixty-five and over, but, more important in terms of the provision of health care and other social services, there are more persons aged eighty-five and over. Currently, individuals who are aged eighty-five and older represent 1.7 percent of the Canadian population. Statistics Canada projects that, by the year 2016, this number will increase to 2.2 percent, and that by 2041 it will increase to 3.7 percent (Statistics Canada 1998:14).

Further, the majority of older persons who are presently aged eighty-five and over are female, and most of them live alone. As

McPherson (1998:99) notes, this situation is compounded by the fact that: "Women constitute a large proportion of the elderly population, especially among the very oldest cohorts. Because of women's greater life expectancy, an unbalanced sex ratio that begins in mid-life becomes exaggerated in later life .... Thus, an elderly woman may live ten or more years as a widow." The growing number of single, elderly women will represent an important challenge to governments and policy and pro-gram planners as they attempt provide services to this subgroup of older individuals.

Functional Age

Functional age is related to an individual's ability to function, physically and mentally, as she/he grows older. Functional age is usually measured in terms of normal physical changes that come with growing older, such as stiffness of the joints, diminished short-term memory, reduced skin elasticity, and diminished aerobic capacity (McPherson 1998:10). Func-tional age measurement is also used to define individuals as the frail, somewhat impaired, or well elderly. Quadagno (1999:12) differentiates these individuals as follows: "The *well elderly* are people who are healthy and active. They are involved in social and leisure activities and are often employed or busy with volunteer work. They carry out family responsi-bilities and are fully engaged in the life of the community" (emphasis in original). According to a Statistics Canada (1998:91) report entitled *A Portrait of Seniors in Canada*, 139,000 Canadian men over the age of sixty-five were still employed in 1995, as were 60,000 Canadian women in the same age group. These individuals clearly fit within the well elderly category.

When defining the somewhat impaired elderly, Quadagno (1999:12) notes that these older persons are in a transitional phase in which they are "beginning to experience chronic ailments and need some assistance from family or community agencies. Although they can participate in many aspects of life, they may need support in transportation, shopping, cleaning, or personal care." In 1990 Health Canada (1993:32) conducted a health promotion survey amongst Canadian elders aged sixty-five and over. Table 3.1 shows the results of their self-rating of their health status. As these results indicate, the majority of persons aged sixty-five and over reported that their health was either fair or good. They would probably be placed under the category "somewhat impaired elderly."

The frail elderly are those individuals who, according to Quadagno (1999:12), "show some mental or physical deterioration and depend on others for carrying out their daily activities. They need more care from

Table 3.1 The Health Status of Elderly Canadians

Health Status (Self-rated)	Males	Females
Poor	8%	7%
Fair	19%	19%
Good	31%	30%
Very Good	29%	27%
Excellent	14%	17%

Source: Minister of Supply and Services, Canada's Health Promotion Survey: Technical Report, 1993, Ottawa: Supply and Services.

family members and may be in institutions." Within this group of older persons would be those suffering from dementias such as Alzheimer's disease. As Lilley and Campbell (1999:31) point out in their excellent publication *Shifting Sands: The Changing Shape of Atlantic Canada*:

> Dementia is among the most distressing and demanding of illnesses encountered in later life. The prevalence of dementia increases sharply in old age, and women are twice as likely to suffer from dementia as men. The 1991 Canadian Study of Health and Aging found that at age 65–74 the rate of dementia is 2.4% of the population, and at age 85+ the rate is closer to 34.5%. In 1991 approximately one half of people with dementia were living in institutions. By 2031, the number of people with dementia in Canada is projected to triple, from 252,000 in 1991, to close to 800,000 in the year 2031.

The frail elderly are most likely to live in institutions such as hospitals, nursing homes, homes for special care, or other residential care facilities. The majority of people (8.1 percent of Canadian elders) who live in institutions are aged seventy-five and over (Statistics Canada 1998:33). Whereas functional age can provide some measure of the biological aging process, of course all individuals age differently and at different rates depending on their lifestyles, attitudes, genetic makeup, and so on.

Age Cohorts

An age cohort is a group of individuals who were born at or around the same time. The assumption is that such persons will share a common background, history, and view of the world. Of course, this need not necessarily be the case, especially in a country as wide and varied as

Canada with its huge rural and urban differences. People who are presently aged sixty-five and over may have lived through two world wars, a depression, the advent of television, video recorders, the computer, and other so called "advances" in technology; however, their individual experiences of these global events could differ drastically from one another.

My (Jeanette's) father's family was born and raised in rural New Brunswick, and my elderly relatives have yet to enjoy some of the "benefits" of modern technology, especially in the field of health care. When certain specialist or surgical procedures are required they must drive or be driven to Moncton, some four hours away. This is not the case for my elderly friends who live in an urban community such as Halifax, where such facilities are more readily accessible. Those who live in Vancouver, British Columbia, have even greater access to health care services. So even though individuals may have been born within the same time frame, where they live their lives and how differs greatly across the country, especially with regard to the accessibility of services that enable them to live, full productive lives.

Older persons from culturally diverse backgrounds can also be seen to belong to age cohorts, especially where they share a common language, customs, and beliefs. The same might be said for lesbian and gay elders as well as those with physical or mental disabilities not related to age.

Life Course, Social Roles, and Age

The life course perspective and the social roles associated with age refer to the ways in which older individuals assume activities based on cultural norms. This perspective draws heavily on a developmental framework, which suggests that there is a socially prescribed timing and ordering with regard to when life events and their associated social roles are to be performed. In general, as Canadians we are expected to be educated at specific times in our life, marry (if heterosexual), have children, find suitable employment, retire, and so on. Of course, we all know individuals who do not act in accordance with their culture's accepted norms. We also realize that age-ranked behaviour is a very individualized phenomenon and that, increasingly, older persons are breaking down some of the stereotypes regarding what they "are supposed to do" as they age. An example of this going against the grain is the increased rate of university attendance amongst people aged sixty and over. In 1998, over 24,920 older persons were enrolled in university courses across the country (Statistics Canada 1998:74).

There are specific social roles associated with growing older, most of which have to do with when individuals are supposed to retire and receive various income security programs, long-term care options, and so on. Atchley (1976:63) defines a role as "the culturally transmitted, general norms governing the rights and duties associated with a positioning in society (judge, woman, retired person, mother, etc.). For Atchley, the retirement role is one that "represents a valid social role which consists not only of rights and duties attached to a social position but also of specific relationships between retired people and other role players" (63).

The concept of social role is also related to the notions of role change, role loss, and role transitions, the emphasis here being on how older people deal with the loss of status and roles associated with being employed, enjoying good health, having adequate incomes, having affordable shelter, having access to leisure activities, becoming widowed or losing a life partner, and so on. For many, retirement brings with it a potential loss of status due to giving up a highly valued work role. With each new role we play as we grow older we are confronted with sets of expectations and, often, the need to perform new tasks (e.g., moving from the role of paid worker to retiree).

The adjustment from living independently within one's own home to living within an institution can be extremely challenging. I (Jeanette) have a friend who is in her late seventies; she presently lives in her own home and is quite independent. She has worked all of her life in the health profession in a fairly high-status position and is currently experiencing hearing loss and some minor difficulties with mobility. Recently, she has decided to move into an assisted housing facility. She commented to me that, whereas in the past a move in residence usually meant a new job, new country, and new challenges, the move to a residential facility seemed like a move to "nowhere." She talked about her loss of status and how, at the facility, she is just another "oldie." She sees the move as entailing a loss of independence and a loss of role. She mentioned that, at the facility, the nursing and administration staff expect her to "sit by quietly" instead of cleaning her own room and assisting with meal preparation. Rather than being encouraged to do for herself, she is being encouraged to let others do for her.

As my friend has been a highly active, very social and independent woman all of her life, this move (and the role acquisition that accompanies it so that she will "fit in" with the facility's expectations) will be very stressful indeed. I can only hope that it will also be challenging and rewarding for her and for those with whom she will come into contact.

Adam Zych (1992:24) has written about the psychological adjustments that older people must make as their social roles change:

> We must realize that these people struggle with the absolute necessity of constant adjustment to rapid economic and social changes and with the difficult problems of loneliness and isolation, which has been referred to as "the scissors of social death." Furthermore, on the collective [social] level one can notice visible changes in the social conditions of elderly people which are related to their altered social roles and status and which reduce the productivity of the final years of the elderly.

AGEISM

Ageism refers to the ways in which age discrimination marginalizes, devalues, and hinders older people from feeling good about themselves and their contributions to the societies in which they live. Like misogyny, racism, heterosexism, and discrimination against individuals on the basis of religious preference or abilities, ageism occurs in all forms of everyday life and social practices. Whether it be because of retirement policies forcing individuals to stop working for pay at certain ages, or jokes found in greeting cards that make fun of the aging body and mind, ageism is pervasive. In a culture that values productivity defined on the basis of financial earnings, the contributions of older individuals who do not work for pay go unnoticed and unappreciated. Ageist attitudes posit old age as a burden rather than as a time of opportunity and freedom.

The term "ageism" was coined by the American gerontologist Robert Butler in 1969. According to Butler (1969:243), old people are categorized as "senile, rigid in thought and manner, old fashioned in morality and skills …. Ageism allows the younger generation to see older people as different from themselves; thus, they subtly cease to identify with their elders as human beings."

Indeed, we have all seen the stereotypes of "crotchety old women" and "dirty old men." We are aware of individuals who do not want to disclose their age for fear of being ridiculed or having to endure responses such as, "Oh, you don't look that old" or "You can't be sixty-five: you look so young."

When I (Jeanette) ask my students to discuss popular images of older persons in the community and the media, they are always able to come up with a large number of them, most of which stereotype older people as "crotchety," "behind the times," "not with it," or "grouchy." They are generally seen as "complainers." Seldom do students invoke positive representations of older persons. Most advertisements, whether on television or elsewhere, show older people in negative ways. Even if one examines publications aimed specifically at those aged fifty-five and over, one finds that they focus on the stereotype of the relatively wealthy older person who is trying to decide which expensive vacation to take or car to drive. In the case of women, the elderly person is concerned with determining which cosmetics most assist her in covering up wrinkles, grey hair, or "unsightly age spots."

When some people aged sixty-five and over are asked about growing old, they often respond that people older than themselves are the "really" old ones. Recently, while on a field trip with my class to a senior citizens day centre, we asked some of those present how they defined "old age." One eighty-one-year-old woman said that she still felt very young and that that was why she was not in a nursing home with "all of them oldies." On the other hand, a sixty-four-year-old woman who had recently had a stroke and was now dependent on others for much of her everyday living needs said that she felt as though "old age had robbed her of her life." So age is a relative experience: it depends upon individual life experiences and circumstances.

In a British film made in the 1950s, starring Dame Peggy Ashcroft (*The Listeners*, Rank Film Productions, 1952), the major character is an old-age pensioner who is so poor that she spends her days in the public library to keep warm, drying off her wet socks on the radiator. One evening she returns home to her small flat with a bag of chips (French fries, in Canada) for her supper, which she shares with her cat. On the radio she hears about old-age pensioners in Britain being so poor that they are forced to eat cat food. As she feeds her cat a chip drenched in salt and vinegar, she says, "Poor old dears." This clearly illustrates the notion that old age is a relative experience and that people who may be deemed to be old (due to physical appearance, behaviour, or receiving old-age security) do not necessarily self-identify as old.

We can observe ageism taking place in media advertisements, newspapers, magazines, and television shows and films that portray older people in stereotypical ways. Ageism can be observed on both the personal level and the institutional level. With regard to the former, there are people who are so concerned that their physical appearance might reflect aging that they are willing to spend huge sums of money on cosmetic surgery; with regard to the latter, older people are discriminated against in terms of retirement policies, employment, education, and other governmental and private-sector initiatives.

Gilleard and Higgs (2000:134) note that cosmetic surgery is not just about subjective fears of aging; it is also about societal values:

> Using cosmetic surgery to determine whether and how to "age" is not just a matter of personal aesthetics. It reflects the public valuing of "agedness." Expenditure of over $15 billion on anti-ageing nutritional compounds in the USA is not just a matter of consumer choice. It represents a massive social dread of old age.

Agreeing with the concept of the "social dread" of aging, Zych (1992:25) has coined the term "gerontophobia" to explain the "aversion to old people and old age with a simultaneous lowering of the social status of old people." Aside from being cruel, unfair, and ignorant, ageism is also foolish, for all people who live long enough will grow old, and, when they do, they will not want to be ridiculed, feared, or stereotyped because of it.

The eradication of ageism requires education at all levels, particularly in all forms of the media, where so much of public opinion is created, maintained, and reinforced. On a recent trip to England, Jeanette was delighted to see a regular column in the London *Times* (March 20, 2001) entitled "Not Dead Yet: The Column That Challenges Ageism and Celebrates Being 50-plus." In this regular feature, *Times* readers send in letters describing ageist comments they have heard or seen or experienced. For example, Coral Thomas, from Baldrine on the Isle of Man, wrote:

> A few years ago, just turned 50, I was asked to model for a hotel brochure. Feeling impressed with myself, I tripped through the hotel foyer and asked the young attendant to take me to a suite where I emphasized I was going to be photographed. He looked quizzically at me and said: "Did you used to be good looking then?"

A photograph of Ms. Thomas in her "model" attire accompanied this item, thereby providing a visual as well as a written account of her experience of ageism. As well as letters from readers, quotations from playwrights and authors are also included in this newspaper column, all of which helps to raise public awareness of ageism.

Ageism and Gender

It should be noted that ageism does not affect women and men equally; this is because, for women, it is combined with sexist attitudes. Simone de Beauvoir (1977), in her seminal work on growing old, which discusses the social and cultural images and expectations of aging women and men throughout history and within different cultures, notes that women have always been discriminated against on the basis of gender and that this unequal treatment is exacerbated by age. Similarly, Susan Sontag (1973) concludes that, in most cultures of the world, but especially in North America and Europe, there is a "double standard of ageing." According to Sontag, the "prestige of youth" afflicts everyone to some degree. Furthermore:

> Men too, are prone to periodic bouts of depression about aging—for instance, when feeling insecure or unfulfilled or insufficiently rewarded in their jobs. But men rarely panic about aging in the way that women often do. Getting older is less profoundly wounding for a man, for in addition to the propaganda for youth that puts both men and women on the defensive as they age, there is a double standard about ageing that denounces women with special severity. (73)

For de Beauvoir, Sontag, and many other writers who discuss the notion of the double standard of aging, the primary social issue is a preoccupation with physical attractiveness and desirability—a preoccupation that hinders women, especially, from being able to present their "true" selves. Sontag (1973:78) reminds us that "women do not simply have faces, as men do; they are identified with their face .... A man's face is defined as something he basically doesn't need to tamper with; all he has to do is keep it clean .... A woman's face is the canvas upon which she paints a revised, corrected portrait of herself."

Ageism further separates women from men, and from each other, as heterosexual women compete for the scant attentions of men in an attempt to feel desirable and worthy of attention, of affection. As Sontag notes, physical attractiveness is equated with age:

> In a man's face lines are taken to be "signs" of character. They indicate emotional strength, maturity—qualities far more esteemed in men than in women. (They show he has "lived.") Even scars are often not felt to be unattractive; they too can add "character" to a man's face. But lines of aging, any scar, even a small birthmark on a woman's face are always regarded as unfortunate blemishes. In effect, people take character in men to be different from what constitutes character in women .... A wom-

an's face is prized so far as it remains unchanged by (or conceals the traces of) her emotions, her physical risk-taking. (79)

Over the past ten years, in a non-scientific perusal of magazines such as *GQ, Modern Maturity,* and *Chatelaine,* it was noted that few advertisements were geared towards the improved physical appearance of older men, especially their faces and hair. On the other hand, hundreds of such advertisements were aimed at older women, suggesting that their faces, hair, hands, skin, legs, and breasts could be enhanced and made to look fuller, less wrinkled, smoother and younger. Sontag concludes her brilliant essay with the following comments: "Nothing more clearly demonstrates the vulnerability of women than the special pain, confusion, and bad faith with which they experience getting older" (80).

OLD AGE AND SELF-IDENTITY

We all have perceptions of ourselves as individuals moving through our lives—perceptions that are honed in terms of membership in and interactions with social groups such as family, friends, neighbourhood, community, and the various activities in which we engage. We are social beings who bring to our interactions expectations, beliefs, and feelings about others and ourselves. If we have high self-esteem, then we feel valued by our peers and deem our contributions to our social networks as also valuable. If we have low self-esteem, then we feel useless to our communities and see ourselves as "done for" rather than as "do-ers." This may be especially true of persons who live within institutions. According to Lassey and Lassey (2001:33):

> The loss of independence and control are among the explanations for the unhappiness of many elderly individuals who are confined to nursing homes or other institutional settings. They lose some of their identity with the diminution of former roles in the family and community. At the same time, autonomy is lost as they become subject to the rules and limitations of institutional personnel who sometimes do not respect them as human beings.

Clearly, if individuals value independence as a correlate of high self-esteem, then it is imperative that institutional settings encourage and support older people in their efforts to remain independent for as long as possible.

Our definitions of self are in direct correlation to how we assume we are seen by others. In 1934, the sociologist George Herbert Mead (1934) introduced the concept of the "looking glass self." This idea was further conceptualized by another sociologist, Charles Cooley (1972). Essentially, the notion of the looking glass self suggests that we see ourselves as others see us and, further, that who we are, and how we are expected to act in the world, is reflected back at us by the cultural norms and expectations of the communities within which we live. It is for this reason that older persons share the same stereotypes about their generation.

Christopher Gilleard and Paul Higgs (2000:1) claim that it is increasingly difficult to categorize what it means to be old because "ageing has become more complex, differentiated and ill defined, experienced from a variety of perspectives and expressed in a variety of ways at different moments in people's lives." Margaret Morganroth Gullette (1997:3) echoes this opinion when she notes that not only is age difficult to culturally define, but that it is also first and foremost created and maintained within a cultural perspective: "The basic idea we need to absorb is that whatever happens in the body, human beings are aged by culture first of all. Everything we know of as culture in the broadest sense—discourses, feelings, practices, institutions, material conditions—is saturated with concepts of age and aging."

In Canada, government services, programs, and benefits are provided to individuals according to the dictates of a seemingly arbitrary chronological marker based upon the year of birth. Most of these benefits are provided to persons once they reach the age of sixty-five. Throughout recent history, a great deal of thought has produced the decision to make sixty-five the necessary age for expediting the provision of such services as Old Age Security, the Canada and Quebec pension plans, housing allowances, health care and pharmacy assistance, and other such programs. Financial subsidies (especially pensions) for persons aged sixty-five and over began in 1844 in Belgium and Holland. At that time they were restricted to soldiers and civil servants. Later, France, too, began to provide pensions to public employees. In 1890, in Germany, Chancellor Bismarck proposed a program of social insurance to protect older citizens from poverty. At that time, "old" persons were those aged seventy and over. This system was in effect in Germany between 1890 and 1910 and was adopted in the United Kingdom in 1908. In Canada, similar legislation was passed in 1927 after years of discussion and parliamentary debate.[2] It must be remembered, however, that not all individuals aged sixty-five and over require financial subsidies. For these people, the designation of sixty-five as the age that defines the beginning of old age is nothing more than a negative stereotype whose consequences they must bear.

Clearly, our culture is ambivalent about growing old: on the one hand, we talk about the "golden years" of retirement as a time to enjoy all of those pleasures that we had little time for while working; on the other hand, we fear old age and do what we can to avoid it. A huge range of products are readily available to us to enable us to "fight" aging—everything from anti-wrinkle creams, to vitamin supplements, to hair transplants, to anti-aging nutritional compounds, to hair dyes and various surgical procedures "guaranteed" to make us look and feel younger. Even though younger people may help to create and maintain the negative images of old age, older people internalize these images, with the result that, all too often, growing older is viewed as a no-win situation.

Seniors Speak about Their Definitions of Old Age

When we met with people who self-identified as old (chronologically speaking), they responded to the question "How would you define old age?" in a variety of ways, ranging from "those who are ten years older than me" to "there really is no such thing anymore." The main themes emerging from the focus groups concerned chronological age, labelling, and identity.

Chronological Age

We know that, according to the lending institutions and the federal government, we become "old" at sixty-five; however, the vast majority of people in our focus groups believed that chronological age was irrelevant to their lives. Margaret, a vivacious sixty-year-old from rural Nova Scotia, commented: "I may have a sixty-year-old body but [I have] a twenty-year-old mind." Lyn, a community activist and rural resident who is in her seventies, explained:

> Old age is a non-issue. I don't believe there is any such thing as old anymore. Because of medical science, educational opportunities and the ability to keep active and interested, support groups, families and better financial planning, people, in my experience, rarely see themselves as old in the sense that they are no longer any use to society or no longer interested in events around them. In my experience, people are integrated and not categorized by chronological age.

In one rural, small town focus group only two out of eight participants would acknowledge their age. They didn't think it was anyone's business. However, for the most part, both the women and men in these groups readily and proudly gave their age. Some eighty-seven-year-olds—and there were a good number of these—were happy and grateful that they had arrived, so well, at this age. Ruth, an urbanite, wife, mother, and grandmother stated: "I used to think sixty was old but now that I'm here I've changed my mind." A vibrant and active seventy-one-year-old named Holly announced: "I'm only seventy-one and I'm not there yet. Neither is my ninety-six-year-old mother who swims daily and loves life."

Eileen Foley, in her article "The Way It Was" (Troll, Israel, and Israel 1977), wrote about Willie, a Black woman who grew up in Mobile, Alabama, and, at the age of seventeen, married the "wrong" man. Willie experienced great difficulties during her lifetime but always seemed to look on the bright side. Even forced retirement due to ill health did not deter her joy at life and her determination to live one day a time. Willie slowed down a bit after retirement but continued to barhop, crochet, and be sexually active: "Except for my health, I am no different than I was at twenty. Until your mind grows old, you are not old" (18).

For the most part, our focus group participants concur with Willie: one is only as old as one feels. Women are living longer than they used to, and many are well educated, with various skills and job experiences. Others, while working in the home, have created an outside life in political parties, organizations, or community groups. Women in general have combined the public and private parts of their lives, and we see a new type of aging woman emerging—one who is no longer dependent upon men for status, survival, or self-identity. How one feels about oneself determines how one feels about aging and "being old." The general belief among the focus groups was "we are what we think."

Not only did the participants in the focus groups feel that age was a state of mind, they also reminded us that being afraid of growing old was ridiculous. Irene Paul (1976:47) expresses this notion succinctly: "When we ask for a chance to live our old age in comfort, creativity and usefulness, we ask it not for ourselves alone, but for you. We are not a special interest group. We are your roots. You are our continuity. What we gain is your inheritance." In other words, the aging process does not involve an "us" versus "them" scenario; rather, as Paul notes, the younger generation should learn from the older. Similarly, Ann Noggle (1986:34), a photographer of aging women, points out that, in North America, there is a phenomenon that she refers to as "Youthenasia"—the idea that older people really "belong in the past ... [that they are] historical objects occupying space." Through her photography she wants "to show who they are and how damned difficult it is as each of us in our own time becomes one of them." The men in the focus groups, like the women, were not interested in chronological age but, rather, in how they felt about themselves and the world around them. Interestingly, though, an eighty-nine-year-old man from the South Shore of Nova Scotia responded to our questionnaire as follows: "Old age is the age of acceptance of physical and some variable intellectual limitations. It is the age of appreciation of tolerance and support of those around us."

John Jerome (2000), in *Life After Sixty-Five*, willingly acknowledges that he is getting older. He examines the physiology of growing older and the emotional, mental, and spiritual aspects involved with recognizing this process. Jerome very much wishes to define old age in "his own terms":

> I recently watched a friend turn sixty-five, receive his first Social Security check and sink into depression: the government had officially declared him an old man. Seeing him struggle was instructive. It had entirely sneaked up on him. I hadn't given sixty-five much thought either. I don't like being blindsided any more than the next guy. (1)

For Jerome—author and active athlete—the whole aging process needed investigation. For him the issue of physical movement was a good starting point. Not being able to move as quickly as he had been, or to get through winters as actively as he had in the past, was a depressing idea for Jerome to consider. Due to physical problems he no longer pursued his passion of skiing, and he got tired of being really "cold." Jerome alluded to the World Health Organization, which, he said, considered him "already elderly"—a category he considered to be insulting: "WHO considers that category to span ages sixty to seventy-five. I'd prefer just to be 'old' but don't reach that designation until seventy-six (7)."

In summing up the idea of chronological age and its lack of relevance in the lives of most older persons with whom we spoke, Mary, who lives in a small fishing village in the Annapolis Valley, said: "I do not know how to define old age. In years I would say over sixty-five. In spirit it could be any age. I am three weeks short of seventy-six. I don't think I am 'old' although I am aged." Most of the older persons with whom we talked were, to say the least, very annoyed with the labels placed on them by society (i.e., government agencies, health care systems, caregivers, and younger people). It was very clear, early on in our research, that each person believed that she/he was an individual and that labels placed limitations on her/him.

Labelling

In a focus group conducted in Halifax, the participants included many retired professionals, a tour guide, a doctor's wife, and a few homemakers. These women were divorced, widowed, or still married. Their ages ranged from sixty-one to eighty-six years, and they found labels of any kind to be both degrading and dangerous. As Nellie, a retired tour guide, suggested:

> I don't like to be labelled anything! How does another person or government agency know how I feel or see myself? I want to do what I want to do when I want to do it! I don't need the bureaucracy telling me when I am sixty-five, or whatever age, that I can only do this, that or the other thing! I know how I feel, and I will do what I can at any given point in time.

A discussion then ensued concerning how advertising tends to suggest that "old" means "sick" or that "life is no longer worth living." Clearly, labelling the old as worn out or in poor health does little to encourage them to live their lives to the fullest. When inundated with these images of the old as ugly, decrepit, and sickly, it is not surprising that the elderly begin to see themselves in this light.

As these women pointed out, the media and magazine/newspaper advertisements portray the old as crotchety, and young people pick up on these stereotypes with the result that older people are often not taken seriously. Their stories, feelings, needs, and frustrations are not heard because no one cares to listen. As one very outspoken seventy-year-old grandmother put it:

> If these young things would simply take the time to listen they might find out something that would be helpful to them— something I have learned through experience and would be happy to pass along. But oh, no, they are too busy and impatient to sit down and listen to me. I might be able to tell them something about living in this old world of ours. Like what is important and what isn't. Like having more patience and understanding. I seem to remember though, when I was young, I

probably did the same thing, although I remember sitting down with my grandmother and listening to her storytelling. We all loved those times. They were precious.

In another focus group this issue also came up. This group consisted of rural, small-town women who were retired nurses, teachers, and homemakers between the ages of seventy-two and eighty-five. Their feelings of anger and bitterness came to the fore when they brought up the issue of labels and stereotyping. Susan, a retired nurse, age seventy-five, commented:

> Society labels us as old in an effort to define the winding down of life with certain limitations. I put no limitations on myself. My ninety-two-year-old husband may put some on me, but I just do what I do everyday. Yes, I may get a little slower doing it, but I still do the same things—cooking, volunteering, and looking after Dick and whoever else comes along.

Another participant, Eve, an eighty-five-year-old retired homemaker who had spent a good part of her life caring for sick men, looked Diane straight in the eye and: "I deeply resent someone else not only telling me what to do and how to do it, but labelling me as incompetent simply because I do things more slowly and with more thought. It is totally unacceptable to me! I can still think for myself!" Eve required daily homecare. Physically, she needed the help; but she was still quite capable of making her own decisions. Some homecare staff members had condescended to her, and, of course, she didn't like it. She mimicked one of them as she said, "Now dear, will we have our bath?"

Others who participated in the focus group discussions suggested it was most annoying to be placed in a certain category simply because they had slowed down. As Eve, a participant from a small town, said: "Thinking we can't do it or that there is a deficit in our thinking process is insulting! I feel really bad when I am treated this way and it makes me forget even more."

Jane Seskin (1980) interviewed various women between the ages of sixty and eighty-something, all of whom had had various life experiences, occupations, and roles. Fanny Rosenau, who was eighty-two when Seskin interviewed her, commented:

> I don't care what they call me—senior citizen, whatever; labels don't mean anything to me. You're what you are—the hell with

the label! Call me a dirty old lady if you want; it wouldn't bother me at all. I'm too secure. My years of experience in living a full life have given me, I feel, the privilege of saying what I think. (34)

Lil Levine, an eighty-two-year-old woman who found her spirituality and her connection with all age groups through her music, told Seskin that she did not believe in labels and that she certainly did not believe in the label of senior citizen. She believed that labels "separate[d] people." Rose Gale, a widowed, seventy-year-old retirement home resident with sparkling blue eyes and a zest for life, also spoke out against labels: "I hate the term 'senior citizen.' I'd rather be called 'aging.' Everybody's doing that" (245). Helen, a seventy-six-year-old student and sportswoman who had survived three cancer operations and had refused to give up on life, stated: "'Senior Citizen'—I hate that term. I think the word 'adultery' is better! Anyway, today's older people are not just sitting around waiting to die, if they're well" (204).

We don't think that anyone could sum up this discussion of labels better than Marjorie Craig, a sixty-seven-year-old physical fitness instructor who has led an active life and who, in her interview with Seskin, stated: "I hate the term 'senior citizen.' If human beings feel good, look good and can carry on their lives, why stick a name on them just because they're ten, twenty or thirty years older than they once were?" (62).

Identity

Most of the participants in our focus groups agreed that the body does age and that we all experience some, mainly physical, limitations as we get older. However, again it was noted that, just because a body gets older physically, it does not follow that the person within that body changes. The participants were explicit about the need to advise their younger counterparts, their caregivers, health care professionals, and families of this fact.

Eve, an eighty-five-year-old woman living in a small town in semi-poor health, described herself this way: "I may have an old body, with wrinkles and yellowish skin. My legs don't hold me up too well and my feet hurt! However, inside I am still that twenty-year-old who loved adventure and doing new things. I still have the need to create and be connected in the world." The other women in this group observed that how they lived out their mid-life was probably how they would live out their older years. Nan, a very active seventy-five-year-old former nurse, noted: "I have spent an active mid-life, working and doing for people in the community. It has been a way of life for me and I can't see that changing. I am still the same person, just a little different on the outside."

In our Halifax focus group the general consensus was: "as we are young, so we are old." These women, although they acknowledged that their bodies were not as subtle or as smooth as they used to be, considered themselves to be the same people as they had been in their youth. The spirit of each person is the same now as it was then. According to Nellie: "I still feel the same inside. I have always needed to be in control and do what I want and what I think is right."

To return to Jane Seskin (1980:259), Hildegarde, a seventy-three-year-old supper club entertainer comments, "I'm not old. I'm young. I just bubble up. I've always been that way!" Hildegarde's story is one of perseverance, of having a positive attitude and living life to the fullest. For her, the years go by and, although she ages chronologically, she does not age mentally. According to Angelina Boccaccio, a seventy-eight-year-old foster grandparent at the time she was interviewed by Seskin: "I see myself looking the way I did as a young woman. I look in the mirror and I'm surprised that I have wrinkles" (247).

In Mitch Albom's (1997) *Tuesdays with Morrie,* the reader is privy to the final journey of a lifelong teacher, Morrie Schwartz, as he struggles to live while learning how to die. This is the story of Morrie and his former student, Mitch, who spends each Tuesday with his teacher during the latter's final days. Mitch, who is ambitious and preoccupied with earning money and gathering possessions, learned valuable lessons from Morrie, who remained his teacher to the end. In the last paragraph of this tale of the poignant journey of two men—one young, the other old—Mitch closes with: "The class met on Tuesdays. No books were required. The subject was the meaning of life. It was taught from experience. The teaching goes on" (192).

Morrie's body changed and finally succumbed, but he was a passionate teacher, and this remained a large piece of who he was as a human being, husband, father, and friend. Although Morrie was old and ill, he was still able to teach and learn from others. In this book, Morrie engages in a dramatic struggle as his energy depletes, and he faces his dying as he had faced his living. The stories of those in our focus groups may not always be as dramatic as Morrie's, but the message is clear: "Tell people we are the same no matter what our outside covering may look like."

Ellen M. Gee and Meredith M. Kimball (1987) look at the double standard of aging from a woman's perspective. As they point out, women are viewed as aging sooner, and are seen as less attractive, than men of the same age and older. They mention L. Cohen's (1984) observation that, as they age, many men see themselves as young, virile, sexually attractive, and married to older women.

In our interviews, it became apparent that many of the women did not see themselves as "old" but, rather, as "getting older." It was interesting to us that some women did not want to admit their age and that others were passionate about staying and feeling young. Obviously, society's view of aging women both creates and reinforces this phenomenon. Women do tend to work hard at maintaining a youthful appearance. For the healthy woman this may simply be a continuation of who she really is and not, at least consciously, a symptom of accepting the double standard of aging.

When Diane was recruiting older persons to participate in the focus groups, she met one woman who stood out as having internalized ageist views. Louise was a seventy-year-old widow, although she looked younger with her dyed hair and bright coloured nail polish (on both hands and feet). She wore the same style of clothes she wore as a younger woman, and she absolutely refused to be part of any "seniors" group. In no way did she want to be associated with the term "senior." She saw herself as young, as "not really" over the age of sixty-five. In wanting to present a self that appeared younger than her chronological age, Louise showed the power of internalized ageism. She recognized that, in her culture, youth was valued while age was not.

In our research we did not find many common denominators with regard to opinions, perspectives, or concepts of aging. While focus group participants living near or in urban settings did seem to be less reflective about the aging process and more interested in keeping socially busy than did those living in rural settings, each had her or his own ideas about aging. Rural elders seemed to be more aware of their limitations as they grew older than did urban elders. We will discuss these rural/urban differences in Chapter 4, but, for now, let it suffice to say that the whole concept of aging is as diverse as are the people with whom we spoke. We found that the concept of aging is very personal and that the view of the individual does not necessarily fit with the view of society at large.

Throughout all of our focus groups the one issue that united all participants was their state of health. Many noted that good health, or at least the ability to keep going and lead fairly active lives, was key to their whole concept of growing old. Many did acknowledge that, if they suffered from chronic pain or breathing disorders, then they would certainly feel "old" or at the least "older." It was acknowledged that severe limitations due to health problems would have an effect on how they viewed the aging process and on how they experienced their ability to put mind over matter. It was noted that many of the participants did suffer from mild arthritis, stomach disorders, and heart problems; none of these ailments curtailed their usual activities.

It is clear from the comments of those in the focus groups that most of them were uncomfortable with specific labels that identify them as particular kinds of older persons. None used the pronouns "nearly" or "old, old" to define themselves or others, and almost all said that they felt that "age was a state on mind" and that life "goes on" regardless of the challenges of aging. Florida Scott-Maxwell (1968:16), writing in her seventies, reminds us that old age, like any other time of life, can be one of discovery: "I want to tell people approaching and perhaps fearing age that it is a time of discovery. If they say 'Of what?' I can only answer 'We must find out for ourselves, otherwise it won't be discovery.'"

THE NOVA SCOTIAN BLACK AND MI'KMAW COMMUNITIES

Imagine what it would be like to live in a community where growing older was a positive and inspiring experience, where younger people would respect, admire, and look up to older people and where there would be no stigma attached to growing old. *In Aging with Grace: What the Nun Study Teaches Us about Leading Longer, Healthier and More Meaningful Lives*, David Snowdon (2001) discusses his research into Alzheimer's disease. For many years, he and his colleagues worked with the sisters of Notre Dame, who live in a convent. He notes that living in such closed communities provides the Sisters with ever-present networks of love and support:

> The community stimulates their minds, celebrates their accomplishments, and shares their aspirations; it also encourages their silences, intimately understands their defeats, and nurtures them when their bodies fail them. From the day they enter the convent, they are members of a congregation that existed long before they were born. On the day they are laid to rest, they are celebrated by a community that will endure long after they are gone. How many of us are held so securely throughout our life? (202)

In our Black and Mi'kmaw focus groups we found a close approximation of this ideal. In both of these communities, members face discrimination and marginalization. Although these are negative realities, they nonetheless bring people together and reinforce familial and cultural ties that bind the generations together in mutual love, respect, and interdependence. To envision what such a supportive community might look like, we need to examine the historical underpinnings and experiences of the Black and Mi'kmaw peoples of Nova Scotia.

Growing Older in the Black Nova Scotian Culture

In 1996 the Canadian census introduced a new question regarding ethnic origin: "To which ethnic or cultural group(s) do your ancestors belong"? (http://www.statcan.ca/Daily/English/980217/d980217.htm). At that time, 17.9 percent (573,860) of Canadians responded that they were Black. In Nova Scotia that year, out of a total population of 899,970, 3.5 percent (31,320) claimed Black heritage. Of this number, approximately 1.5 percent were aged sixty-five and over (figures obtained from the Senior Citizens Secretariat of Nova Scotia, personal communication, May 28, 2001). Nova Scotia had the highest proportion (69 percent) of Canadian-born among the visible minority population, a result of earlier generations of Blacks who settled in this province. Nova Scotia and New Brunswick were the only two provinces in Canada in which the majority of the visible minority was Canadian-born (ibid).

In 1605 Mathieu Dacosta, a Black seaman, arrived in Nova Scotia and acted as a French and Mi'kmaw interpreter. He was the first recorded Black man to reach Canada. (Black Cultural Centre for Nova Scotia Web site: http://www.bccns.com). African–Canadians have a rich and diverse history of settlement in Nova Scotia, from 1749 when the first groups of Black people were enslaved in the province through to the arrival of the United Empire Loyalists between 1775 and 1782. The first Black refugees arrived in Nova Scotia after the war between the United States and Britain (1812–16), and, finally, a wave of immigrants from the Caribbean landed in Nova Scotia between 1890 and 1920. Black Nova Scotians have a proud history; they have achieved much in the face of adversity.

We wanted to know if the experience of aging as a Black elder was different than that of aging as a Caucasian elder, and, if it was, we wanted to know the extent to which culture affected these differences. As well as holding focus groups within two of Nova Scotia's Black communities, we also drew upon data gathered from other sources. In the summer of 2000, when Jeanette was the president of the Gerontology Association of Nova Scotia, she organized a conference entitled *The Cultural Diversity of Growing Older in Nova Scotia*. As part of that event a panel of Black elders discussed their experiences. That same summer, the Multi-Cultural Health Council held a similar workshop in Halifax, and once again the needs of

Black elders were addressed. In 2000, Jeanette invited a group of Black elders to speak with her cross-cultural aging class. Later on, we shall present the results of all of these events as well as the focus group discussions.

Gerry Browning (who asked that her real name be used), a Black Nova Scotian activist, introduced Diane to two Black communities in Nova Scotia. One is situated in East Preston and is located close to Halifax, and the other is a community in Bridgetown, in the Annapolis Valley.

In the semi-rural community of Bridgetown, ten women, ranging in ages from sixty-one to eighty-four, took part in a focus group. They insisted that old age was not necessarily associated with chronological age. They made statements such as, "you're are as old as you feel" and described growing old as occurring once a person lacks interest in living. Mary, an eighty-year-old widow, put it this way: "You are as old as you feel. When you decide not to be interested in anything, I guess that's when you are old. I don't feel old. I keep too busy. I belong to the church choir, this community group. And we are always busy."

Eighty-four-year-old Betsy described her life this way: "I have some freedom now after all the children have gone. I try to adjust to what I can do and try not to dwell on what I can't do. There seems to be more contentment in my life, as I get older. I don't seem to get as angry as I used to when I was younger."

Most of the participants agreed with these two women. They were all actively involved in their community and didn't really dwell on their ages. The Bridgetown group has recently recorded a gospel tape that has been used as a fund-raiser for their hall, and they felt that their contribution to the community was ongoing and that it was not related to age.

In Jeanette's class some members of the Black community noted that their experiences of growing older seemed different from those experienced by members of the mainstream White culture. As one eighty-four-year-old woman remarked:

> I really feel that we are more respected in our community. I think it has to do with the role of the church and the fact that we older people are so strong there. We were the ones who got to work hard and make a life for our people here, and the youngsters appreciate and respect us because of that. I don't see that happening in the White community.

Another member of this panel noted that the Black community had faced many upheavals while living in Nova Scotia (especially as a result of the provincial government's attempt to resettle Black families, moving them from Africville to various places throughout metropolitan Halifax). This time of adversity brought the community closer together than ever before. As she put it:

> The Black community really pulled together to fight the government over Africville, even though they managed to get us off the land, we stayed close and still celebrate that place every summer. Everyone in the community knows how hard the older people worked then and now to keep us together, and they all appreciate what we did for them. The older ones are really respected because we did the fighting and the keeping it all together.

Participants in the focus groups were not familiar with the science of gerontology, but they did agree that doctors, nurses, care givers, social workers, and governments could benefit from gerontological studies, perhaps discovering issues important to older citizens and finding ways to alleviate some of their challenges. They did not, however, see the study of gerontology as affecting their lives. As one widow in her seventies put it: "Black voices are really never heard. No one really listens to us. We have to do for ourselves. We are the only ones who will. Not only are we older, but we are Black—the double whammy!"

The East Preston focus group consisted of twelve women and two men, ranging in ages from sixty to eighty. It was significant that, as we went around the circle introducing ourselves, we found that the family of the average group member consisted of ten children (some families had three offspring, while some had twenty). It seemed amazing that, in spite of having so many children—far more than the normal 1.8—these women were also able to be so involved in their communities (working for church activities and choirs, raising their children, working in and outside of the home to provide for their families, etc.). What was also clear was the amount of support that women provided to each other so that they could accomplish all of this work. One of the women in this group described old age as follows: "I will be old when I can't wear high heels anymore." Another woman, this one in her seventies, declared: "I guess you are old when you have to go into a nursing home!" None of the members of this group included her- or himself in the category "old."

Only one person in the East Preston group had heard about gerontology, and she was a retired teacher and social activist. While the members of this group did not see the study of gerontology as having an impact on their lives, they did mention nutrition and skin care as issues. It was at this point that we discovered race-based difference of perception. The discussion turned to skin care and the colours of various products, such as Band-Aids, lotions, and so on. Some of these products are advertised as skin tone, or flesh-coloured. One eighty-year-old widow asked, "Whose skin are they talking about anyway? Do you ever see any brown Band-Aids?"

This theme was mentioned earlier, at the gerontology association conference, when a Black nurse noted that, in hospital settings, the cream normally used for treating bed sores was not helpful in treating the sores of Black people because it was too oily. This same nurse noted that many Black seniors in nursing homes have trouble with their hair because those with Afro styles cannot get access to Vaseline, which is needed to keep the hair from breaking. Those who want to wear dreadlocks experience similar problems. This nurse also noted that most Black families do not institutionalize their elders because to do so would not be culturally acceptable: "They took care of us all our lives, now it's our turn to take care of them."

No one in either of the focus groups had heard of, or knew anything about, theories of aging, nor had they attended any courses, workshops, or conferences dealing with the topic of gerontology. They were not on any mailing lists that might supply them with information about such events. As well, they doubted whether their concerns would be addressed at such gatherings unless they were specifically asked for their input.

When disengagement theory was explained to them they objected to it. Indeed, many participants reacted strongly to the whole idea of "disengaging" from anything. As Betsy, an eighty-four-year-old woman in the Bridgetown group, exclaimed:

> The only thing I disengaged from was paid employment. I wouldn't call it that either. I left paid employment and am now a full-time volunteer in my church, my community club and in various organizations around the province. I am always working to have our voices heard. I never stop. We may change our direction but we don't disengage!

One widow described her experience in this way:

> After my husband died I did retreat for a while. I felt like I was
> in a cocoon. I guess I did disengage for some time. I had to heal.
> I spent a lot of time alone, thinking things through. But I came
> back, it was only temporary. I am busier than ever now. I have
> discovered new freedoms now; I have a new lease on life. I just
> needed a time out.

In both focus groups participants strongly connected with continu-
ity/activity theory, and, as we listened to them describe their daily lives,
it was obvious that they felt lucky to be as healthy as they were, actively
involved in their communities and with their children and grandchildren. A very strong family connection was evident.

Placing labels on people became an issue as we discussed the aged as
a subculture. The participants did not see themselves as members of a
subculture because they were older but, rather, because they were Black.
As Betsy said: "Others may put those labels on us but we don't put them
on ourselves. We are in a minority as Black people, and perhaps some
would describe that as a subculture. I don't see age having much to do
with this."

A widow from the Bridgetown group offered the following:

> There recently was an article in a newspaper on shopping
> locally. It encouraged people to frequent the local stores and
> support local people. This article made me cry. I went to bed and
> cried and cried. I finally got up and had to write something
> down, expressing my deep hurt. We Black people have been
> "forced" to shop locally, in our own communities, because we
> weren't welcome in other communities. We weren't allowed to
> shop in other places. So for us this article was another insult to us
> as Black people. It brought back the memories of having to "stay
> within our own." I got my response published and felt better!

As White people we had not anticipated this kind of response. It was an
eye-opener.

Again, as in other focus groups, exchange theory was not popular.
Some felt insulted by it, and others simply said that they had more to offer.
It was generally agreed that, as we get older, we gain experience, wisdom,
patience, and coping skills. As one mother of twenty children said:

> As we get older we gain patience and more understanding. We
> don't get as angry as young people. We have learned how to

cope. We have been too busy trying to feed our children I guess. I used to have to chop and carry my own wood for fires to keep everyone warm. Everyone in the family had jobs to do, all geared to feeding us. Even the small children gathered berries from the fields. Our lives were made up of valuable exchanges, each member of the family doing their part. We didn't see one as more valuable than another. As we get older we can offer our experiences. We have learned to cope with discrimination over the years. We can teach the others non-violent ways of coping.

Members of the East Preston focus group described their lives as exciting and challenging. They believed that each person had a choice with regard to how to live. As one participant noted: "You can decide! I chose a long time ago to be active, get lots of exercise, be involved, look after my health and work on my spiritual growth. I share my life with others in mutual love and respect. My family and my church sustain me and help me keep positive." As Dot described her feelings, others nodded their heads in agreement.

When discussing modernization theory, both groups had diverse responses. Some felt utter frustration with bank machines and telephone "button pushing." One woman described some members in her community as follows: "I don't mind learning new things. But for some in our communities, they are illiterate to some extent and fearful to tell anyone that they don't understand. They feel isolated when they can't talk to another human being. The lack of personal contact is missing and people get left by the wayside." Others were enthusiastic about learning computers and getting on the Internet: "I have lots of fun. We have a Cap Site [Community Access Program] here and people are learning how to operate the computers. It's fun."

In discussions of age-stratification theory, it was generally agreed that, within the Black community, the hierarchy of importance was not as evident as it was in other, predominantly White, communities. According to a retired teacher:

Here in the Black community there is more respect for the elders. It is remembered what we have done and are still doing. Because we are so close-knit and work closely with each other there is more love and respect. The community helps raise the children, so everyone knows everyone else. There are many shared experiences as the children grow up in this community. It is true that they usually leave to gain employment, but the roots are there. They come back. In the rural communities we see some disintegration as the young people are forced to go further away to find jobs. But as I said, the ties are there and the memories remain.

It was fun discussing what successful aging looked like. Participants had many ideas, and most took full part in their exchange. One enthusiastic community worker put it this way:

As long as we have stable minds, and relatively good health, stay active and are financially stable, we can keep going forever! Yes I have to accept that I can't do everything that I used too, or at least not as quickly, but I can still do most things. I think the key to it all is "acceptance." Accepting that changes will come and adjusting to those changes without getting "down."

Maggie, sixty-seven, described her life this way: "I need to take care of myself first now. I spent years looking after others. Now I realize I need to care for myself so I can keep going and doing the things I love to do. My children and my grandchildren give me great joy. I am peaceful now."

To reiterate, in general (with the exception of continuity theory and activity theory), the participants did not see that theories of aging affected their lives to any great extent. They did, however, hope that governments, health care systems, and caregivers would consider some of these theories. And they felt strongly that *From the Inside Looking Out* would help put a face on the reality of aging not only for Nova Scotia in general, but also for the Nova Scotian Black community in particular.

Health issues were a priority for these groups, with arthritis and memory loss being two particular challenges. As one gregarious widow in her eighties commented: "I get so anxious when I forget things. I have always been able to manage independently, but, as my memory leaves me, sometimes I do get anxious. I guess I am going to have to make lists for myself and start laughing about it. The more upset I get the more I forget!" Most of the participants live with some kind of arthritis. However, they seemed to continue their activities in spite of this, adjusting to their situation as the need arose (e.g., through acquiring electric can openers, raised toilet seats, etc.).

Habitation, transportation, and independence were three other challenges mentioned. Some families still live in extreme poverty, and most of those present spoke about situations with which they were familiar.

One such story came from a retired teacher in her seventies: "There is a widow lady down the road that lives in a little house with no insulation. Her health is not good. Some of the neighbours help but it really isn't enough. Her children have moved away and there she is. Too proud to ask for help. She manages, but sometimes I wonder." The importance of good housing was not a matter for debate.

The availability of transportation and independence is much higher in East Preston than it is in Bridgetown. In East Preston, which is close to Dartmouth and Halifax, many of the participants' children still live in the community and travel to the cities to work. Thus the older persons living there still often have their families to assist them in living independent lives. If the older people can't drive, then there is usually someone around to drive them. Younger people are available to shovel snow and cut grass. Shopping trips were easily arranged with other family members. Although the loss of one's driver's licence was a big concern for the members of both groups, those in the East Preston group had access to more help in this regard. Not only did they have family and friends to help, but they also had access to good public transportation.

In Bridgetown, which is further away from job opportunities than is East Preston, older persons have different experiences. Mary, who is in her eighties, explained:

> The young people in our community, for the most part, have had to move away to get jobs. Many of them are better educated than we are and need to travel away to take advantage of their education and to earn a living for their families. In this community we are left to help each other to some extent. That is good except that we are all getting older. Transportation is more difficult. Some of those who can no longer drive don't like to ask for help and sometimes they don't know where to ask. We need to help people have access to services that are available.

Thus, it is apparent that it is possible for older people to remain independent for a longer time in a community that is close to working opportunities and that has adequate public transit (e.g., East Preston) than it is for them to do so in a community that does not have such amenities (e.g., Bridgetown).

After the focus group was formally over, some of these women brought up the subject of elder abuse, and, while no specific details were forthcoming, it was obviously part of their experience, whether in their own families or in the families of others. Frustration, lack of income, and lack of control were some of the issues that were invoked around this problem. They acknowledged that women were survivors and were able to cope in a positive way, but they expressed concern for the men in the community. Here is what Betsy had to say:

> I don't know what it is with these men. They retire and don't know what to do. They have kept their feelings all bottled up inside for so long, they can't seem to express themselves. Depression quite often follows retirement. They become "stick in the muds." You will notice many Black women doing things on their own. The men tend to stay home.

With regard to health care, Mary expressed her concerns as follows:

> Many seniors here are lonely. A lack of compatibility seems to rear its head here. Women have been actively involved in community and church. Many politically as well. Working to create a better place for their families to live in. Men, on the other hand, go to work, come home, period. When they retire, couples discover they have little in common. It is a problem for some families. As well, homecare is not adequate here. There are very few Black caregivers. People need help with lawn care, snow shovelling and more intense housecleaning. Some folks have very little pensions. For those of us who worked outside the home, things are better financially. However for most elderly women, the old age pension is the only pension they have. It is not easy. Our club members try to help but we can't do it all. We aren't spring chickens anymore either!

It was noted that, while there are few Black caregivers, it was more important that homecare people be of the same gender as those they are tending and that they treated the elderly with love and respect.

Many noted that Medic Alert helped seniors stay independent longer. Spring and fall clean-ups by Homecare Nova Scotia (which provides services to eligible persons aged sixty-five and over) were also beneficial. For most participants in the focus groups, social solutions to their challenges would involve more homecare, more outside help, expanded services, a resource directory, and the recruitment of more Black caregivers.

In the East Preston group it was noted that, upon retiring, only five out of fourteen participants had work-related pensions. A retired teacher commented: "Before 1960 Blacks in Nova Scotia did not have the right to an education. So many of us had 'day work' and then worked at home, gathering berries, housecleaning, providing food for the family. Women and children were responsible for collecting wood for the stove as well." By "day work" she means cleaning other peoples' houses; others described this as "working out." One eighty-year-old woman with twenty children described her existence: "I had to feed my children; I carried wood on my back. The day I gave birth to one of my children, I carried wood that morning. We hardly stopped our daily routine to have babies."

We discussed how elderly Black voices are not being heard by politicians and the general public. When asked about expressing their needs, one participant said:

> What's the point? From our past experiences we have learned that very few people are interested. That is why it is difficult for some seniors to speak out now. What is different now? We experience racism and ageism together from people outside the community. I think it is political lack of respect. Politicians come in here to be seen but they don't listen.

A retired teacher in the East Preston group belongs to the Halifax Regional District Seniors Council. Her club sends two delegates to the council meetings to discuss issues of safety, policing, pensions, and prescription drugs. Several members of the East Preston group also belong to the Seniors Secretariat. For the most part these women and men are active in their own communities. A few venture forth to voice their opinions, but, for the most part, there is enough work to do within the communities themselves. It was agreed that politicians need to come to the Black communities and ask "how they can serve." With respect to the Victorian Order of Nurses (VON), it was also suggested that representatives from the VON and Homecare need to ask the Black communities what they need rather than telling them what they can have.

Spirituality is crucially important to many of the people in these two focus groups. Their history has proven to them that "the Lord loves them when no one else does." The church, its music, and preaching all help to lift their spirits not only in times of trouble, but also in times of joy. Seventy-year-old Maryann exclaimed:

> Oh, how I love to sing! We always used to sing. I can remember the stories of my ancestors talking about the days of slavery.

> When all else failed, they would sing and praise the Lord. No one could take their spirits from them. They could whip their bodies but not touch their souls! I sing and dance around to praise the Lord. It is a reminder that we are worth something. That Jesus loves us!

Betsy told the story of a preacher who came to town when she was a little girl. His words have stuck with her throughout the years: "This preacher came to a camp meeting when I was small and could he preach! I will always remember his words, saying, 'Be a Singing Church—the devil doesn't come near a singing church!'"

Dorothy, who as been an activist for many years and who was involved in education, denounced the province's new policy on school board members. This last year (2000) each district was asked to elect a Black representative as well as regular members. For Dorothy, this was a slap in the face:

> Why can't I run on my merits, not because I am Black? I do not agree with this policy and so I did not run as the Black representative. Needless to say, I lost. However, sometimes one has to stand up for what one believes. I wanted to be elected for my proven abilities in the past, not just because I am Black.

While group members agreed that gerontologists should work with seniors, they believed that what was most important was for politicians, health care providers, and senior members of the Black community to all come to the table and sit in equality and respect, sharing ideas and really listening to each other. These older persons told us that this was the first time any White person had come into the Black community with an interest in listening to their stories and hearing their voices.

The video *Black Mother, Black Daughter,* produced by the National Film Board of Canada in 1989 and directed by Sylvia Hamilton and Claire Preito, gives a vivid picture of the bonds created in the Black community—bonds with family, church, and community. In addition, this video demonstrates the strong ties between mothers and daughters. Sylvia Hamilton, a Black Nova Scotian filmmaker, speaks about learning, at a very young age, about the interdependence between family, church, and community. Pearleen Oliver speaks about the loss of culture when Africville was torn down and replaced by a park. Other members speak of a loss of heart and soul when the church was demolished. However, the people of Africville survived through their family and community ties. Oliver goes on to say that she remembers the words of the Honourable Joseph Howe, the then premier of Nova Scotia, who had said "the Province of Nova Scotia owes you people a debt of justice." She says that debt was paid with interest when Corrine Sparks became the first Black female judge. She speaks about the long way women have come from the days of slavery, when they were their masters' property. She recalled the story of the slave woman who stole ribbons from her mistress and was given thirty-nine lashes in public. Some of these slaves committed suicide, believing that was the only way to freedom. Many of the Black Loyalists who landed in Nova Scotia in May 1783, were seamstresses and/or cooks. According to Oliver, "The average woman had to do the work of a man." Little is known about the Black Loyalists who settled in Shelburne and Birchtown as it is only recently that the Black Cultural Centre of Nova Scotia has begun to investigate their stories.

In *Black Mother, Black Daughter*, Marie Hamilton spoke about the early days, when the White settlers had little respect for the Black settlers. The attitude seemed to be that the latter were lucky to be free and that anything was good enough for them. Needless to say, the original Black settlers had very little and certainly were not treated as equals.

Today, notably through groups like Four the Moment,[3] Black women's stories are being sung. The women of today are "still standing" because of the women who went before them. Hamilton recalls an incident that clearly exhibits racism. Apparently she was going to church and saw a little boy fall off his bicycle. His mother came up to him and said, "Hurry up, we need to go to church." He didn't want to go, and his mother, looking at Hamilton, said to him, 'If you don't hurry that lady is going to get you!" Hamilton immediately told the child she would not "get him" and asked his mother, who was carrying a prayer book, if she were going to or coming from church. Before the woman could answer, Hamilton cut her off with: "No matter which, you certainly left God behind today."

She went on to explain that the boy's mother had effectively instilled in him a fear of Black people. And so it goes. Hamilton concluded by talking about how she had "wanted to be a nurse." "But in those days they didn't accept Black women into nursing school so I had to become a teacher. I really wanted to help people in the community learn. Most parents were illiterate and the children were so eager to learn."

The church is the centre of the community and, as one woman in the video said: "A community that has no church is not a community.

When you hear that you realize the damage done in taking down the church in Africville!" In the video, Sylvia Hamilton speaks about her mother taking her to church and to the Women's Institute meetings at the East Preston African United Baptist Church. The women would meet twice a year to celebrate their faith and each other. Recently, one of these meetings was held in North Preston, and the older women were celebrated; it was a time to "honour the elders." These women were the pioneers, the ones who had gone before and who had made the path easier for their daughters.

The caring and nurturing went beyond their own families. *Black Mother, Black Daughter* also introduced Cleo Whiley and her husband, who had twenty-two foster children because they loved to hear their laughter and talk. "So many lonely children needed a home so we just took them in."

Edith Clayton, the last of the original basket weavers in her family, spoke in the video about her mother:

> My mother taught me to weave baskets when I was eight years old. I remember the morning my mother died. It was 5:00 AM and she asked me to get her a drink. She took three sips and said to me, "That is all you can do for me now, God will bless you." And she died. My mother raised twelve children alone and I was the youngest. I didn't like being poor.

Edith's daughter explained her journey: "I always watched the other girls. They were getting an education and I wanted to do the same. I finally did. I went to Dalhousie but it was the examples set before me that kept me going."

Daurene Lewis, who is a weaver and was the mayor of Annapolis Royal—and one of the first Blacks to be elected to municipal politics in Nova Scotia—spoke about her history:

> My mother would get up at 4:00 AM to weave so the children wouldn't get in her way. We got used to the click, click, and click of the loom. I learned how to weave by osmosis. The story of Rose Fortune, who was my great grandmother five times re-moved, we heard so many times. Her story has been passed down to us from generation to generation. Rose was the first female policewoman in North America, in the Town of Annapolis Royal. She started the Lewis Transfer Business by carting garden produce by ox and cart to the ferry where it was transported

across the harbour to the City Market. From there the business grew and is still operating today. Her story is my inspiration—to know we can do whatever we put our minds to.

Marie Hamilton gave a last bit of advice to today's young people when she said, "In the struggle, anger will only stop you from going ahead. That negative energy gets in the way." Indeed, the stories of mothers and daughters so vividly documented in *Black Mother, Black Daughter* moves the viewer and provides her with new insight into the struggles faced by Black Nova Scotians.

The three-hundred-year history of Blacks in Nova Scotia involved hardship, discrimination, and prejudice; it also involved facing adversity and overcoming it, creating supportive communities, and making significant contributions to the life of the province. For many years Blacks have not had any positive role models in mainstream society. This is changing, as younger Black people are becoming educated and are being integrated into that society. Consider, for example, people like Sylvia Hamilton (the filmmaker who made *Black Mother, Black Daughter*), George Elliott Clarke (playwright), Delvina Bernard (singer/songwriter), and Wayne Adams (in 1997 the first member of the Black community in Nova Scotia to be elected to provincial politics).

Black communities need to have better communication/transportation systems, and they need to have access to resources that will help elders live independent lives for as long as possible. It would be extremely traumatic to move elderly people out of the communities within which they have grown up and to which they are both socially and spiritually rooted. Whereas aging obviously has many similarities in both the Black communities and the White communities, racism adds yet another burden to those living in the former.

Growing Older in the Mi'kmaw Culture

There are many similarities and close ties between the experiences of Black Nova Scotian elders and Mi'kmaw elders. It has been noted that, when Blacks first arrived in Nova Scotia, Aboriginal peoples "helped us to survive through the long winters, showed us how to hunt for food, build shelters, and stay warm and welcomed us onto their lands" (Nova Scotia's Black Heritage. wysiwyg: 120/http:// Halifax. about...lifax/ library/weekly/aa020201a.htm). In 1996, the percentage of Aboriginal people over the age of sixty-five living in Nova Scotia was 0.3 (Senior Citizens Secretariat of Nova Scotia, personal communication, May 28, 2001).

On a sunny day in May 2001, we took the six-hour drive to Cape
Breton, where we had been invited to hold a focus group with a number
of Mi'kmaw elders from the Eskasoni reserve. This reserve is one of the
largest in Nova Scotia, and those with whom we met made us very
welcome. As in the Black community, organizers were both pleased and
surprised to learn that we wanted to include the voices and experiences
of their elders within this book. As with the Black communities, we
were the first White researchers/writers to want to do so. Amongst those
with whom we met was the well known and admired poet Rita Joe, the
"bard of Eskasoni" as she is lovingly known amongst her people. Rita
Joe not only read us one of her poems, which she especially selected for
this occasion, but she also gave us permission to quote from it (and one
other) in this book. The first piece she chose expressed her feelings about
being included in *From the Inside Looking Out*:

> How Soon Will I See Greatness?
> My fears unveil my longing
> To possess the very important view
> In showing you my world.
> No longer made important
> —this year of the jet.
>
> How soon will I be allowed
> to be as great as I was.
> My back as broad and tall as trees
> —the speed, my run.
>
> How soon will I see greatness?
> Even my dead you shun
> I want as much or greater than you.
> The need to share like I've always done.
> I want ....
>
> How soon will I see greatness?
> The major point of my life
> The weary uplift of my soul.
> Let me have my say.
> The perspective will be my own.

Imagine what it might look like to grow old in a culture where you
felt respected, cared for, and important. Where you still felt useful and

needed, as vital to your family, friends, neighbours, and culture as you ever were. So it was with the elders of Eskasoni. While there, we were most fortunate in being invited to supper at the local Roman Catholic convent, where we spoke with the nuns, some of whom were aged sixty-five and over. Here we met Sister Adele (not her real name), who, at age ninety-two, was as much needed by her community as ever. Sister Adele was an excellent cook and pastry chef, and she prepared for us a meal fit for queens. Even though she was hard of hearing, Sister Adele was fit and healthy and felt very much an integral part of her community life. She was inspirational, an excellent example of what it is like to grow older in a setting within which one feels loved, needed, and productive.

We did not go into many details about gerontology with the Eskasoni elders because, at the outset, they made it clear that they were not familiar with it as a discipline or as a set of practices in their community. They said that they had never heard of it. Although one of the workers at the health centre explained it to them, they had no experience of it and little interest in it. Consequently, we spoke mainly about old age, successful aging, and how aging in a community such as theirs is different from aging in a Caucasian community. In discussing these issues, recipes and stories of herbal medicine cures were shared. Storytelling is a crucial element of Aboriginal culture; it is one of the means by which traditional values are passed down through the generations. In Mi'kmaw culture elders are the transmitters of historical and cultural change, and storytelling is the forum within which such experiences and lessons are shared. When we asked what it felt like to be old, or what old age looked like, these were some of the stories we heard.

Maggie, a community activist who is in her eighties, described her experience: "I feel like a sixteen-year-old but my body feels rotten. I feel that my bones are rotting away. I try to keep happy and positive. There are so many things I still have left to do but sometimes my body won't let me!" Willie, seventy-four and the father of fourteen children "or thereabouts" described his experiences of growing older:

> I have arthritis something terrible. Sometimes I can hardly get out of bed in the morning. I suffer from prostate cancer as well. I brought it on myself though. In my earlier years, drinking, smoking and sleeping outside certainly didn't help my body parts. I am paying for it now. I stopped drinking twenty some years ago but the damage had already been done.

Sixty-seven-year-old Doris, who lives alone, described her feelings as follows: "I had four children and I live alone now. My bones feel old. I don't want to be old. I have lung cancer and only one kidney. I try to walk everyday. I learned to make baskets and quilts from my mother-in-law. I still try to do a bit of that work."

Maggie, also known as "Doctor Granny" because she recently received an honorary doctorate from the local university (in recognition of her community activism and storytelling), has had many interesting aging experiences. At eighty-six she has been a counsellor and has taught arts and crafts, basket-making, and beadwork. She has literally kept the old crafts alive and has been a role model for many of her people. She lived in a wigwam as a child, and she shares these experiences with the younger people. Rita Joe expressed her gratitude to Maggie for the help that she has extended to her over the years.

Eighty-one-year-old Betty, who arrived at Eskasoni as a war bride from Holland in the early 1940s, described how she felt about growing older in Eskasoni:

> I have always felt so welcome here. When I first arrived, we got off the train in Sydney and had to start walking to Eskasoni. It was so different for me. It was not easy but my mother-in-law welcomed me and I have always felt part of the community. As I get older I feel safe. Safer than if I was in a city. I know my friends and neighbours keep an eye on me and I am not afraid to live here by myself. This is my home.

When asked how they felt about growing older or what has changed in their community since their grandparents' time, several different impressions emerged. Betty felt that there was still a great deal of respect for the elders and that the young people still asked them for advice. Willie disagreed:

> Things have changed. There isn't the same respect, the same sharing, the same need to rely on each other. When the government programs and welfare came into being, people became more independent and don't have to depend on each other so much for food and shelter. We have become disconnected somehow. It isn't the same anymore. The hunting and gathering way of life is no more. We are told when we can fish and hunt and where. We can be fishing along a river bank or lake and have someone come up and ask, "Do you have a licence?" There is no incentive to do anything on our own. We are discouraged from

doing anything! I think it was James Watts in the States who said, "You don't have to go to Russia or China to see communism working. You just have to look on the reserves!" We all get the same cheques and have to follow all the economic rules.

Rita Joe disagreed with Willie's assessment of the situation regarding the respect younger Mi'kmaq had for elders on the Eskasoni reserve. She noted that there are many negative stereotypes about, and misunderstandings of, Aboriginal life, and she related this personal story:

> I was going around talking to non-Natives about our culture and way of life. This one little boy came up to me, felt my arm and said, "You feel the same as my grandmother." We are the same. Another young non-Native came up to me and asked, "Do you get pogey?" I said, "What is pogey?" It was then explained to me that it was welfare. I responded by saying, "No, I travel around and teach and write books and poetry. I earn my living." These stereotypes are everywhere. We have to share our stories and break down these myths that none of us work and earn our living.

Many of the elders agreed that the hunting and gathering activities of the past were over. Pollution, logging, and restrictions on where to log, when and where to fish, where to hunt—not to mention competition from non-Aboriginals for natural resources—have caused the demise of this way of life. Fish, rabbits, and other game are not as plentiful as they once were. Willie expressed concern that younger people had no incentives to work or to become more highly educated because they had the feeling that they could always rely on government programs and services. As well, he felt that traditional values had been replaced with capitalist consumer values.

Our conversation then moved to the concept of community and to what the elders felt was distinctive about Mi'kmaw cultural practices. According to Rita Joe: "One of the cultural differences here is that, for the most part, we don't believe in nursing homes for our elders. We usually find a way to care for them in their familiar surroundings. There is always room for one more in our homes. To move people away from the land and their communities is almost like killing them."

Agreeing with Rita's comments, Leigh, a seventy-four-year-old elder, told the story of how she and her family had coped with looking after her husband, who had cancer:

The doctor said we needed to move him to a nursing home. That we could no longer look after him. I gathered my six children around and we discussed the problem. The kids agreed that "you guys looked after us, now it is our turn to look after you"; we took turns looking after my husband. It was hard but we did it and he died at home.

Willie responded to this story by exclaiming: "I am going into a nursing home when I can't take care of myself any longer! I will not be a burden on my kids! I don't want them to have to look after me that way!"

There were clearly great differences of opinion as to whether or not institutionalization was a desirable option with regard to caring for one's elders. However, there was general agreement that, if the nursing home were located within the community, then this could be an attractive option.

We asked what happened in the community after a person died. According to Sister Veronica:

After a person dies, traditionally, family members prepared the body; however the funeral director provides that service now. After the funeral service and a shared community meal, neighbours bring items to auction off along with personal items of the deceased. The money is then used to help with burial expenses. This is one of the traditions that have not been lost. People share what they have.

Sister Veronica later took us on a tour of the church and explained that sometimes, if the home of the deceased was too small to hold a large crowd, the wake would be held in the church basement.

It was noted that approximately 90 percent of the Mi'kmaw community is Christian, and we asked how this came to be. Willie suggested that many Christian beliefs were familiar and were similar to Mi'kmaw beliefs. His people believed in an afterlife and in the Creator, and so the one-god concept was acceptable. While the subjects of colonialism and the imposition of Roman Catholicism were not discussed in detail, the following story, told by Doris, clearly indicates that the transition from the traditional Mi'kmaw belief system to that brought over by the missionaries was not a smooth one.

There was a girl who drank a lot but when she became pregnant she stopped. The baby was baptized but died at three months old. The woman began to drink again and carry on. In the end she had seven children and they all died at three months old. She got very sick with TB and asked for the priest to give her last rites. The priest refused to come, saying she was no good. In two or three more days, they asked again, and again the priest said no. After the third time of asking she died. When they told the priest, he said, "Bury her on the other side of the graveyard, she goes to hell." And so they buried her on the other side of the graveyard. The people saw a light going up into the air, sort of like the northern lights or a fiery aura. They were afraid she was in hell. This story is a true story and took place in Antigonish about one hundred years ago. The bishop was told the story and agreed to come and look. The bishop picked up the priest and together they went to the grave. There they saw seven angels, kneeling, holding candles. The bishop gave the priest hell, telling the priest, "You never judge. God judges. You pray for the people. You pray for her. You help her prepare to die." As the story goes, they dug up the woman's body and buried her in the graveyard. She lost seven children, and seven angels appeared to take her home.

Very little was said about the Jesuits or the residential schools, even though several of the elders were products of these institutions. This silence surrounding what is known to have been an extraordinarily painful experience was most eloquent, as was the general silence around issues of poverty, violence, and alcoholism. It must, however, be re-membered that we were White visitors to a First Nations community; that we did not pursue these issues; and that, quite understandably, the people wished to emphasize the positive aspects of their lives.

When we were speaking of traditions and spirituality the issue of sweat lodges came up. Willie insisted that "these were a Western idea." Rita, on the other hand, suggested that, according to her reading and research, sweat lodge cleansings were a long-time Mi'kmaw practice:

> I have studied this and our people have had sweat lodges for many years. Today there are several people in our community that practice fasting as well. They go out for four days fasting before going into the sweat lodge. It is a way of healing and getting in touch with the Creator.

The community of Eskasoni has approximately 250 families. Maggie described what it was like when she was younger: "There were only seventeen families in Eskasoni when I was growing up. I was about twelve, some seventy-two years ago. Now there are about three thousand people. Young people are staying in school longer. Some are going to college and fit in anywhere." She went on to tell this story:

> There was an old woman dying in the community. People went to sit with her and ask her questions. She remembered her childhood back to 1910. The further back she went in her history the more she taught those listening to her stories. In her dying she was still teaching about the old ways. She described driving in a horse and buggy. She was still respected and revered as she died. She was never made to feel useless.

Lil mentioned that an elder is usually invited to tell stories at most of the public functions held in the community. It was suggested that the younger generation do not listen to stories as much as they used to. It was evident to us that some of the elders believed this to be true, while others hoped the stories were still being heard and respected.

One of the traditions still followed in many Aboriginal cultures involves the use of herbal medicines. Blueberry root is used to make teas; alder is gathered to make a tea that can bring down fevers. According to Maggie, the ability to recognize and gather wild flowers, roots, and herbs is a "dying art." Nonetheless, even though, due to modern farming and agricultural practices many wild plants, trees, shrubs, and herbs are no longer grown, there are still elders who know where to find medicinal plants. Pat, who is sixty-nine, explained her knowledge of herbal medicines:

> I learned from my sister-in-law. She would gather herbs and make an ointment. This is all written down so we can pass it along. My Uncle Roddy had a huge cancerous sore. This ointment was applied to it daily and finally it cleared up. It all seemed to lump together, terrible stuff came out of it, but in the end he was cured. I remember her keeping everything in different containers so they wouldn't get mixed up. She has everything described so people will be able to recognize the different herbs and roots.

Another elder mentioned bear oil as being very popular not only in healing, but also in keeping hair beautiful and black. Even though it is hard to come by, apparently it is still in common use among Aboriginal people in both Nova Scotia and Newfoundland.

Rita told the story of going home from the hospital after having a baby: "I was still bleeding and an old woman in our community came to me with a bottle of herbal medicine. I asked what it was, and she replied, "Never mind what the heck it is, just drink it." I did, and all my problems cleared up. I remember it tasted sweet. I was about twenty-five or twenty-six then."

Brit, a seventy-five-year-old widow with eighteen children, talked about the need to keep productive and busy in old age:

> I can't do anything about getting older, we all do it. I have to keep busy. Next week I will be planting potatoes. I am used to working all the time. I was in the residential school for five years. I am old all right, with tumorous things bothering me, but I just keep going. I'm not sure if I am cured yet or not. My oldest child is fifty-four, and my youngest thirty-two. One lives in London, Ontario, the others in Eskasoni. I lost two boys. My first baby died at nine months of whooping cough, and I had two miscarriages. But life goes on.

In response to Brit's story, Rita emphasized the courage of her people: "We never stopped trying. We had to overcome obstacles and we did. We had to keep going."

In summing up our conversation we asked the elders if there was anything they wanted to share with our readers. Sister Veronica stated, "Tell the people our way of life has not stopped. We have had to adjust to what is expected. We have no fear of death."

Rita Joe (1969) dedicates *Song of Rita Joe: Autobiography of a Mi'kmaq Poet* to "my children and their children's children, and to all people who read about and identify with my life. Alasutmay ujit kilow [I pray for you]." She reiterated these sentiments to us as we drove her home and visited her house.

We were both deeply moved by our talks with the Mi'kmaw elders; and the poetry of Rita Joe and her life story touched our hearts in a way that cannot be described in words. Rita has had a hard life. She was orphaned at five and spent many years in a series of abusive foster homes. She requested that she be sent to the residential school in Shubenacadie in order to escape from the foster care system. She survived that experience as well as an abusive marriage. She found her voice when she began to express her feelings through writing poetry, and, as she found her voice, she began to speak her truth (i.e., to share with others the abuse in her marriage, her childhood experiences at the residential school, and so on). During the last years of their marriage, Rita and Frank found new understanding and love. Rita forgave. Her grace through all her trials and tribulations is indeed remarkable. She has many lessons to teach us about love, forgiveness, and cultural harmony. As she says, "Regardless of skin colour or race, we are all the same. We breathe the same air, we feel the same, and we hurt the same." In her autobiography she states:

> I am an elder in the community, and it feels good to be respected and admired. Even today, I would not trade the best place in the city for the home I now have on the reserve. Many of the elderly people are my friends, and the younger crowd—as I call everyone who is even a year younger than me—is always visiting. Helen Sylliboy and her three sisters visit and on Sunday, after church and the family meal, a group of women come over. We play cards, gossip, and compare recipes, trade secrets, joke and talk about everything happening in the community. There is nobody in Eskasoni who is an enemy. I love people, and the love bounces back. (167-68)

Rita is very involved both in her community and abroad, and she is a great ambassador for the Mi'kmaw people. She is very concerned about the education of younger Mi'kmaw people and is involved in the discussions between the federal government and the Nova Scotian Mi'kmaw communities. With regard to her life in Eskasoni, she says:

> My life is in Eskasoni, with my friends and my children and grandchildren. The more my grandchildren come to visit, the more I love them. And it is not only my own grandchildren—all the children call me grandma. Even older people call me Su'kwis [Auntie]. I love that. Who could ask for more? Being a survivor has made me build a brave heart—what we would call a kinap. Our tradition tells of the men who are kinaps, but I think there must be women kinaps, too. I leave behind the memory of an orphan child, picking herself up from the misery of being nobody, moving little grains of sand until she could talk about the first nations of the land. (169)

In one of her poems, Rita Joe (1988:16) praises and celebrates the aging experience:

Old Woman

Mi'kmaq woman
Face of old heartache,
Betraying hurt
Her thoughts of children far away.
Crying spirit tears.
Her fingers restless
Desiring to create
Pretty things for grandchildren
To share dreams, love, happiness.
Look into her heart,
Walk with her
Before life ceases.

Our visit with Eskasoni elders taught us many things: the importance of growing older in a place where one is respected and welcomed within the community; the necessity of sharing friendship, reminiscences, and values through storytelling; the need to come together in supportive and nurturing communities; the need to respect diversity and to celebrate difference—to be open to new people, ideas, and values. Many changes are occurring in Eskasoni. For example, the chief, a younger man, wants to open a nursing home on the reserve; this would alter traditional ways of caring for the old within the community. Business opportunities are being pursued, especially call centres. Fishing disputes with non-Aboriginals are threatening a traditional way of life. If the Eskasoni fishers decide to own boats and licences, this will mean the introduction of regulated fishing practices. Elders are coping and adapting fairly well within the community. They are still given a position of honour and are treated with respect. The chief and other band administrators want to create jobs and to provide better education and health care to the people just as, in theory, do all municipal, provincial, and federal politicians. The greatest challenge the elders face involves being able to accept change.

NOTES

1. http://www.statcan.ca/english/Pgdb/People/Health/health26.htm
2. For a more complete overview of some of the philosophical bases for various financial aid programs geared to those aged sixty-five and over, see early works such as de Beauvoir (1977), Bromley (1966) and Estes (1979) as well as more recent works such as Tulle-Winton (1999), Dychtwald (1999)

and Gubrium and Holstein (2000) among others.

3. Four the Moment was a very popular women's a cappella singing group. These women wrote and performed songs and music celebrating Black culture in the Atlantic region, focusing specifically on the experiences of Black women. Sadly, they disbanded in 2000.

Chapter Four

The Social Problems and Realities of Aging

There appears to be unanimous global agreement amongst researchers, academics, governments, and older persons that (1) there are several areas of life that become more challenging as we grow older and that (2) we may need assistance in dealing with them. Workshops, conferences, international symposia, text books, popular literature, government reports, newspapers and magazines, television and radio programming—all address, to a greater or lesser extent, certain worldwide "problems" of aging.

All programs, services, and assistance packages provided to older persons must be affordable (in terms of direct costs to the consumer [i.e., older persons and their important ones]), accessible (to wheelchairs, walkers, etc.), and available (regardless of whether one lives in a rural or an urban area and regardless of income).

There is a close link between affordability and accessibility in that, although services and programs may be available within any given community, people with low incomes may not be able to afford them. Or they may be reluctant to seek assistance in acquiring the necessary funds, or transfer payments, to purchase them.

There is an interconnectedness between all of the needs of older people, so that, for example, even though an individual may have sufficient income, if he is in poor health, then he is not able to enjoy many of the benefits of that income. Similarly, adequate income but lack of local resources means that the older person cannot purchase what she needs in order to improve or to enhance the quality of her life. These needs, although not exclusive to older persons, are crucial to their ability to age successfully. They include the right to accessible, affordable shelter and living arrangements; adequate incomes, including financial supports; transportation services (locally, nationally, and globally); leisure/recreation opportunities; education and lifelong learning opportunities; the right to practise their sexuality and have intimacy, including within institutionalized settings; the right to practise spirituality and religion; the right to practise cultural values, to take pride in their race and ethnicity, and to be provided with services in their own language; health care services, including options regarding where to die (e.g., palliative care programs or hospices); and opportunity for contact with others.

Related to all of the above are (1) differences between rural and urban communities (in terms of the provision of goods and services) and (2) gender differences (which can affect program accessibility). Whether or not individuals have mental or physical disabilities also affects their use of, and requirements for, special needs services within their communities.

All of the above-mentioned topics are discussed more or less thoroughly in most textbooks on aging and gerontology. Mark Novak and Lori Campbell's (2001) *Aging and Society: A Canadian Perspective*, does a particularly good job. Textbooks usually address these topics according to what services, programs, and forms of financial assistance are available to older persons, based on criteria such as means tests (e.g., to ascertain financial situations) and/or health assessment techniques. Provincial and federal publications also provide this information (see, for example, *Seniors Guide to Federal Programs and Services* [Health Canada 2001; also available on-line at http://www.hc-sc.gc.ca/seniors-aines/pubs/guide/2001/intro_e.htm]). All provincial governments in Canada have similar guides available, as do local and national seniors organizations (e.g., branches of the Canadian Pensioners Concerned, One Voice, and the Canadian Association of Retired Persons).

Rather than reiterating what has already been said, we want to hear what the people in our focus groups had to say about the "problems," or challenges, of growing old and how they have attempted to resolve them. We will cover each of these topics by briefly discussing the resources available within some Canadian communities and then listening to our focus group participants.

SHELTER AND LIVING ARRANGEMENTS

If we were to list our priorities with regard to accommodation, we would mention things like comfort, affordability, access to shops and services, transportation, places to walk, safety, attractiveness, and so on. As we grow older, and especially if we suffer from declining health and reduced income, these needs may change.

At present, in Canada there are a variety of shelter options available to older persons. These shelter options range from one's own home, to institutions (such as nursing homes), to long-term care facilities, to boarding or guest houses, to assisted-living residences. As well, as has been mentioned, older persons may live in granny flats/garden suites—

independent living units normally attached to the main dwelling of a relative or friend. The majority of Canada's seniors live independently in the community, and some require assistance with everyday living activities. They seek this assistance from organizations such as the VON and/or provincial homecare programs.

According to the Facts on Seniors Web site (http://iyop-aipa.ic.gc.ca/English/m_facts.htm), which was created especially for the International Year of Older Persons, in Canada a large majority of persons aged sixty-five and over (92 percent) live at home rather than in institutions. However, 29 percent of older persons live alone, and, within this group, "senior women, especially those in the very oldest age groups, are even more likely to live alone. In 1996, 38% of all senior women, and 50% of those aged 85 and over, lived alone" (ibid).

According to the Canadian Council on Social Development (1998) the majority of persons aged sixty-five and over (59 percent) live in areas with populations of 100,000 or more, whereas 24 percent live in areas with populations of less than 100,000. A minority (17 percent) live in rural areas, but there are vast differences across the country:

> There are large differences in the proportion of seniors living in Canadian cities. In Victoria, seniors account for 18 percent of the total population, and in St.Catherines-Niagara, for 16 percent. But in Calgary, Edmonton, St. John's and Halifax, seniors account for 10 percent or less of the population. (4)

Regardless of where they live, older persons consider location, design, and facilities when choosing accommodation. Older people who reside in large cities and towns are likely to have more shelter options available than do their counterparts who reside in rural communities. On the other hand, as some in our focus groups pointed out, living in small rural communities often results in closer-knit, more supportive neighbourhoods than are possible in large cities. Irma, who was seventy-three and is now a rural resident on an island in British Columbia, noted:

> When I lived in North Vancouver I hardly knew a soul. Occasionally I spoke to my neighbour across the hall in the apartment block where I lived. I used to wonder what I would do if I ever needed help. Even though I don't have neighbours close by any more, I know that just a phone call would bring them here at any time. People look out for each other more in a small community, especially other seniors.

Even though older persons say that they prefer to live close to key services such as shopping and public transportation, they also prefer housing that offers personal security (e.g., a place within a shared, user-friendly, and supportive community).

Even though the majority of older persons own their own homes, most of these were built before 1940; therefore, they are expensive to maintain. For many, their homes are their only source of equity. Also, they are often places of past memories—memories that connect them to their families and their history. This being the case, there is a great need for services that allow older persons to remain in their own homes for as long as possible. According to the Web site mentioned earlier, those who do own their own homes need help with the following activities associated with daily living: housework (36.9 percent of men and 35.4 percent of women); yard work (26.6 percent of men and 32.4 percent of women); meal preparation (34 percent of men and 19.6 percent of women); grocery shopping (29.7 percent of men and 32 percent of women); transportation (20.2 percent of men and 41.3 percent of women). Other assistance required included the management of money, personal care services, and emotional support.

In a publication produced by One Voice: The Canadian Seniors Network (Canada Mortgage and Housing Corporation 1991:1), the executive summary notes that "housing has been identified as one of the top five issues of concern to seniors in Canada." The Canada Mortgage and Housing Corporation sponsored this publication, which was the result of a series of national workshops attended by over two hundred seniors concerned with identifying their shelter needs. Those present at the workshops identified ten major concerns:

1. Seniors want to be involved in the study, planning, design and implementation of housing programs.
2. Seniors want to be as independent as possible.
3. Seniors need affordable housing options at all income levels.
4. Seniors need physically accessible structures.
5. Seniors need access to accurate information. Private developers, housing societies and governments all need to pay attention to the way that they communicate with us.
6. Seniors want to be able to exercise choice. There is no single type of housing and services that fit all their circumstances.
7. Housing for seniors must be adaptable to fit changing needs.
8. Seniors housing programs must be sensitive to quality of life.

9. Seniors want more effective working relationships among all levels of government.
10. Seniors see housing and services as an integrated package that requires holistic planning. Programs to support us need to integrate all these factors to make *housing* add up to *home*. (7–10, emphasis in the original)

The message clearly presented by these seniors is that housing involves more than bricks and mortar; it "encompasses design, forms of ownership, support services, living arrangements and other elements" (32). With an ever-increasing population of persons aged sixty-five and over in Canada, there will be a need for a greater array of housing options, whether they are integrated within the community and subsidized (like those built with the assistance of Kiwanis and Rotary Clubs, Royal Canadian Legion auxiliaries, and housing cooperatives) or whether they are segregated, age-specific dwellings (such as retirement villages). Housing that supports seniors' independence will also be required, such as:

> Granny flats, home sharing, congregate housing, emergency response systems, home–equity conversion plans, accessibility modifications to existing homes, retirements communities, and facilities that offer a continuum of accommodations and services from meals in communal dining rooms, to full–time nursing care. (7)

A range of shelter assistance programs exist across Canada, and they are aimed at helping older persons to repair, renovate, and maintain their own homes. Many programs, such as the Access a Home Program in Nova Scotia (which enables existing homes to be adapted so that they are wheelchair accessible), are provided through provincial governments. Also, there are provincial housing emergency repair programs that provide one-time grants to assist in major repairs (e.g., roof replacements). The federal government provides financial assistance through the Parent Apartment Program, which helps people to create granny flats/garden suites for elderly family members.

The majority of older persons who participated in our focus groups or who completed questionnaires lived in their own homes. Some had recently relocated due to health problems or financial constraints. For example, Lillian, a seventy-two-year old retired bookkeeper who lived in British Columbia and responded to our questionnaire, spoke of her circumstances as follows:

When my husband died I had very little money and had to make some very difficult decisions about where I was going to live. There aren't a lot of choices here, especially if you don't have money. But since I have moved into the co-op life has felt much better to me. It is very handy to the park and the community centre, and I don't have to worry that my rent will go up because I never have to pay more than a third of my income in rent. My income is never going to change now unless I win the lottery!

While the economic base of the two focus groups from Wolfville was higher than the norm, considerable thought was given to community-based housing. It was noted that a retirement village of sorts had been constructed in this town, with separate bungalow-type housing available. This housing costs around $145,000 per unit and is, therefore, out of the reach of many seniors. Concern was expressed for those in middle- and low-income brackets who had less access to shelter choices because of reduced incomes.

Seniors need affordable housing that will support an integrated lifestyle. Many believed that segregated housing was a detriment rather than an advantage. As one retired seventy-something schoolteacher living in a small university town explained:

I don't want to be segregated from all other age groups when I need to move to assisted housing. Right now I am okay, and I can stay where I am. I now live in a neighbourhood that houses seniors, middle-aged families, and those with young children. I truly enjoy the diversity in our neighbourhood. My house is all on one level, with wider doorways and such in case I need a wheelchair down the road. One of the reasons we moved here was the diversity of the population in this residential area. I think I would become very bored and stagnant if I had to live with others the same age as myself and older.

Another retired teacher, a man in his late seventies, said:

I have a concern about people falling through the cracks. If we had community-based housing right in our own neighbourhood we would not lose the continuity of our lives. The familiar surroundings would still be there—the churches, the grocery store, the pharmacy and the familiar neighbours. The idea of sticking assisted housing or long-term care facilities in one

central place, away from smaller communities and neighbourhoods, doesn't seem right somehow. Isn't it bad enough people
have to leave their own homes at some point? But to have to
move out of the neighbourhood as well is the final insult! The
final blow! Somehow we have to find a way to pay for community-based assisted-living where we can all help. Where neighbours, friends, and family can still drop in and volunteer around
the premises to make it feel somewhat still like home!

Anne, a retired yoga teacher in her mid-seventies, talked about some
of the problems facing people who try to set up small guest houses in
their own communities. Her experience was with a family on the South
Shore of Nova Scotia that had opened up its home to elderly seniors.
One could note the frustration in her voice:

These folks are wonderfully kind, caring people. They have
made their home available. However, they can't advertise because of all the rules and regulations. This red tape gets in the
way of people trying to help others. I know we have to have
some standards, but couldn't the whole process be more flex-
ible? Could not each residence be based on its own assessment
rather than having to fulfill all the requirements written up in
somebody's manual or something? These folks are having a hard
time keeping going and may have to shut down because they
can't get the financial help they need.

Polly, a seventy-two-year-old divorced mother of five living in a small
community on the South Shore, put it this way:

My problem is that I have this old house and my kids aren't
around much. My income is very small and I am really feeling
panicky about what I am going to do. Sometimes now I have
great difficulty getting up in the mornings. I have arthritis and
am in terrible pain. I can't do any of the repairs needed, and I
seem to fall through the cracks in seeking help financially. I
really don't know what I am going to do! I am not ready to go
into a nursing home or long-term care facility. I am really
confused right now and don't know where to turn.

Several members of the group who have known this woman for many
years had not realized her situation, and her comments affected them like

a light bulb going on. Several had some ideas about how they might help her. In the meantime, I (Diane) told her about a story I had heard while at university. Somewhere out west, a group of women who had been friends over the years and who had kept in contact with each other came together to discuss their aging process and some of the problems they were encountering. It seems that many of them were having some financial difficulties and were concerned about how and where they were going to live out their aging years. About the same time, it came to their attention that there was an older house for sale in the neighbourhood. It needed some repairs, but it had six bedrooms and seemed to be a possible solution to their housing situation. To make a long story short, they bought the place, fixed it up, and moved in together.

As I was telling this story, I could see Polly beginning to think about her different options. It was during this brainstorming session that ideas and hope began to take shape. When I left this group, I felt in my heart that they, together with Polly, would come up with a community-based solution to her problem.

It was in this same focus group that we discussed a Chinese village type of living arrangement. The Yee Hong Centre for Geriatric Care is located in Markham, Ontario, and it was featured in a five-page ad in the *Globe and Mail* (Monday, April 23, 2001: Y1-6). The Chinese community in Markham has built a culturally specific community-based living complex. This village consists of a long-term care facility, assisted-living apartments for seniors, and units that may be rented by family members. Playgrounds, gardens, and recreational complexes form part of this village. Members of the long-term facility help each other get breakfast in a common area, then they go down to the fifth floor to pick out vegetables for lunch. The women then move back upstairs and prepare the vegetables. Even though, for hygienic reasons, these vegetables can't be used, preparing them gives these women a sense of continuity because it allows them to participate in familiar activities. (It has been noticed that many women suffering from dementia make noticeable improvements when taking part in familiar activities.)

There are plans to construct several more such villages in Ontario, some of which would house non-Chinese families as well. While these villages are expensive to build, once they are up and running the costs are competitive with those of other long-term care facilities. Using culturally sensitive health care techniques that honour the roles of older persons within their community, the Yee Hong Centre hopes to provide an alternative model for shelter arrangements for the elderly, especially those who suffer from dementias.

A number of older persons who responded to our questionnaire suggested that communal living or shared accommodations would be more acceptable than would living in institutions or assisted-living arrangements within an all "older" community. One widowed woman in her seventy-sixth year commented: "I haven't given it too much thought really. But maybe communal living or shared accommodations with others in the same boat. You would have to be congenial though."

Several participants in our rural focus groups spoke about the problems they experienced, particularly during the winter months. Dot, a widow in her eighties, explained:

> I love my little house. I don't want to move but this winter in particular I noticed I didn't want to go out on the ice. It was so very slippery around my house, and it is difficult to get people to salt it for me. Everyone is so busy. All that snow as well. It is the winters that I find hard. Too bad there wasn't somewhere I could go for four months of the year and come back to my little house for the summers.

Not all rural communities have snow-removal programs (nor, for that matter, do some urban ones). Four years ago when I (Jeanette) lived in a large urban city in Nova Scotia, my daughter Ceilidh had a newspaper delivery route. One very cold winter day, after weeks of heavy snow, we received a call from a seventy-six-year-old woman who lived in a nearby apartment block. It appeared that she had recently had a hip replacement operation and had no family living nearby. She received no home assistance program and was scared to leave her house in case she fell on the ice (which the landlord had not removed). She wondered if Ceilidh could pick her up some milk and bread and deliver it with the paper one day. She offered a rather large sum of money for this service. Disgusted that such a situation was occurring one block away and that no one knew about it, Ceilidh hurried to the store and picked up the bread and milk and delivered it, refusing any reimbursement. For several days we then collected groceries for our neighbour.

Karie, a sixty-one-year-old woman living in a South Shore community, related the story of a neighbour who wanted to live at home but couldn't get the night-time care she needed. She was forced to move in with her son and daughter-in-law, and the situation was not going well. There were many conflicts between the mother and her relatives, and the fact that she did not willingly move in with them has not helped. The neighbour asked: "Why is it we can't get overnight help? That would solve so many problems—even someone coming in for three hours—say from 12:00 AM to 3:00 AM to check on things and make sure all is well. Even that amount of checking would relieve families and the client as well."

An article written by Brian Dunning of *Stirling News-Argus* (vol. 120, no. 24) describes a study conducted by Dr. Marion Lynn (a professor at the centre of Feminist Research at York University) entitled "The Housing Factor Project: Housing Needs of Mid-life and Older Women." Lynn presented her findings to a packed audience at Hungerford Hall in Tweed. The research had been carried out by the Older Women's Network and involved looking at six communities. Because 263 questionnaires were returned from Tweed, this is the only community Lynn mentioned, remarking that "[its] return rate of 130% was the highest of the study communities." From this study it was remarkably clear that people wanted to stay in their own communities. As Lynn stated:

> An overwhelming portion of these women (73%) state that it is very important for them to remain in the community. The problem is that they will require different forms of housing. There are not enough retirement homes in the area and with an inadequate sewer system, building restrictions are in effect. (3)

Lynn spoke about one finding that "shocked" her: 25 percent of the respondents expressed the fear of being homeless. Many older women live on fixed incomes, and maintaining their homes constitutes a financial burden. Senior women are generally not well off as many left the workforce to raise children and had to take low-paying jobs when they returned (ibid).

In the same study, Leona Dombrowksy, the MPP for Hastings-Frontenace-Lennox and Addington, mentioned that seniors are a "wonderful resource." She noted that the real brain drain occurs when a community loses the life experiences of seniors who are forced to move. She also pointed out that, "over the next fifteen years the number of seniors will double," and she suggested that "governments should be putting the infrastructure needed to look after them in place now" (ibid.). Finally she posited that "most resources have to be directed to helping people remain at home" (ibid.). The study went on to say that many older women just need some help with home maintenance and transportation (now the only homecare available to them is personal care). This study reiterates the experiences of many of the participants in our focus groups.

INCOME AND FINANCIAL SUPPORTS

Researchers and policy planners generally agree that the incomes of Canada's older population have improved "drastically over the last twenty years." Further, it appears that "their incomes have risen more quickly than those of younger people, whose incomes have remained relatively stable over the same time period" (Lilley and Campbell 1999:23). The higher rates of income are said to be the result of improved private pension plans, seniors benefits at both federal and provincial levels, and taxation policies. Even so, poverty amongst older people still exists, especially for older women. The Division of Aging and Seniors, Health Canada (http://www.hc-sc.gc.ca/seniors-aines/seniors/english/whatsnew.htm), notes that:

> In general, Old Age Security (OAS) benefits, including Guaranteed Income Supplements (GIS), continue to provide the largest source of income for seniors. As in other groups, female seniors have lower incomes than their male counterparts, and unattached senior women have considerably lower incomes than unattached senior men.

In an attempt to discover the present rates of financial assistance plans available to persons aged sixty-five and older, Jeanette spent two full days making a number of telephone calls, both locally and long-distance. Interestingly, one of these calls was to the provincial government's programs for seniors, which did not have the numbers. They suggested that we go to various Government of Canada Web sites to find the information. Eventually, after much searching, we were able to locate that Web site, which does not provide present rates. Jeanette then sent an e-mail to the Human Resources Development Commission, specifically requesting this information. Jeanette is an experienced researcher, yet she encountered these kinds of difficulties. Consider what such a task would be like for an older person, especially one unfamiliar with how to seek information, without the income to make long-distance phone calls, and without access to the Internet.

As of May 1, 2001, the maximum rate of the Canada Pension Plan (CPP/QPP) is $775 per month. For those receiving Old Age Security (OAS), the basic rate is $433.52. The Guaranteed Income Supplement (GIS) is available to low-income individuals who also receive OAS, but the rate is determined by marital status. Other federal government sources of income support include Spouse's Allowance, Widowed Spouse's Allowance, Canada Pension Plan Survivor Benefits, Canada Pension

Plan Death Benefit, and the Canada Pension Plan Disability Benefit (personal communication, e-mail, Human Resources Development Commission, Government of Canada, May 2, 2001).

According to Statistics Canada (1977), the majority of persons aged sixty-five and over (97.2 percent) are in receipt of the OAS and the GIS. As well, 80.1 percent receive some form of the Canada/Quebec Pension Plan. According to Lilley and Campbell (1999:24) Canadian senior couples receive about "40% of their income from government pensions and benefits and 60% from private pensions, investments and earnings. Senior women who live alone rely on the government for 62% of their income." Low-income seniors, especially women, are more likely to have no source of financial aid other than that provided through government income assistance programs. And, as Lilley and Campbell note, "In 1996, government transfers were the *only* source of income for nearly half (44%) of senior women, whereas that was the case for only one out of five (22%) senior men" (ibid., emphasis in original).

Because women comprise both a higher number of persons aged sixty-five and over and a greater number of those living below Government of Canada low-income guidelines, the financial situation facing them has frequently been referred to as part of the "feminization of poverty." As more women enter the age eighty-five and over cohort, many of them may be facing a high risk of financial insecurity. Although the current generation of young women is more likely to be well educated and to have pensionable employment (which may result in investment opportunities and private pension plan contributions) than is the current generation of old women, this is of no particular help to the latter.

It is important to know not only the income levels of older persons, but also on what they are spending their money. According to the material produced by the Government of Canada for the International Year of Older Persons (http://www.hc-sc.gc.ca/seniors-aines/pubs/poster/seniors/page7e.htm) in 1996, seniors spent a total of $69.9 billion dollars on the following:

Housing	14.0 billion
Clothing	2.3 billion
Recreation	3.1 billion
Health	3.6 billion
Home Supplies and Furnishing	5.1 billion
Other expenses	5.3 billion
Gifts and Charity	6.1 billion

Transportation	8.3 billion
Food	9.6 billion
Personal Expenses	12.5 billion

This Web site notes that "seniors play an important role as consumers in Canadian society. In 1996 households headed by seniors spent $69 billion dollars on goods, services and taxes, representing 13 per cent of all expenditures."

Interestingly, seniors without limited access to funds are more likely than those in any other age group to provide charitable donations. As the aforementioned Web site further notes:

> Households headed by seniors spend a larger share of their total income on gifts and charities than do younger households. Over one-fifth of all households headed by seniors spend at least one-tenth of their after-tax income on gifts and charities compared with seven per cent of all households headed by people aged 35–54 years.

Five years ago, Jeanette and a colleague (Paula Chegwidden) at Acadia University conducted research that examined retirement issues faced by older female faculty and staff.[1] Overwhelmingly, the women we interviewed spoke of the need for adequate pre-retirement programming aimed specifically at their needs. Several informants had taken time out from post-secondary education to marry and raise children. They re-entered the workforce after child rearing and so took up full-time employment later in life than did their spouses; the pensions they received reflected their absence from the world of full-time work. Many of the women with whom we spoke had become widowed after retirement, and this placed an additional strain on their limited financial resources.

As Joan, a retired senior administrative secretary noted:

> Well I assumed that after I had worked twelve years at Acadia we would have enough to live on. Then George became ill with cancer and I took care of him until he passed on. It was an expensive time because I had to have in-home help to take care of him and it was very costly. I never thought that I would be living so close to poverty in my old age.

After completing a PhD in her fifties, a dream she had always wanted to fulfill after her difficult divorce, Pat, a part-time faculty member who had spent the past ten years of her working life teaching courses at three different universities in Nova Scotia (making a total of $15,000 per year), spoke of her lack of financial resources:

> When I got the house in the divorce settlement, rather than any sort of cash settlement I thought that if I could tie down a full-time job somewhere I would be set for life. Ha, I must have been joking, no one nowhere hires 50-year-old women to start teaching careers in universities. Now I just make do with what little I have and just hope that the roof never leaks!

Poverty comes to older women, regardless of the types of professions they held in their working lives; and more needs to be done, both by governments and the private sector, to recognize their fundamental needs (especially with regard to pension reform).

Most of the participants in the focus groups were middle-income elders. However, one of the serious concerns brought forth during our discussions with them had to do with long-term nursing care and the financial burden this placed on families, particularly on female spouses. In Nova Scotia, a three-year financial assessment is mandatory when placing a family member in a long-term care facility. Recently, various articles addressing this issue have appeared in Halifax's *Chronicle-Herald*.

In response to one of the articles, Con Desplanque,[2] from Amherst, Nova Scotia, wrote to the newspaper with concerns about nursing home costs and pension reform. In responding to Joe Fitzpatrick's article advising women to pay more attention to their retirement needs and recommending that they receive a better deal from pension plans (*Chronicle-Herald*, March 19, 2001), Con introduced himself as having been a member of the executive of the Cumberland County Branch of the Federal Superannuates National Association since 1983. He stated that, during that time, he had developed an interest in pensions, and he agreed that women get a raw deal:

> When I worked as a federal civil servant I had first deducted from my gross salary 6.5% and later on 7.5%. From what I had left my wife got household money and thus contributed as much as I to my pension. But the outcome is that when I die, she will get 50% of my pension plus what has been deducted because of the Canada Pension Plan, which will bring her income to about 60% of what I would still get if she dies before I do. This is in my opinion not a fair deal.

Con goes on to explain the actuarial reports in the books of the Public Service Superannuation Account:

> For instance, in the latest actuarial report as at March 31, 1996 the actuaries calculated that for paying the pensions of the actual contributors $27.4 billion should be in the fund as an asset, for retired personnel $24.2 billion and for surviving spouses only $3.1 billion would be required. The total liabilities on that date were estimated to be $56.3 billion and the assets $66.1 billion. Thus for equalizing the pensions of survivors only 4.7% of the assets should be required. In the previous actuarial report of December 31, 1992 this percentage was 5.2% in 1989 and 5.77% and in that year. Thus there is plenty of money available to right this wrong.

In his letter to Fitzpatrick, Con states:

> The fact is that the percentage of persons belonging to pension plans is steadily decreasing, as you write, for males from 57% in 1980 to 42% in 1998 and for females from 48% to 40%. This is most likely due to the fact that companies regard their personnel nowadays as inventory that can be disposed of at any convenient time, to the benefit of the shareholders. Too many people today have permanent temporary jobs with minimum wages and no pensions. And this trend is propagated by Canadian Alliance and the Alberta Government which is bad news for the present generations. Most of the other political parties seem to shy away from this potential problem, not daring to bell the cat. If things were right everyone should be a member of a pension plan which should be portable from job to job, providing an indexed pension, equal to subscriber and spouse. Such pension can be based on the average life expectancy of Canadian workers, which is around 76 years for men and 82 for women. If each person has to set up a pension fund on its own one has to take into account that one can live to an age of 100 or more, requiring a larger amount of savings, which most likely is not spent and is left in the estate, from which the taxman can take its share. Not to speak of the inroad that inflation can make on the buying power of the savings. A pension fund can be seen as a cooperative effort that will provide to its members the means to make one's last years less worrisome.

Con also sent Diane a copy of his response to Cathy Nicoll's article in Halifax's *Sunday Daily News*, April 15, 2001. The article was entitled "Seniors' Home Economics," and in it she wrote about the potential problems seniors can encounter should they need to be admitted to a nursing home. Con is very passionate about this subject, and he wanted us to include his stories and experiences in this book. In his words: "Mr. Fitzpatrick brought forward the confiscatory practice of the Nova Scotia Department of Health, taking every asset they can lay their hands on and leaving the stay-at-home spouse destitute. This spouse has to keep body, soul and home together with the Old Age Security pension and this forces the person to apply for a Guaranteed Income Supplement."

Con also discussed the high costs of nursing homes in Nova Scotia and elsewhere:

> The cost of nursing homes is said to range between $90 and $147 per day, thus every married person who does not have an annual retirement income substantially higher than $33,000 to $54,000 and has to go into a nursing home, that person will leave a destitute spouse at home. I am not aware that anywhere an account is given of the real cost of nursing homecare. It might be possible that those who can be robbed of their assets are forced to pay also for those that cannot be robbed. In Ontario about 57,000 persons are guests in the about 500 nursing homes and homes for the aged. The cost of a bed in a public long-term care facility includes both the resident's portion and the provincial government's portion. The Ministry of Health set in August 1999 the accommodation resident's portion for wards at $1,277.95/month, for semi-private at $1,521.28/month and for a private room at $1,825.45/month. Even the latter rate of about $22,000/year is substantially lower than the lowest rates in Nova Scotia. The fact that in Ontario the medical costs are covered by the Province, is perhaps the explanation of the fact that the Public Service Health Care Plan does allow $10,000 per year on nursing costs as long as that is not provided in a nursing home. This means that this provision is of little use for plan members residing in provinces where this is now the case.

> Some of the nursing home costs, the medical and nursing portions can be claimed as medical costs. It is said that this forms about 75% of the costs. But those who have to pay these costs fall mostly in the 25% bracket for their federal income taxes. But

the Non-Refundable Tax Credits calculate only 17%, giving the Federal Government an 8% bonus calculated from the cost of one's misery. The Province gets only a 5% bonus on top of it.

As well as being concerned about the high costs of nursing homes, Con was also concerned about the situation faced by those in receipt of registered retirement savings plans (RRSPs):

> Not very well known is what the province can do with spousal RRSPs and RRIFs. Any lawyer who advises how to make a testament the easiest for the executor will tell you that joint bank accounts are the best thing to do. But if one has to go in a nursing home the province will take all of it. In Ontario if one gives some of the assets to one potential heir, these remain theirs if one ... has to go to a nursing home [one year later]. But in Nova Scotia this term is three years. As it can be noticed it is very difficult for middle income couples to stay solvent in their retirement if one can no longer stay at home. The best advice seems to be that if this is likely to occur either one hopes to die simultaneously or divorce. In the latter case the spouses get half of the assets. The Canada Pension Plan has the humane ruling that its pension can be split between spouses, but this is not the case for other pension incomes. Talking steps to protect finances before entering a nursing home is well nigh impossible when the only thing one can do is designate one's home, which will be hard to maintain if no money is left over for property taxes and maintenance.

Con's concerns reminded Diane of a friend who is legally separated from her husband. She is receiving approximately one-half of his monthly pension and would maintain survivor benefits should he die before she does. But what happens if he has to go into a nursing home? What happens to her RRSPs (which she retained under the separation agreement) one of which is still a spousal RRSP? The other difficulty she has is that all her mother's income is held jointly with her only child. They were advised, after her father died, to do this for estate purposes. Her mother is eighty-six and in poor health. Her monthly income, with interest, is approximately $2,300. If she went into a nursing home this year, then any money she has given her daughter during the last three years would be considered part of her investment portfolio; and if her money ran out, say if she lived to be one hundred, then the daughter would have to give her the money that had been given her as a gift. The money this woman has given her grandchildren over the last year or so would also come under the same category. This woman still has a fair number of investments, and they should cover a normal stay in a nursing home. She has not given away her money in order to ensure that the government has to pay for her care; rather, she gave those she loved a gift while she was still living on her own, in her own apartment.

We have known people who gave their money away three years in advance simply so that their care would have to be subsidized; but should we all suffer for this? Is divorce the only way Diane's friend can protect herself? Does she have to lose survivor benefits? She and her mother have worked hard over the years to invest their money so that the latter will be cared for in her final days. Do they have to spend every last cent? Will the daughter have to sell her home to cover some of the money given to her as a gift?

This is not an isolated case; we frequently hear of such situations in our work with and for older persons. Because very little, if any, information is made available to older persons and their families in advance of situations such as the need for residential care, many find out the hard way that their plans for a successful transition from home to nursing home are fraught with trepidation and can often result in a loss of family income.

Since Con wrote the above-quoted letters, he sent Diane the following e-mail (May 3, 2001, 4:18 PM), which he gave us permission to share with the readers of this book:

> I just had a talk with Mrs. Marjorie Fisher of the N.S. Depart-ment of Health, (Home Care) Tel. 667-6470. I asked her about how the payments for a nursing facility are to be made. She assured me that the rules have changed since 1999, when Helen Murray scared us to death at a FSNA meeting. At present all income of the two spouses are split to pay for the admittance of one of them, thus no longer leaving the other spouse in the cold. However I asked her if these rules were somewhere in black and white but that seems to be not the case. But she was quite adamant about the whole affair, thus I have good hope that the NS Government finally saw the light.

Perhaps the older citizens of Nova Scotia are finally getting their message across. However there are many things, including the three-year rule, that remain troublesome. Several other letters have appeared recently in Halifax newspapers. In the *Chronicle-Herald* (April 27, 2001, C2), several letters appeared in response to an article about nursing home costs. I.C. Boutilier, of Halifax, wrote:

> I have a friend who, after selling his home, had to be placed in a Halifax nursing home due to a serious change in his health. He shares a room with another man and each of them pays $4,414 for a 31-day month. From May to December, 2000, his portion of the cost of the room was $31,000 plus additional charges for haircuts, cutting toe and fingernails and medications. This room has two beds in it and each person has one chair, a bureau and a closet and there is no room for a TV or anything more. The total cost of the room alone, for eight months is $62,000. That's a lot of money to pay for one room. There were no private rooms to be had at this or any other nursing home at the time of his application and acceptance into the home. My advice to seniors, from this experience, is to sell your home, go rent an apartment to live in, have a good time with the money from the sale of your property, and travel if you're well enough or share it with your family. It could be later than you think. By the way, my friend's home was his primary and only place of residence. He had no insurance or investments of any kind; he is just a person who worked hard all his life. The care at the home is excellent, but expensive, and he is being well looked after and that is the main thing.

Another letter on the relationship between income and shelter needs was entitled "Degrading Scrutiny" and was written by Shirley Beamish of Halifax. It also appeared in the *Chronicle-Herald* (April 27, 2001, C3):

> Who are the people who contrived the application for nursing homes that they should know everything down to the last sheet of toilet paper? To whom can we appeal as they try to obtain verified copies of all assets? The scrutiny is degrading to individuals and families. People are in shock as their lives are dissected. For people who have worked most of their lives for a pittance, paid their dues, and tried to save for their golden years—it all disappeared in an hour. So the applicant is left waiting for the unknown, the family behind stunned and wondering what's next. Where is the justice? God help people to accept a very distasteful system. Catch 22 is correct. Why can't

people, if they have been saving for many years, be able to proceed with their intentions?

Many of the focus group participants believed they had planned properly for their old age. However, not many discussed the possibility of nursing homecare and what that would do to their long-term savings and to their families. As we can see, this whole area of finances and care is both troublesome and controversial. Much needs to be done in the area of care and pension plan reform.

Most of the participants in the focus groups, and most of those who completed and returned questionnaires, did not respond to the topic of finances in general; however, they were very specific with respect to the connection between finances and the ability to pay for nursing care if and when necessary.

TRANSPORTATION

Most of us take affordable, accessible transportation for granted. The majority of Canadians think nothing of getting into a car to drive to the grocery store, go to the movies, visit friends and family, and so on. The automobile seems to be a way of life. Those fortunate enough to live in urban areas are more likely to have good access to buses, trains, taxis, and assisted-transportation systems than are those living in rural areas. Lilley and Campbell (1999:30) state that having access to transportation allows seniors to

> maintain social relationships, avoid dependency, and to keep a sense of control over their lives. In 1991, two thirds of senior Canadian men had driver's licenses, and 75% reported that they drove more than three times a week. In contrast, fewer than one quarter of senior women had drivers licenses, and of those nearly two thirds said that they drove more than three times per week.

I (Jeanette) have a neighbour who is a seventy-seven-year-old woman with limited mobility due to severe arthritis in her knees and lower spine. Her only child, a son, lives in Alberta, and she seldom leaves the house to walk or to participate in social activities. In our semi-rural community there is a bus service that runs once an hour from 7:15 AM until 8:15 PM each day (except Sunday, when the first bus leaves later in the morning). This bus is Elsie's only form of transportation, and it is not accessible to her due to its high step up to the main seating area. She could utilize the access-a–bus system provided locally, but she doesn't want to "bother anybody" (although she will book it in advance for medical appointments and, twice a year, she does take taxis to the airport to visit her son and his family). Her days are spent looking out of the window, reading, listening to the radio in the daytime, and watching television at night.

Her groceries and other supplies are delivered by local merchants for a limited fee, and when she really needs something in addition to these she will walk the four houses down the road to me and ask if I could pick up such and such. Elsie does have friends who visit occasionally, but she feels that, since her husband died some five years ago, they only visit because they feel "sorry for her." Elsie could, at no cost, participate in the "friendly visitor" program provided by the local VON, but she doesn't feel comfortable having "strangers" in her house. Elsie is a typical example of an older woman whose social networks are diminished as a result of a lack of accessible, frequent transportation.

Seniors are, according to Lilley and Campbell (1999:30), the heaviest users of public transportation:

> Where it is available, mostly in urban areas, many seniors depend on it to remain independent and maintain their day-to-day routines. In rural areas and small communities where public transportation is not available, seniors are more dependent on others and are more likely to be physically and socially isolated.

When Jeanette was conducting research into the respite care needs of family caregivers living in various rural areas in Lunenburg county in Nova Scotia (Auger 2000b), the issue of transportation was paramount and was invoked frequently both by older persons and by their caregivers. This was especially the case for individuals in the over-eighty age group who, although still able to drive, were constantly worried that poorer eyesight and ill health might prevent them from being able to pass their driving tests. Joanne, the eighty-two-year-old primary caregiver of a husband suffering from Alzheimer's disease, spoke of this dilemma:

> I am very afraid that I might not be able to renew my driver's licence this time around. I can tell that my eyesight is deteriorating due to the diabetes and I cannot imagine what we would do. I have to take him [spouse] everywhere and we would be lost without use of the car. There is no bus service here and it would mean getting taxi cabs all the time and we just can't afford that. (Auger 2000b:9)

In keeping with this theme, Lilley and Campbell (1999) note that, "over the next decade, as the over-80 age group continues to grow rapidly, the need for public transportation is likely to grow as well and is expected to remain high in subsequent decades as 'baby boomers' age. In 20 to 30 years, roads will become increasingly populated by seniors" (30).

Recognizing that transportation for older persons ought to be a government priority at all levels, Lilley and Campbell conclude:

> Although age itself does not reduce ability to drive, increased age does increase the possibility of diminished hearing, vision, and reflexes, conditions that do affect driving skill. Flexible, low cost, and convenient alternative means of transportation will encourage those with diminished driving skills to avoid driving. (30)

Without access to appropriate transportation services, and as they grow older and lose their drivers licences, seniors will be forced to become reliant upon family, neighbours, and friends, thus once more reducing their opportunities to remain socially active, contributing, and integrated members of their communities.

Most people in the focus groups had access to their own forms of transportation, but they did express such concerns as: "what will happen when I can no longer drive?" "How will I get around?" and "How will I make appointments without a car?" Eve, who is eighty-six and who recently moved into an assisted-living apartment in a small town, commented:

> I want to continue to drive my car. My daughter and my doctor don't think I should. I know I am dizzy when I am walking, but sitting down I am fine. They tell me I am taking 13 different types of medication and because I don't always feel my feet under me they say I shouldn't drive. I can see wonderfully well and I do compensate. I drive slowly and carefully. Oh what I would give to be able to drive to the grocery store! There is no public transportation within walking distance. I do call the Kings County Assisting Transportation people when my daughter can't pick me up for a doctor's appointment but it isn't the same. I feel so dependent and not free anymore. I feel closed in and not worth much.

Another older woman, Dot, who lives on Salt Spring Island in British

Columbia and who responded to our questionnaire, commented: "Driving one's one car is so important. I suppose I will have to get a cataract operation pretty soon so I can still get my driver's licence." Dot moved to Salt Spring Island five years ago to live in a home collectively purchased and built by her children and herself. At that time she was mobile and very active. Since then she has had a fall, has experienced knee surgery, and has found her mobility to be somewhat impaired. Her home is about ten minutes away from the centre of a small town, where all local goods and services are available. Without access to her own form of transportation she would be isolated and lonely.

On a recent visit to British Columbia Jeanette spoke with Dot, who explained to her the importance of transportation to older people on Salt Spring Island:

> We have no bus system here. There are cabs, but who can afford them? Neighbours are helpful, but who wants to always be asking for help, especially when you want to be spontaneous and just pop into town on a whim? When I first moved here I loved the isolation of the house, but if I am ever not able to drive I wouldn't be able to stay here. I'm not sure where I would go and I don't want to move again. When you are younger, and fitter, you never think about things like this, you take so much for granted. Having access to a good form of transportation, preferably your own car, is a lifeline that connects you to the rest of the world.

Dot so adequately describes the experiences of many older people (especially women, who are more likely to live alone than are older men) of the crucial need for public transportation services that enhance the social networking opportunities of older, especially rural, persons.

Polly, who was in the Seabright focus group and who has very little money, explained that she and her daughter bought a car together. She is managing at the present time, however: "What happens when I can't drive anymore? There is no public transportation along the South Shore, and most older persons live in a rural setting so what are we to do?"

Some of the women in several rural focus groups explained that they carpool fairly often. There are several women in the area who no longer drive but, being long-time residents, they have many contacts in their own neighbourhoods. Usually once a week women who are still driving pick up several of their non-driving friends and head off to town.

In the Halifax focus group, participants had access to good public transportation. In fact, several of them chose not to own an automobile, having purchased their condos in downtown Halifax because it was close to all amenities, including a very good bus system.

Transportation meant freedom for most focus groups participants/questionnaire respondents. Many dreaded the day that they might have to give up driving and sell their cars due to poor eyesight (or some other physical disability), the ever-increasing cost of gas and insurance, or for some other reason.

LEISURE AND RECREATION

The needs of older persons for affordable, accessible forms of leisure and recreation are as varied as they are for any other age group, regardless of whether they live in urban or rural areas. When planning formal leisure and recreation programs for older persons, one needs to recognize the special needs of some (e.g., mobility impairment and physical limitations).

As with people of all ages, older persons have a variety of reasons why they engage in leisure and recreation activities. Some of these include the need to have fun, to meet new people and to become reacquainted with old ones, to enhance social networks, to learn new skills and to brush up on old ones, to alleviate loneliness, and so forth. As well, being engaged in leisure/recreation activities enables us to assist the communities and neighbourhoods in which we live, engage in fitness programs in order to stay healthy in body, mind, and soul; and to have a sense of connection with others. Some seniors say that they participate in specific leisure activities, like quilting bees and needlepoint groups, in order to maintain old skills. Louise, a seventy-nine-year-old woman living in a rural Nova Scotia community, spoke to us about her involvement in the local quilting bee organized through her local church.

> I love to quilt. When I was raising the children I didn't have the time or the patience. When the kids were gone and my husband retired I needed to get out of the house, was so bored, so I started taking it up again. We have such a laugh together, we can talk about the grandchildren, even have a little gossip, but mostly it keeps the hands moving and the heart full.

For Louise, as for others with whom we spoke, having a hobby and participating in leisure activities is a good way to keep in touch with friends while also keeping active and contributing to the community. Most of the quilts that Louise and her sister quilters produce are sold at local fund-raising auctions to assist a variety of non-profit organizations.

Many people become involved in leisure and recreational programs in order to alleviate job stress. As Jeanette has learned while conducting pre-retirement workshops for federal public service employees, often the activity one chooses in order to deal with job stress becomes less interesting once the stressor (i.e., the job) is no longer part of one's daily routine. The challenge then becomes determining which hobbies or activities to pick up in order to provide oneself with a new sense of pleasure. Many individuals with whom Jeanette has spoken in such workshops say that, at the beginning of their retirement, they didn't want to engage in any activities; however, once they had established a new pattern of life, they became bored with having nothing to do. It appears that it is important to take up activities that we enjoy for their own sake rather than because they function as stress-reduction techniques. If we do this, then, when more free time becomes available to us, we can enjoy such activities more than ever.

According to the official Web site of the International Year of Older Persons, seniors generally have more leisure time than do people in younger age groups. "In 1992, people aged 65 and over had an average of 7.7 hours of free time each day, two hours more than the 15–64 age group" (http://iyop-aipa.ic.gc.ca/english/facts.htm). This Web site notes further that seniors devote an average of almost "an hour and a half a day to active leisure pursuits such as sports, socializing, hobbies and driving for pleasure. Seniors also spend a significant amount of their leisure time traveling" (ibid).

On the Internet a variety of travel sites are aimed specifically at seniors, as are publications such as the Canadian Association of Retired Persons *Fifty Plus*, which provides a travel service for its members. Airline companies often provide older persons with discounts, and tour agencies and programs such as Elderhostel provide not just leisure and recreational opportunities for travel in many parts of the world, but also encourage lifelong, continuing education opportunities.

As part of their leisure and recreation activities, seniors, more than those in any other age group, are highly active and committed volunteers. The institutions to which they devote their time range from schools, churches, political parties, seniors centres, and charitable organizations to programs such as Meals on Wheels, palliative care visiting, and so on. In the previously quoted Web site the authors note that "an estimated 23% of Canadian seniors contribute some time each week as unpaid volunteers. Many other seniors look after children. In 1995, just under 20% of seniors looked after children at least once a week" (ibid). Linking the financial value of such services to neighbourhoods, family, and community, the authors go on to state: "The economic value of the volunteer work done by seniors is estimated at between $764 million and $2.3 billion annually. As caregivers to spouses, family, friends and neighbors, seniors are also a vital force in reducing health care costs" (ibid).

Whereas it may be true that older persons have more free time to devote to voluntary activities than do those in other age groups, they also do so as a way of "giving back" to the community. Joyce a sixty-nine-year-old retired nurse from a small rural community, put it this way:

> I have been blessed with a job I enjoyed and friends I admire. I have had a rich and varied life. I am happy to give a little something back to the community for all the support and encouragement I have received over the years. That's what it should all be about, receiving and giving.

Many in our focus groups are very active volunteers at both local and global levels. Most of them volunteered with many different organizations, ranging from the Victorian Order of Nurses Support Services (where they take part in friendly visiting, foot clinics, and palliative care) to the local health boards, school boards, and church organizations. They take their volunteerism seriously and conduct it as a part of their lives. Many of them had always been volunteers, while others were starting fresh after having had busy careers. One very active seventy-year-old from a small university town put it this way:

> I wonder what society would do without senior volunteers? I am on the District Health Board, the VON Board and belong to various organizations in my church. I would bet that seniors make up the largest percentage of volunteers in the whole country. I love giving back to my community. I have been so blessed in my life it is time to give back.

John has retired from his position as a librarian at a local university; he is very active in voluntary activities in his community, especially those involving fund raising for health-related agencies such as the Canadian Cancer Society and the Canadian Red Cross. He spoke about his work in the following way:

I really felt isolated when I left my job. At first I relished the freedom it gave me—no routines, no schedules. But then I started to get bored at home, even though my wife left many instructions of what I should do before she came home from work [laughs]! I met Jill in the post office and she said that the cancer society was always looking for people to do fund raising, and so I went to see them about it. I really enjoy meeting new people and they are quite kind and friendly. I feel connected again because of my volunteer work, and I recommend it to everyone. It really is a lifesaver.

Seniors who are not physically able to volunteer their time and expertise to their communities are able to make charitable donations. Colin Lindsay (1999:92) notes: "In 1997, 80% of all seniors made at least one charitable donation. This was about the same as figures in younger age groups; seniors however, made larger contributions, on average than people in other age groups. That year, seniors donated an average of $328 each to charities." Overall, older persons continue to volunteer as long as their health and mobility enable them to do so; when they can no longer physically contribute to their communities, they financially contribute.

The majority of the people with whom we talked treasured their leisure and recreational time. For many, it was the first time in their busy lives that they have been "allowed" the time "to practise" all the activities they longed to engage in during their earlier, working years. For the most part, the older persons who had worked outside the home for many years are now enjoying "roaming the golf course" and "curling up a storm." Indeed, for the more affluent members of the retired workforce golf and curling, along with travel, seem to take up a large amount of their leisure time. Several people from Wolfville addressed this issue. Lyn, a fifty-seven-year-old retired nurse, enjoys baking, curling, and working with the mentally challenged. With reference to her curling activities, she said: "I just love getting on the ice. Once you start to curl it is so much fun. And the people I meet. It is one way of making connections while having fun at the same time. I am not that competitive but I certainly do enjoy having the time to curl whenever I feel like it." Bill, sixty-three, retired from the retail business, describes himself as Lyn's gardener. He is also an avid golfer: "It is great getting out on the golf course, wandering from hole to hole, challenging oneself to do better. But simply walking the course is so relaxing. I try to get out as many times a week as I can, probably three or four times at least. I never had the time before. Now I can play!" Betsy, a sixty-six-year-old retired home economics teacher, loves to garden, walk, curl, golf, and travel: "Now we have the time to do these things. With both of us having a pension it helps: we can do these things. We are very fortunate."

Maryann (a retired nurse) and Dick (a retired clergyman) love to entertain. They recently bought a house in town in order to be near their family and to practise their "gift" for entertaining. Dick, seventy-two, loves to watch baseball, travel, and help Maryann entertain. Maryann, seventy-one, puts it this way:

> I have spent most of my married life working outside the home as well as entertaining various groups of people involved with the church. It seems to come naturally to me and I love doing it. I like making people feel at home. I like creating the atmosphere where people can get to know each other. We have moved here recently so this focus group get-together is great for us to have a better chance to get to know our new acquaintances.

While many of the focus group participants enjoyed live theatre, concerts, and the like, those in the Seabright group were especially involved with these pursuits. Mary, who came to Canada from Scotland in 1939 and is an avid bridge player and reader, is now learning how to speak German. She is very enthusiastic and tackles life with gusto: "We still play a mean hand of bridge. Some of my partners are eighty and ninety-one years old and we get along just fine. Yes, I am learning how to speak German along with some other friends. It is always good to learn new things." Margaret, a retired nurse who is now seventy-nine, spent thirteen months in the army during the Second World War. While in the army she served the people detained in Canada's prisoner-of-war camps. She flies with her husband and is thinking about taking flying lessons. She enjoys music, but her first love is the Lunenburg Family Resource Centre. Margaret is on the board of this new centre and is very enthusiastic about what it might be able to accomplish. She loves travelling to Wolfville to catch the plays at the Atlantic Festival Theatre: "I love the whole atmosphere in Wolfville and travelling to the AFT is a day out. Their events are very professional and so enjoyable. As well, I am really excited about this new Family Resource Centre. To be in on the ground floor is so exhilarating. I have great hopes for helping people at this new centre."

Billy, who is sixty-three and one of the two men in the Seabright focus group, is a former Department of National Defence employee.

Billy, who served in the RCAF for ten years and is an avid gardener, is content to be out of the "rat race": "I could never get used to the bureaucracy in government. I was totally frustrated most of the time. Now I can garden at my leisure, I do some carpentry work but I just love doing needlepoint. It is so relaxing. I especially enjoying recreating the flowers I love so much. Life is great right now."

Ellen is married, sixty-five, got her nursing degree at McGill in 1958, and helped put her husband through graduate school. They worked in the United States for most of their lives but are now back in the Glen Haven area. Ellen is a VON volunteer, and she loves to sing in the choir: "We certainly moved around a lot but we love Nova Scotia. I love to sing so I joined the Church Choir—it's a good place to sing! I also love the symphony and going to the plays at Neptune Theatre [in Halifax]. Of course I love to read. I can't imagine not being able to do that!"

Anne, a vibrant seventy-four-year-old, explained her passion for palliative care this way:

> It is so rewarding to care for people preparing to leave this world. I am very active and interested in the palliative care and hospice movement in Nova Scotia. I believe it helps one's peers to have a person in their own age bracket visiting and discussing their passing on. We have much in common, and a special bond is formed early in the relationship. I have always volunteered and faced life's challenges. I took yoga when I was younger, and it helped me so much I started to teach it. Soon I was teaching all the new things I was learning—especially a new way of eating! This is a special time in our lives. A time to sit back and reflect on living every day. We have earned the right to slow down and figure out what is important in life.

Several others were avid bridge players. Eve, who has now moved to an assisted-living apartment, arrived on the scene with her cards and score card in hand. It wasn't long before she encouraged people to play with her. Some had been reticent to engage with others, but they could not resist Eve, and the first thing they knew, card games were springing up all over the place. According to Eve: "It was so awful. No one was doing anything. I couldn't stand it. I had to get people moving. We all just couldn't sit around waiting to die. I still want to live the best I can, even though my health isn't all that good. I am going to keep plugging along." The older persons with whom we talked were varied in their likes and dislikes, but all agreed that it was time to do the things they hadn't had time for earlier in their lives.

EDUCATION AND LIFELONG LEARNING

Many older persons return to university and college either for educational upgrading or simply to pursue subjects that they did not have the time, finances, or interest in taking during their younger years. Throughout Canada, the United States, and Europe many seniors enroll in university-based educational programs either for credit or not. Many Canadian universities provide free tuition for persons aged sixty-five and over; some even provide special programming, especially during the summer months. When Jeanette taught at the University of British Columbia, every year hundreds of seniors would enroll in the Summer Program for Retired Persons.

Topics of interest range from astronomy and geophysics to English literature and medieval history. At Acadia University in Wolfville, the Continuing Education Department provides Elderhostel programs, which offer a variety of subjects to both local and international students, as well as a lifelong learning curricula, which provides year-long courses (covering a range of topics from financial planning to study tours of France) to persons aged sixty-five and over.

At the University of Manitoba the Creative Retirement Program offers an educational program run by and for seniors; it offers more than one hundred courses to over two thousand older people each year. As well as a range of courses, this program also produces a newsletter and regular course schedule.[3] Although there are usually minimal fees for these programs, arrangements are often made to assist low-income seniors who want to take these educational and information courses (personal communication, assistant director of Continuing Education, Acadia University, May 7, 2001).

While the vast majority of seniors engage in educational pursuits for pleasure, some also do so in an attempt to acquire literacy skills. According to Statistics Canada (1999b: 45), in 1996, 2.6 percent of persons aged sixty-five and over had no formal education; 36.9 percent had attended grades one through 8; 34.8 percent had attended grades nine through thirteen; and 25.6 percent had received a post-secondary education.

Lower levels of education, are, as Lilley and Campbell (1999:20) point out,

> associated with poorer health, institutionalization, and greater dependency in later life. There is also a strong relationship

between education level and low income. Seniors who did not finish high school are more than twice as likely to live in poverty than those who have some post-secondary education.

In a recent conversation with a local provincial homecare program assessment officer, Jeanette learned about an elderly couple living in her community. George is a seventy-eight-year-old man who suffers from a heart condition. He is the sole caregiver to his wife Lyn, who is seventy-six years old and is suffering from Alzheimer's disease. George received no formal schooling, as he grew up in a small rural community in northern New Brunswick where, as he told his assistance worker, he was "needed more on the farm than in the schoolhouse." Although he is able to care for his wife and is extremely reluctant to have her institutionalized, his lack of literacy skills compounds his frustration at attempting to make the system work for them. He is stymied by the need to complete forms, to read prescriptions and contraindications on medicine bottles. He cannot read the phone book, so he does not know how to find out who to contact for information about what services might be available to them. He cannot read the literature that comes to him from the local Alzheimer society, nor can he read the mail from his wife's sister in England inquiring as to her health. He lives, as he told his assistance worker, "in a kind of fog without an end in sight." He was always reliant upon his wife to take care of anything having to do with literacy skills. He asked why there wasn't any place that someone like him could go to learn to read and write "just enough to get by." This is a very good question. In spite of numerous calls to a variety of social service and educational establishments, Jeanette was unable to locate any programs that could assist George.

Lilley and Campbell (1999:21) note further that the present age cohort of seniors (as well as that coming into the next decade), which did not benefit from universal access to education, will continue to have low literacy and education skills. However, they also note that

> the next wave of seniors, coming of age in the second decade of the new millennium, will consist of the postwar "baby boomers" who had greater access to the education system. This population of seniors will have had substantially higher education and literacy levels, and the education gap between men and women will be much smaller .... These seniors may be more receptive to health promotion and prevention messages, and more able to navigate the health and social support systems.

If literacy skills are challenging for some older persons who were born and raised in Canada, then it is positively frightening for seniors who are immigrants or refugees and who speak neither of the official languages. When, as part of the Multi-Cultural Task Force on the Needs of Nova Scotia's Ethnic Elderly (in 1986), Jeanette conducted needs assessment research in the ethnically diverse communities of metropolitan Nova Scotia, she discovered that one of the principal needs of such elders was educational and literacy programs (Auger 1989, 1993). When conducting similar research in Vancouver, British Columbia, between 1982 and 1983, she obtained similar results (Auger 1983a; Auger and Kyles 1982-83).

In most cases, regardless of where seniors lived (but especially in Nova Scotia), very little, if anything, was provided in the way of literacy skills programs for older immigrants/refugees. The general assumption seemed to be that younger people would need such training so that they could enter the workforce, educate children, and be literate consumers of Canadian goods, services, and commodities. It appeared then, and it appears now, that family members or others who sponsor immigrants/ refugees to come to Canada will somehow take care of "their" elderly. There was not then, nor is there now, any overt recognition of the need for seniors to learn English, to enhance their literacy skills for their own intrinsic need to be independent and accepted as fully functioning contributors to their new homeland.

ELDERHOSTEL

Elderhostel is a United States-based program committed to the principle of lifelong learning, and it provides "high quality, affordable, educational opportunities to people aged fifty-five and older. Presently, Elderhostel programs are offered in every state in the USA, in Canada and in 93 countries around the world." Elderhostel recognizes that learning takes place at all ages and that age is not a matter of mere chronology. As President Stephen H. Richards notes:

> I have met Elderhostelers who, at 80, are more vibrant than many 40 year olds. Education matters because it keeps our minds sharp and our hearts open. What better reason for learning is there than because you want to learn, to pursue a passion, and to discover new ideas? …. We question and we learn. (Letter from the president of Elderhostel, http://www.elderhostel.org/ AboutEh/Letter/2001-0409.htm)

Many of the participants in our focus groups spoke about their continuing education goals and were eager to learn how to operate computers. In a small fishing village on the Bay of Fundy, the historical society, in conjunction with the provincial government, has set up a Community Access Program (CAP) site. Jane, an enthusiastic seventy-eight-year-old, spoke of her interest:

> I am anxious to learn how to use the computers. I am taking a beginner's course at the CAP site this spring so I can learn how to turn the thing on! I want to learn how to e-mail so I can keep in touch with my grandchildren. I don't have a computer but I can drop into the old schoolhouse and use their computers. I can hardly wait!

Many others have taken part in Elderhostel programs all over Canada, England, and the Caribbean. Most were very enthusiastic about them. One sixty-two-year-old explained her trip to the Sorrento Centre near Kamloops, British Columbia:

> We rented a car in Calgary, drove over the Rocky Mountains, and ended up at the Sorrento Centre in the centre of Samquash Country. We learned about the flora and fauna of the area, the history of the area, and I learned how to weave baskets from a Native woman who was very patient with me. It was a grand experience. We also travelled with the postal boat and saw hieroglyphs on the rocks. It was very moving.

Some participants have audited university courses in literature, history, and religious studies. Diane related her experience with late learning:

> I always wanted to have a college education. I enrolled at Acadia University in 1957 but changed my mind and stayed in Ottawa and got married. After three children and many ups and downs I went to Mount St. Vincent University when I was fifty years old. My first course was on personal development with Professor Goulet, who was a former Jesuit priest. A whole new world opened up for me. The next two years I took courses in psychology, women's studies, and a course on the Old Testament. When I lost my ten commandments what a shock! I had believed in the literal truth of the Bible for many years. The last two years I went to school full-time and received my bachelor

of arts with distinction in religious studies (minor in psychology). I then enrolled at the Atlantic School of Theology in the
Masters of Theological Studies Program. While there I was
undergoing a total change of perspective. I began to see a new
way of practising my spirituality. I completed ten subjects in this
program before I decided I needed to move in a new direction.
This was the first time I had not completed anything I under-
took to do. It was a big step for me to say, "It is all right to
change my mind in mid-stream!" I have continued to take
courses, learn new things, computers, e-mails, et cetera. I took a
three-level course in therapeutic touch and practise on family,
friends, children, and animals. At this time I also took a palliative
care volunteer course. At sixty-two I am still anxious to learn
and grow in all areas of my life. It is exciting to be alive in these
times. More opportunities are available than ever before. The
only thing that limits us is "myself." It is so true that one can do
whatever one puts her mind to regardless of age.

As has been mentioned, one focus group participant is taking German
lessons, and another is going to try to fly. Truly, the sky is the limit with
regard to one's efforts to enjoy life to the fullest.

SEXUALITY, INTIMACY, AND EROTICISM

At the Atlantic Sexuality Conference, entitled *Reframe and Celebrate* and
held at Mount Saint Vincent University in Halifax in 1992, Jeanette
presented a workshop entitled Sex and the Elderly: Moving from Myth
to Reality. She began the interactive session by saying that there were
three "isms" that hinder older persons from feeling free to express their
need for sexuality and intimacy regardless of their sexual orientation.
These "isms," which older persons themselves sometimes choose to
accept, are detrimental not only to older persons, but also to everyone
who hopes to continue to affirm a love of life through sexual expression.
They are:

1. Ageism. This results in negative attitudes that suggest that older people
    cannot, do not, and will not have any interest in sex. It ensures that
    when researchers and medical personnel do discuss the topic of sex and
    the elderly it was (and still is) from the perspective of the "limp dick"/
    "dry vagina" syndrome, which envisions sexuality in a dysfunctional
    light rather than as a continued celebration of self-expression, love of
    one's own (and another's) body, and a source of delight.

2. Sexism. This results in the idea that older women aren't interested in, or capable of, sexual fulfillment because they are "old hags," "ugly," and "asexual" and that older males are "dirty old men" who are "impotent" and "sex mad."

3. Heterosexism. This results in the assumption that all people are heterosexual, that heterosexuality is "normal" and that any deviation from it is "unnatural," "disgusting," and "immoral."

There is, in fact, no relationship between chronology and sexual activity; and even though some older persons may experience challenges in terms of expressing their sexuality (due, for example, to diminishing health or the loss of a partner), they may still enjoy satisfying and intimate sexual relationships until they die.

The Web site of the Sexual Health Information Center (http://www.sexhealth.org/sexaging/) notes:

> We are all victims of the harmful attitudes towards older people in our society. As we age, we will have to deal with the preconceptions which now exist. Now is the time to address harmful stereotypes and insure that elderly people in the future do not have to live with the prejudices that affect them today .... Sex is an expression of the satisfaction gained from the present. It expresses the closeness of our deepest relationships and is an important measure of the quality of life.

Having said all of that, the topic of sexuality and intimacy is still one that older persons, in particular, seem to have trouble articulating. In 1981–82, Jeanette was the principal investigator for a needs assessment of over 200,000 seniors living in British Columbia (sponsored by the Social Planning and Review Council of British Columbia). Among the many questions on a survey were a series that asked about sexuality and intimacy in later life. Most respondents chose not to answer these questions and made comments such as "it's none of your business," "that's too personal a question," and "I would rather not respond to these questions." We found some of the same responses when we attempted to deal with these questions with our current focus groups, some nineteen years later.

However, in 1984–85, while working as a researcher/consultant for the CBC television program *The Best Years*, Jeanette organized a live program dealing with the topic of sexuality and the aged. In this program, older persons spoke freely and openly about their feelings and behaviours. Therefore, it would not be true to say that all older persons have difficulty talking about these issues; in fact, it would appear that they have no more trouble doing so then do those in any other age group.

Much of the literature dealing with the topic of sexuality and intimacy in later life does so from the perspective of the challenges faced by older persons as the result of menopause (in older women) and erectile dysfunction (in older men). However, even though many older people may experience sexual problems, this is not true for all older persons. And even when it is true, several over-the-counter prescriptions may provide help. A lack of estrogen in women and a lack of testosterone in men does not mean that they cannot adjust to these bodily changes as they age, and it certainly does not mean that they cannot enjoy sexually fulfilling lives.

Because many older people (84 percent of all people aged sixty-five and over and living at home, according to Lindsay [1999:65]) are taking medications prescribed by physicians, it is possible that some of these drugs inhibit sexual functioning. As well, alcohol, diabetes, and endocrine, vascular, and neurological disorders are prevalent in this population, and this may also affect sexual desire (see http://www.umkc.edu/sites/hsw/age).

Throughout this text we have suggested that older women experience more negative labelling than do older men, particularly regarding sexual attractiveness and desirability. As Browne (1998:40) notes:

> Society in general, however, continues to have a difficult time seeing older women as sexual. Paul Newman can be a heartthrob in his 70's and star opposite a forty-something Melanie Griffith, but what about the roles for women in their 70's? With age, older women can have the same needs for companionship and sexual response as younger women can.

For all women, especially those who are heterosexual, the loss of a partner often signals the end of sexual intimacy. Usually, when men are widowed they remarry; this is not usually the case for older women. In fact, the 1996 Canadian Census shows that "80% of women aged 85 and over were widowed, as were 58% of those aged 75 to 84 .... Senior men are much more likely than senior women to have remarried" (Lindsay 1999:48).

Further, of those aged sixty-five and over, 48.9 percent of females are widowed, in comparison with only 13 percent of males (ibid.).

According to Novak and Campbell (2001:246), widows outnumber widowers for three primary reasons: "1) Women live longer than men; 2) women marry older men; and 3) men, more than women, tend to remarry after widowhood."

Browne (1998:40) and others argue that masturbation is not an option for today's old woman (although it may well be for the old women of future generations) because "there was a great stigma attached to it when the present cohort of older women were younger. Many were raised to believe that intercourse was functional primarily for procreation purposes and religions also played an important role in these beliefs." Interestingly, in light of the heterosexist attitudes that abound in our culture, middle-aged and older lesbians have been found to be "healthier, more career conscious, better educated, and closer to families and friends" than are their heterosexual sisters (Browne 1998:40). As well, lesbians have been found to "enjoy continuing and fulfilled sexual lives throughout their later lives" (ibid.).

Sexuality is the result of a complex set of social relations that transgress social expectations, roles, and rules; how we feel about our bodies and our physical appearance, and whether we consider ourselves worthy of love and intimacy, plays a role in our sense of ourselves as sexual beings. As we grow older, we may feel like attractive, desirable sexual beings, or we may absorb the social pressures and stereotypes directed towards the aged and so feel unattractive and sexually undesirable. Sexuality, like many things in life, is an ever-changing and complex process. As Marilynn Scott (http://socsci.mcmaster.ca/soc/courses/soc3k3e/stuweb/scott/scottm4/htm) notes in her article "Sexuality and Aging: Myths, Attitudes, and Barriers":

> Sexual expression among the elderly is a predictor of general health .... Sexuality, the mix of physical and relational behaviors, extends well beyond the reproductive years, and a normal factor is self-esteem and satisfaction .... Touching, smelling, hearing, tasting, and visual sensations are important components of sexuality. Hugging, fondling, caressing, cuddling, kissing and hand holding all bring about a sense of romance that can best describe closeness, even if or when sexual intercourse is not possible.

One day we will all become old. Sexuality is "part of life with no clear beginning much less a clear ending. Our collective failure to deal with these sexual issues is a very denial of our own self" (ibid.). One of the reviewers of an early draft of this book remarked on the absence, in literature, art, and film, of eroticism pertaining to old age. Our editor wondered whether we shouldn't explore the "erotic possibilities of old age," and we decided to attempt to pursue this topic further. Sadly, after a great deal of searching through various literary databases and Web sites devoted to issues of sexuality and/or seniors issues, we could find no material dealing with this subject. It appears that, within the popular media, old age is not considered to be erotic. We wondered what role the seeming absence of erotic material had on sexual practices in old age. We have, as yet, not been able to answer this question.

While we were contemplating this fascinating topic, an article appeared in the *Globe and Mail* (September 5, 2001, A1 and A8) under the title "Porn Calms Danish Seniors, Staff Say." Apparently "pornography and prostitutes have a greater calming effect on elderly patients than traditional medical treatments such as drug therapy" (A8). In response to the Danish example, the *Globe* quotes two Canadian nursing home staff members. The one from British Columbia commented, "Oh my God! That's interesting. A number of years ago there was a couple that got together and they were often caught in various places." The one from Nova Scotia commented, "Oh, get outta here .... I don't know how well that would go over here" (208). While Diane was collecting data at a local nursing home in Nova Scoria, a volunteer co-ordinator of support workers told of the following incident.

While working at a nursing home an elderly couple were found having sexual intercourse in the woman's room. Staff contacted the children of the woman involved. The children were of the opinion that their mother would consent to taking part in this activity; however, they had to sign papers and talk to many case workers and staff before their mother was "allowed" to continue this exchange of affection. It is clear that staff members were very reluctant to allow this public display of intimacy. This scenario raises questions about the level of custodial care and gate-keeping that nursing home staff inflict upon older persons, who, on the one hand, are told to view the institution as their home, and, on the other, are subject to having their activities heavily policed.

Members of our focus groups were reluctant to speak openly about sexuality. When we asked, "Do you think gay and lesbian people have different problems as they grow older than do heterosexual people?" participants were generally reluctant to volunteer much information. They did believe, however, that the problems of aging are basically the same for everyone. Some admitted that loneliness might be a bigger problem for gay and lesbian people than it is for heterosexual people. As Beth, a seventy-something woman from a small fishing village, put it:

I think it would depend on how family members and friends accepted their sexuality. They might be more isolated than the rest of us if they haven't had a support system around them during the younger years. Every person's circumstances are different so it is hard to say. I don't have much experience in that area so I really can't say.

These sentiments seemed to hold true for most people in the focus groups. It became clear that we needed to talk about the relationship between sexuality and intimacy. Physiologically, we may not be able to "do" all the sexual acts we used to perform in our younger days. For some, intimacy grows stronger as they age and a different way of "being together" is created. One retired clergyman in his eighties described a couple he knew:

These two people had been married for over sixty years. They could be in the same room together and not speak for an hour. However, when one was with them or walked into their home, one felt the intimacy, felt the connection between the two. Not a word had to be spoken. They connected on a deep spiritual level, and in that was their intimacy.

Carolyn Heilbrun (1997:112) speaks about sex and romance. She believes that, after sixty, these phenomena might be better experienced in the form of friendship. She mentions that, in *Writing a Woman's Life,* she divided men into two categories—lovers and husbands. She states that "one may feel overwhelming desire for a man with whom the relationship can 'dwindle' (that is develop) into friendship." However, she goes on to say that if obsessive desire and skillful technique are the only bases for a relationship, then eventually these feelings will become "less compelling." She suggests that the elderly leave romance to the young and welcome friendship.

She goes on to say:

Am I able to suggest a substitute, unromantic adventure for women's later life? Alas, I am not, although I have considered the matter long and hard. I do believe, however, that as we women reach our later years, sex, if it is part of our lives, is a by-product, not the dominant element. Like happiness, or beauty in a work of art, sex after sixty cannot be the object of any undertaking, though it may sometimes be a wonderful and unsought-for result. (113)

There would be many older women who would disagree with Heilbrun's experience and understanding of the situation. When putting together the panel for *The Best Years*, Jeanette met a woman who, at age seventy-six, decided to put a "want ad" in a local newspaper to find a new man. Donna had been a widow for the past thirteen years and, as she put it, "I was too young to be waiting around on the shelf." Ron replied to her advertisement, and they then began a "hot and heavy romance" that lasted until they married two years later. Donna pointed out that at their age "no one thought you could do anything so we thought we might as well do everything. Sex is wasted on the young" (personal communication, May 1985).

We know from previous studies of the psychology of aging that seniors are still, for the most part, sexual beings. Some body parts may not work as well as they used to, but their minds and emotions generally remain intact. While the development of friendship is certainly a high priority, over the years we have heard many stories that lead us to believe that, when health permits, people are sexually active into their nineties and beyond. Again, how we describe sexuality and the "sex act" is important here. Many couples find new ways of being together—touching, caressing, speaking words of endearment, mutual masturbation, or whatever is comfortable and acceptable to that particular couple, whether lesbian/gay or heterosexual. Diane offers the following story:

> An acquaintance of mine, who was widowed at sixty-five, began to really live after her husband died. She learned to play the violin and played in church orchestras for many years. At eighty-six she moved into an assisted-living apartment. There she met a wonderful eighty-nine-year-old man. After a short and whirlwind courtship they had a beautiful church wedding, with all their family and friends in attendance. They were like two teenagers in love. They couldn't take their eyes off each other and they were always holding hands. They didn't need to say a word. Everyone who was around them could feel their love for each other. I do not know of their "sex life," if you will, but I experienced their intimacy and their zest for living and living together. They were rejuvenated in their love.

Another story that was related to us concerned two high school sweethearts who lost track of each other after graduation. It appears that both parties married other people and went on to have their families. Dick was widowed when he was in his late seventies, and Betty lost her husband when she was seventy-four. One afternoon, while on a car trip with a friend, Betty decided to see if she could find this fellow (they were visiting in the town where he had lived out his life). His daughter answered the phone and immediately invited them to stay for dinner. (She knew all about Betty!) In Betty's words, "It was like we had never been apart. We hugged and both knew. It was the most wonderful feeling I have ever had."

For several years they commuted between residences, about a two-hour drive each way. In the fall of one year Betty arrived and didn't leave again. Her daughter closed up her apartment, and the two "loving companions" had five wonderful years together before Dick died. Betty explained that "she had all the usual sexual feelings," but, since Dick had prostate cancer, they found other ways to show their affection. Hugs, kisses, and cuddles were the acts of the day. They spent many hours talking over old memories and things they used to do. Dick had never forgotten Betty. He even remembered the dresses she wore. Their relationship was a joy to them both and to those who saw them together. Some people never attain this level of intimacy. Again, as Betty said, "We don't have to say a word. We smile at each other and know."

"Eroticism" has been defined as the viewing of any sexually explicit material that results in increased sexual desire. Not only did people in our focus groups not wish to discuss many details of their sex lives, but they also chose not to mention the subject of eroticism. In looking into this phenomenon, we discovered that material on eroticism and the older person was non-existent. In our society we do not see any videos, films, magazines, or literature depicting eroticism and the elderly. Nowhere do we see naked older people posing or taking part in sexual activities. One man in his sixties agreed to answer the question, "Do you think it is necessary to view sexually explicit material to be 'turned on'?" His reply: "No, not really, I haven't looked at Playboy for years! I just need to see the woman that I love, and I am ready! It doesn't seem as important to me as it used to."

Recently, while surfing the Net, we came upon an article written by Scott Thomsen of the Associated Press and entitled "Active Older Adults Are Playing Around." Thomsen noted that in Sun City West, Arizona, officials have reported over a dozen senior couples being caught having sex in a public place. This information surprised a good number of people. These activities took place in parks, swimming pools, and even spas in this suburban Phoenix retirement community. As one spokeswoman for the recreation centre commented: "This is not God's waiting room. We have very active seniors. And seniors are human beings and have all the same urges and desires as all other human beings" (http://www.canoe.ca/CNEWSFeatures0106/26_old-ap.html).

The article argues that this constitutes evidence that seniors are rediscovering their sex drives, perhaps due to healthier lifestyles and performance-enhancing drugs such as Viagra. Thomsen goes on to say that, in 1999, the American Association of Retired Persons conducted a Modern Maturity Sexuality Survey of people over forty-five. It was discovered that two out of three respondents who had partners were extremely or somewhat satisfied with their sex lives. As well, it was found that 10 percent of the men and 7 percent of the women used Viagra or some other medicine to enhance sexual performance. It was also agreed that better health improved peoples' satisfaction with their sex lives.

On the downside, in 2000 it was reported that the number of sexually transmitted diseases infecting senior persons is on the increase. This article reports that, in 1995, Arizona's Department of Health Services recorded thirty-seven cases of gonorrhea among people fifty-five and older and that by 2000 the figure had risen to fifty-four. Similarly, in 1995 there were no fewer than five instances of a person over sixty being diagnosed with the HIV virus; in 2000, this figure had jumped to nine.

While authorities are not too concerned over this information, it has been noted that more sexual education and counselling should be directed towards seniors. As the director of education and counselling for planned parenthood, Joseph Feldman, suggested: "Too many seniors don't take precautions, most women are past menopause, so they don't fear getting pregnant ... women outnumber males, giving those men many partners from which to choose." As Feldman says: " It's almost like being a kid in the candy store. Why would you want to be with a woman who wants you to wear a condom when three others don't." The article noted that anyone with a new partner(s) should use a condom.

While this information concerns activities in the United States, there is no reason to believe that Canadian seniors are any different than their American counterparts. One eighty-six-year-old widow with whom Diane spoke admitted: "We were still trying to do it right up until my husband died. Our interest was always there. It seems it got stronger as we got older. The children were gone and we were freer. Even after our health deteriorated, we never gave up trying."

Another story told by a support worker suggests that more seniors than we realize may use sex toys and tools. On many occasions, a friendly volunteer visited a widow in her late eighties. They became very good friends. One day, this visitor arrived and noticed her friend was troubled. When she asked about it, she received this reply: "Dearie, do you think you could get my 'friend' fixed?" With that, the older woman handed the visitor a vibrator that needed new batteries.

Whereas those who live independently can engage in whatever sexual and intimate relationships they choose, this is not necessarily the case for those who are institutionalized. In 1987, Jeanette worked with a Vancouver psychotherapist on a series of workshops aimed at assisting nursing home staff to discuss and deal with issues of sexuality in the "home." What became very clear during these sessions was the discomfort that staff members felt with regard to their patients being sexual or intimate. The attitude seemed to be: "if I think about patients doing it at their age, then I wonder about my parents and grandparents and that makes me uncomfortable." These types of attitudes are not exclusive to this particular nursing home; we have heard them often since. However, they do represent a societal norm that strongly suggests that sexual expression is the prerogative of the young. According to Benjamin Schlesinger (1983:269):

> We have very little data about sexuality among the aged in institutions. We need to deal with the following questions: 1. What part does sexuality play in the institutions for the aged? 2. Is the staff trained to deal with this aspect of the lives of the aged in their care? 3. How can we facilitate the satisfaction of the sexual needs of the institutionalized aged? (This may include sex education, masturbation, prostitution, homosexuality, and heterosexual intercourse.) 4. Are we really dealing with a population that has little or no interest in sexuality as described in the widespread stereotype?

If we assume that we shall remain sexual throughout our lives, then we must ponder Schlesinger's questions.

SPIRITUALITY AND RELIGION

We have suggested that everyone is a sexual being and that we need to be able to express our feelings of sexuality and intimacy throughout our lives. This is also true of our spirituality, whether we choose to express it through a formally recognized religion such as Christianity, Buddhism, or Judaism or by walking through the woods and contemplating our connection to the universe. For the purposes of this book, we define religion as a set of symbols and beliefs practised (usually in public) in order to demonstrate one's faith; and we define spirituality, following Victor Frankl (cited in McFadden 1996:11), as "the human drive for meaning and purpose."

Canadian seniors are very involved in religious activities. According to Lindsay (1999:113), in 1996, "37% of people aged 65 and over attended church or other religious functions at least once a week. This was about the same figure as for those aged 55 to 64 (36%), but well above the figures for people aged 45 to 54 (21%), 25 to 44 (16%), and 15 to 24 (12%)."

Jeanette was raised as a Roman Catholic, and although she no longer participates as an active member of this church, she does recognize the importance of faith and spiritual fellowship for her elderly family members. Four years ago, her uncle died unexpectedly, leaving behind his wife of forty-odd years. Her aunt was devastated by this loss. The couple had no children and, as well as living together, had worked together everyday. The local parish priest became a regular visitor to the home, as did other members of the church, who brought casseroles, muffins, and cakes. It is true to say that, without the ongoing assistance of both the priest and parishioners, Jeanette's aunt would have led a very depressing existence. Because of her faith and the spirit of community that church-going provided her, she was able to deal with a crucial loss. Recently, Jeanette's aunt moved into another community; at age seventy-seven she has had to adjust to a new home, neighbourhood, and lifestyle. Her priest has made connections for her with the new church and minister, and, although she is lonely and still very much saddened by her losses, Jeanette, her only living biological relative, takes refuge in knowing that her aunt is being helped by her faith.

Lindsay (1999:113), among others, has noted that senior women are more likely than are senior men to attend religious activities on a regular basis: "In 1996, 42% of women aged 65 and over, versus 30% of senior men, attended such functions on a weekly basis." Women not only attend religious functions more often than their male counterparts, but they are also more active in church events. Yvette, a French-Canadian member of the Lunenburg caregiver group lives in Yarmouth, Nova Scotia, and she explained the importance of church activities in the following way:

> We have always been very involved with the church. After my husband died I did a lot more for them. I always baked a lot and helped out with the special teas, but now I do the flowers for the altar every Sunday, I take care of the little ones during the church services, in the daycare place in the basement. I really

love this part of the job! I organize the outings for the seniors centres and the nursing home too. There is nothing I wouldn't do for the church. It has given me so much that I must always want to give it back.

Seniors are also the most likely age group to make a contribution to their church or synagogue. In 1997, "40% of all seniors made a financial contribution to their church, synagogue, mosque, or other place of worship" (Lindsay 1999:113).

As we live in the Annapolis Valley, the Baptist bible belt of Nova Scotia, the majority of the people in our focus groups were Baptist, with a smattering of Anglicans and Roman Catholics. Others would not define their spirituality within a religious context. Most have a belief in a greater power, a creator of all things. For some, spirituality entails living out their lives with a sense of connectedness to and with their natural surroundings. The way we live demonstrates how we feel about all living things. Our relationships with others demonstrate our philosophy of living together. While we found that religious activities slow down as we get older, most people maintain a positive religious attitude.

We experienced many versions of spirituality as we travelled around the province collecting data. Here is what some people in the focus groups had to say. Beth, a seventy-seven-year-old retired nurse, active churchgoer, and volunteer from a small town, described her experience:

> I have always gone to church. As a little girl my family was very active. It was just a natural thing to do. The social events held by the church were community based and it was our social life. We lived in a farming community and everyone went to church in the good times and the bad. Without my faith in God and a life hereafter, I wouldn't have been able to get through some of the trials in my life. I have always had a steady faith that God is with me. I believe we all must do all we can to help others.

Annie, a seventy-eighty-year-old from a small rural community, opens her house to everyone. It is nothing for four or five extra people to show up for a meal; Annie simply goes to the freezer, adds another potato, and feeds whoever shows up. She sees this hospitality as part of her Christian life, as part of who she is. Annie lives in a rural area, where the bond between church and community is very strong.

Eve, an eighty-one-year-old woman from a small town no longer goes to church. She explained her faith this way:

My mother died when I was six. Two nights before she died, I had nightmares and jumped into bed with her. During the night I felt that I saw someone standing at the bottom of the bed with a light in his hand. The light was pointed to my mother! I have always believed in a life after this one. I grew up Anglican and when I had pneumonia as a teenager and had to stay in bed for weeks, I read the Bible all the way through. I have had many traumatic experiences happen in my life, but I always knew I wasn't alone. I felt the presence of God with me. And when things were particularly bad, I would have "ancestors" visit me to reassure me. I know there is more than we are conscious of in this world. I don't go to church much anymore, but I pray every night and I have very special hymns that give me comfort.

Anne, who is in her late seventies and resides on the South Shore, lives out her spirituality through her connection with palliative care. Anne did not speak of a connection with organized religion, but her life experience and activities spoke for her. She arrived in Canada, a refugee from the Second World War, with her husband. They had four children and Anne became interested in yoga. From there she practised good nutrition, making dietary changes in her lifestyle. It wasn't long before she was giving workshops on the well-being of body, mind, and spirit. She believed that there was a connection between all three and the world around us. For many years she helped run a spiritual retreat on Nova Scotia's South Shore. Anne is now very interested in the philosophy around palliative care and hospices. She sees a connection between this life and how we live it and what she assumes will be the next life. To help another human being exit from this life in a caring, loving, and dignified manner, free from pain, is Anne's "calling." In her words:

It is very important for us all to remember how we live the last years of our journey here will help us in the next journey. We need to care for each other. We all get older and we all die. If we can make a small difference in someone's life, it is all worthwhile. We need to make more noise so that the politicians hear us. We must never give up. The acute care hospitals cannot do this job.

Anne belongs to the Hospice Consultation Committee, which is attempting to erect the first free-standing hospice in Nova Scotia. She lives her spirituality everyday.

As we enter into mid-life and beyond, some of us take another look at what we believed as children and young adults. We begin to ask questions. Sometimes those who were once involved in organized religion turn towards a way of living that perceives the Earth and everything in it as sacred. For these people, their cathedral may be a hemlock grove in the forest or a brook in the woods. They see god in all their surroundings. At this point, Diane would like to share her personal journey towards her current faith.

As a young girl I always went to Sunday school. My father's parents were Baptist missionaries in India. Dad was born there. My mother's parents were Anglican. In 1936, when they were married, that combination was difficult for my Baptist grandparents. However, in later years they grew to think Mom was "okay." In my teenage years, singing in choir and during quiet times in the church by myself, I always felt the presence of what I believed to be the spirit of Jesus. I would feel warm all over. I fled to church whenever I felt sad, lonely, or upset. I always found solace there. I grew up, married in the Anglican tradition, had three boys who were all Sunday schooled and confirmed! I sang in a gut bucket band in church for five years and subsequently took a lay readers course and did my fair share of preaching and administering the sacraments. During this time I belonged to the Anglican Renewal Movement and experienced "praying in tongues." This language still comes to me in times when words or thoughts cannot express my prayers. At this point I was "in the spirit" and thought everyone else should be too! I had a lot to learn about judgment and each person's individual journey.

At fifty, I was literally "moved" into going back to university. It happened in a small Anglican church near Digby, Nova Scotia. As I was praying, the image of a nun came to me and, with it, the idea for more education. Mount St. Vincent University used to be run by the Sisters of Charity, and that is where I landed! My first course was on personal development, and the doors for self-reflection were opened. Then came courses in the Old and New Testaments and women in the Bible. My whole world was turned upside down! Up until this time I had believed in the literal truth of the Bible. All my beliefs were shattered. It was a time of great turmoil and anger. When I discovered the Inquisition and the witch burnings, I was beside myself. Why had I not been taught these things before? As I have stated before, I graduated four years later and attended the Atlantic School of Theology, taking the masters course in theological studies. After ten courses and more soul searching I decided not to finish as I had too many questions about the "man-made doctrines" we were supposed to believe! During the time at the Mount I took a course in death and dying. I had just lost my father after a very lengthy illness, and I was deeply moved by the stories and videos Sister Betty La Fontaine showed to us. Hence, the beginning of my love affair with palliative care. I enrolled in a volunteer course in 1994 and have been involved since that time. As I questioned the doctrine of the virgin birth, the physical resurrection of Christ, and so on, I set forth on a new quest to find the connection that I needed to live out my life in a way that fit my soul.

I discovered Native spirituality, and the drums spoke to my heart. In meditation I found several power animals, the dolphin and mother bear. I began to see the world around me in a different light. And as I grew in my consciousness, I realized I had been judgmental of others in wanting people to have the same journey as my own. The light came on. I am so grateful that I persevered in my questioning and today I am still on the journey. I discover something new every day.

Several years ago, I had a terrific pain in my neck and head. I was taken to emergency at the local hospital and kept in overnight. They suspected an aneurysm. I was all alone on a steel gurney. A nurse came along and said, "Oh, my goodness! We can't leave you like that all night!" She left, found blankets, and wrapped me in them. I was in too much pain to help her. She tucked me in, gave me a pat, and left. The most wondrous warm energy encircled me, and it was at that moment I realized that "Universal Love," "God," "Christ"—whatever name we give to it—surrounded me and, through that nurse, spoke to me. A feeling of well-being surrounded me, and I knew at that time I would be all right. Many such moments have happened in my life, and I am aware I have many helpers in the "other" world helping me in this one. In my palliative care work I have been blessed to share journeys with those who are dying.

One such case was a forty-five-year-old woman with ovarian cancer. When we first met, there was an instant connection. I had to explain to her that I only had six weeks to be with her. We agreed we would make the most of that time. She loved candles, nature, and growing things. So did I. She loved sunsets, water, and bonfires. So did I. I will never meet another human being that gave me so much. She was in the later stages of the disease and desperately wanted to stay at home. The palliative care team pulled together, and it was only in the last two weeks she had to be taken to hospital so her daughter wouldn't see the last stages of her pain. However, in the meantime we shared drives, sunsets, and the water. She was vomiting nearly all the time. But when I said to her, "Come on, bring your bucket and we will go to the Harbour" (Hall's Harbour, where I live), she was ready to go. During the time she spent at the Harbour sitting in front of my window watching the sunsets, she was never sick. At least for several hours she would have some relief. A mystery? A spirit connection, I believe. I have been blessed to know her and to remember her today. Whenever I have a bonfire on the beach I remember her. She asked that I would, and I do.

Another client, from whom I learned a lot about spirituality and connection, was also dying of cancer. He spent a lot of time doing needlepoint and talking about life in general. As he began to trust me he spoke of other things: his disease, his rehabilitation, and now his final disease—the cancer. About one week before he died, we were talking a bit about what the next journey might be like. He quietly said to me, "I had a visitor last night." When I appeared not to be unbelieving ... he went on to say: "My brother came to me last night. He was looking over my left shoulder and told me it would be all right. Not to worry. It would all work out. At first I thought it was a dream, but I don't know. Anyway, I think I feel better."

I shared some of my experiences with him, and our friendship and spiritual connection deepened. It is this kind of trust and bond that is so rewarding in palliative work. A deeper level of understanding and connection occurs. I have found in my palliative care work that the wisdom learned or shared from older persons in the stages of living while they are dying is contagious. The connection between one who is facing death and one who is caring for that individual narrows down to the total reality of the situation. Masks fall away and truth can be forthcoming. When this happens, a soul connection is made. The Divine is present.

It has also been my experience that even people suffering from dementia can be moved spiritually when hearing a familiar piece of music or a familiar prayer. An eighty-year-old woman suffering from Alzheimer's disease was taken out to the activity room where a hymn sing was in session. She usually is not responsive, but on this particular day, as she was wheeled into the room, she looked directly at the singers and smiled. She remained alert for the rest of the program.

My faith journey has taken me to meditation, vision quests, and to asking for help from those on the other side. At the same time, my connection to the Bible is stronger than ever, as I realize it is a faith story, the story of a people's faith, and not literal truth. The sacraments and ritual of the Anglican tradition are still ingrained within my being, integrated with that of Mother Earth and Father Sky. I see the Divine as androgynous and not father. My knowledge of the Goddess helps make me whole in my faith. The journey continues. I am still exploring the questions: Why am I here? What did I come back to do?

People live out their spirituality in many different ways. In a recent edition of the Halifax *Chronicle-Herald* (April 21, 2001, E9), there was an article by Bob Harvey entitled "Nursing the Spirit." It told the story of a Franciscan nun, Sister Mangalam Lena, from Ottawa, Ontario, who is providing at-home spiritual care for the elderly and lonely. In this article Harvey explains that Lena believes spiritual care is an essential part of health care both inside and outside the hospital. This article explains what she is doing. Lena has launched possibly the first ever home-based spiritual care service. She has worked as a hospital chaplain and as a practical nurse, providing for the physical needs of her clients. She goes on to comment: "There is pastoral care in the hospitals and home-care provides nursing, counseling, and physiotherapy for the homebound. But who cares for their spiritual needs in the home?"

This new service is an example of the connection between spirituality and health-related well-being. Harvey goes on to say that, several years ago, researchers from Duke, Harvard, and Yale universities reviewed more than 1,100 studies and found that faith had positive effects on everything "from the suicide rate to blood pressure." Apparently (according to this article) a large number of American medical schools now include courses on religion, but Canadian schools only have courses on ethical issues, which include sections on religious sensitivity. Lena has persuaded the University of Ottawa to research the need for such care. The assistant director of nursing, Dian Prud'homme, put it this way: "People who are spiritually healthy are also physically healthier … you see less depression and less infection because spiritual health has an effect on the immune system. It also has an effect on the prevention and treatment of rheumatic diseases." She goes on to explain that volunteers who visit the homes do not have the training needed to deal with the spiritual needs of the sick and elderly. Lena points out that, while she was attending the physical needs of her clients, even though they had no way of knowing she was a nun, they would invariable ask her, "Do you believe in life after death?" and "Where is God in all my suffering?" Most of these clients lived alone and had no relatives, community connections, or church affiliations. As she explained, the longer people live, and the more the traditional pool of unpaid help (usually adult daughters) dries up, the more the number of elderly needing care will rise. Lena said that her clients usually talk about "loneliness and death." As she explained, "I discovered this working with them and I suffer for them" (E9).

For this sister of the Franciscan Missionaries of Mary, a life's work has been found, and, as she ages, she connects with those she visits and cares for both physically and spiritually. It should be noted here that Lena has hit upon a large crack in the health care system. How many communities have a spiritual service? If you belong to an affiliated church community, then you may have a visit from the clergy. But what happens to those who do not? We are all spiritual beings, and this should be recognized as programs are put into place to help keep people home, happy, and well.

Maxwell Jones's (1988) *Growing Old: The Ultimate Freedom* had a profound impact on Diane. Jones, a good friend and mentor of Jeanette prior to his death at the age of eighty-three, was the founder of the therapeutic community approach to care of the mentally ill in the United Kingdom. A retired psychiatrist, he explains that the aim of his book is to question the validity of many of the Western stereotypes of growing older. He points out that society tends to view retirement from paid employment as "an unpleasant topic instead of a time to look back on life and to build on the positive areas of interest which were previously sacrificed to the god of work" (1). He goes on to say that it is his intent to explore our "latent spirituality." Seeing retirement as an opportunity to slow down and to discover, Jones describes his journey and that of others in his (and Jeanette's) discussion groups, which, for many years, were held in Wolfville. While recuperating from a serious heart attack—a time during which many of his physical activities were curtailed—he "experience[d] more interest and excitement than ever before."

Maxwell Jones attempts to look at intuition, at deeper levels of consciousness, and at relationships to another world. He questions our education system and suggests that more attention be paid to human relations: "This change would entail a new significance accorded to group interaction between people in all walks of life so that everyone would come to realize the need for a support system which could be trusted and turned to as required" (4). He goes on to say that he sees this as everyone's responsibility. He sees the value of these phenomena for all age groups, but particularly for the elderly. Jones questions whether our education has served us well, and he suggests that it has not. In contemplation and meditation he has discovered another world: "I am now free to live my life as I please, having slowly withdrawn from the rat-race of professional life as a psychiatrist and social ecologist. My interest in group and community work has moved from hospitals to the general community" (6).

Jones notes that, in a recent poll conducted by the National Opinion Research Center of the University of Chicago, sixty-seven out of one hundred Americans claim to have experienced extrasensory perception at some time in their lives. He contends that there is a latent potential for spiritual growth and renewal in everyone, and he challenges us to discover this in ourselves. He suggests that we stop equating the concept of retirement with old age and, instead, see growing old as a time to experience various freedoms:

> Freedom to read, to interact socially and to learn; freedom to change one's lifestyle and set priorities based on contemplation and absence of social pressures; freedom to question cultural stereotypes or the politics of fear and greed ... freedom to explore "absurd" ideas, fantasies and dreams which may in time come to reflect the limitations of our current concept of reality. (7)

Jones maintains that, in celebrating our later years, we have the opportunity to search for whatever we may take to be the meaning of life. He suggests that maintaining a social network is very important to one's well-being. The "poor-me syndrome," in which many seniors engage, can lead to isolation. He believes that when we cease to have social contact we become sensory-deprived and, perhaps, delusionary (27). He maintains that education plays a role in moving people from self-interest to a more global spiritual perspective (59). He believes that the elderly could become role models for both each other and the younger generation (134).

Jones says that, in his eighties, study and contemplation have become a substitute for sex (82). He talks about experiencing joy and energy rather than anxiety, and he expresses his excitement at discovering a new world, a higher level of consciousness. He marvels at his freedom to explore the spiritual world as he comes closer to the end of this life and begins contemplating what he presumes will be the next life. He advocates self-awareness:

> It is this self-awareness that has been largely lost in our western world and must be regained if we are to rediscover our lost potential. Surely we must try to tune in to the impressions and feelings all around us, which we tend to ignore .... This self-awareness opens our minds to the wider field of intuition and our latent ability to get beyond the reality of the scientific rational world and find a new reality in spiritual experiences, intuition and the mystery of life itself .... We are vaguely aware of this need to search for the truth if we are to escape from the illusion we call reality. To find a deeper reality which most of us have only sensed momentarily if at all is the major theme of this book and I believe, a major purpose of life. (134)

It is within this context that Jones speaks of outer and inner energy. We all know how easy it is to pick up negative energy from negative situations, people, or thoughts. Here he describes the joy in creative energy and how we are energized as we create new understandings in our lives. He encourages us to live out our later years in self-reflection and contemplation, which, in turn, can produce great creativity and joy, even in the face of physical limitations.

What Maxwell Jones does not discuss in his book is the fact that he was most fortunate in having a wife (his third) and children who fully supported his work throughout his life. His wife Chris was his sole caregiver at the end of his life, and she shared his spiritual journey until his death. Her work continues as she brings together Jones's work as a legacy for others.

While researching psychology in Acadia's library, Diane came across *The Handbook of the Psychology and Aging*, edited by James E. Birren and K. Warner Schaie (1996). She noted that Chapter 9, written by Susan H. McFadden and entitled "Religion, Spirituality and Aging," spoke about some of the issues we have been discussing. McFadden suggests that, from a gerontological point of view, emotional security stems from a belief in life after death. During our research and discussions with older persons the question of their own mortality often came up. Usually, upon reflecting on their lives and their search for meaning, they discuss matters of religion, spirituality, and faith. McFadden suggests that, because religion is multifaceted (i.e., because it has different meanings for different people), psychology attempts to look at how it affects how older people live the last years of their lives, coping with losses and the oncoming knowledge that they, too, will die.

As people examine their own mortality, they often find that a belief in a life after death brings them meaning and hope. Ritual provides them with a sense of stability and security as they attempt to cope with the changing world around them. When Diane visits Fundy Villa, a nursing home complex in Berwick, Nova Scotia, she notices that many residents find regular church services and Bible studies to be very meaningful. There is also another group of residents who are not regular church goers but who find their spirituality in nature, in making connections with others and with their plants and gardens. These residents are somewhat neglected in the care facility, and it needs to be pointed out here that their needs must also be explored by future care givers and care providers. As one resident said:

> I know it is important for those who are used to going to church to have all these programs but what about the rest of us? I am a very spiritual person. I feel the presence of God in my life every day. My connection with living things around me. The birds, the plants, and the people I meet. They say here they don't have time to do the gardening, and as we get older we can't do it, so therefore there aren't many gardens around. I really miss this. We have a few flowers out front but one woman claims to own it so the rest of us can't touch it! I feel really badly about this. I have gardened all my life.

McFadden mentions the approach taken by Moberg and Brusels (1978). Asking a series of questions they determined that spiritual well–being has two aspects: (1) a vertical connection with God and (2) a horizontal connection with people and ordinary life experiences. McFadden points out that this model is not borne out by her experience; however Diane believes that her experiences with palliative care support this concept or model. What this indicates is that there is no one way of assessing spirituality. What works for one does not necessarily work for another, and vice versa.

McFadden also cites Bianchi (1994), Gubrium (1993), and Rubenstein (1994) with regard to spirituality and its importance in promoting creativity, concern for others, and hope amidst the daily trials of life in a nursing home or senior retirement facility. As psychologists are finally broaching the complex study of the relationship between religion, spirituality, and aging, it is becoming evident that this is something that many seniors are attempting to address. Our research indicates that, in the effort to care for an aging population, it is crucial to take a holistic approach to successful aging.

CULTURE, RACE, AND ETHNICITY

Culture refers to the process through which we share language, art, food, clothing, rituals, symbols, folkways, and (sometimes) religion. It involves sharing meanings with people who have similar backgrounds to our own. For Jeanette, whose culture of origin is English, having a cup of tea and a biscuit every day between 3:30 PM and 4:00 PM is part of a cultural tradition, as is having bangers n' mash for supper (not dinner), listening to the Queen's Christmas message on the radio (not watching it on TV), and enjoying an ice-lolly (not a popsicle) in the summer. All of these activities, which just happen to be primarily concerned with food, are comforting rituals from a familiar and loved culture. Jeanette knows that they will accompany her into old age.

Race is the term we use to describe persons who share such similar inherited attributes as skin and hair colouring, facial and physical features, and descent and ancestry.

Ethnicity refers to the sharing of a common national origin, race, culture, language, and (perhaps) religion. According to Henderson and Primeaux (1981:14), ethnic groups are generally identified by "distinctive patterns of family life, language, and customs that set them apart from other groups. Above all else, members of ethnic groups feel a sense of identity and common fate." However, people who share an ethnic background may not be homogeneous; for example, people living in Mainland China may have very different ethnic traditions. Similarly, people living in Canada may have ethnic traditions whose roots may be traced to Africa, Europe, and so on.

According to the 1996 Canadian census, 27 percent of persons aged sixty-five and older were immigrants. Of that number, 61 percent came to Canada prior to 1961; 14 percent came in the 1960s; 11 percent came between 1971 and 1980; and 14 percent came in the 1980s and 1990s (Lindsay 1999:17). Almost all immigrant seniors have become Canadian citizens: "Indeed 88% of all immigrants aged 65 and over living in Canada in 1996 had taken out Canadian citizenship" (ibid.). Most immigrant seniors in Canada are from Europe (71 percent), 16 percent are from Asia, 6 percent are from the United States, and smaller percentages are from regions such as Africa, the Caribbean, and Central and South America (ibid.).

In 1996 Aboriginal elders comprised just 4 percent of the population, representing North American First Nations, Métis, and/or Inuit peoples (20). A relatively small proportion of seniors are part of the visible minority population, most of whom identified themselves as being of Chinese descent (40 percent), then South Asian (19 percent), then Black (13 percent) (19). Although the majority of Canada's older population speaks either English or French, a small minority (4 percent) does not. Only 1 percent of those aged between fifteen and sixty-four do not speak either English or French (20).

When Jeanette conducted research into the needs of the ethnic-minority elderly living in Metro Nova Scotia in 1989, one of the key issues that faced older persons was the need for language training (the rest of this section is adapted from Auger 1993). In this province English as a second language courses were provided free to new immigrants but not to those aged fifty and over. As no programs (not even those that charged a fee) were available to members of this age group, they could not learn to speak the same language as their grandchildren; consequently, they were not able to feel a connection to others in their new neighbourhoods.

Other key challenges facing ethnic-minority elders included the following: first, they are often marginalized both inside and outside their own and so-called "mainstream" cultures because of age and the socio-economic/gender factors associated with aging. In less populated regions of the country, such as the Maritimes and Newfoundland, ethnic-minority seniors are invisible to service providers because they do not represent a substantial number of consumers or voters within the total community. Often the consumer needs of non-White seniors are met by family and friends, and access to Canadian health services is sought only when absolutely necessary—culturally traditional medicine and modes of healing being preferred where available.

Second, due to an imperialistic ideology and limited health care budgets, which set up an *us* (the host society) versus *them* (the newcomer, immigrant, refugee population) dichotomy in the provision of programs, ethnic-minority seniors do not receive services in their own language or based upon their cultural expectations, values, and understandings. In the us-versus-them mode of service and program delivery, "we" are tolerant of "their" needs. When programs are requested, we ask them what they need from our existing system rather than facilitating their telling us what might be added to that system in order to more adequately meet their needs. Access to such services is deemed a privilege rather than a right. Indeed, there is an element of institutional racism at all levels of Canadian society; however, this discrimination particularly affects people from visible minority groups. With advancing age, and with economic and social circumstances that require family members to work outside of the home, more ethnic-minority seniors may have to enter long-term care facilities where their cultural/ethnic needs may not be met.

Third, ethnic-minority seniors experience a lack of cultural/religious sensitivity on the part of professional service providers. This affects their perceptions of health care, income security, and other assistance programs. Fourth, ethnic-minority seniors are not educated about cross-cultural health care and Canadian beliefs about the roles and expectations of the aged.

This research, which involved hundreds of interviews and focus group sessions with ten different ethnic-minority groups in the Halifax, Dartmouth, and Bedford communities of Nova Scotia, concluded that what was needed to help ethnic-minority elders become more at home in Nova Scotia were (1) language services, (2) education programs, (3) cultural awareness, and (4) attitude changes.

Language services: These should include translations and should be provided by all levels of government, banks and other financial institutions, and service and community organizations. This should be done with the cooperation and assistance of multicultural groups within the province (where applicable). As well, cultural translators, who already exist in some institutions, need to have their role supplemented so that they can provide even further assistance, especially for those without immediate family assistance.

Education programs: These should deal with aging in other cultures and should be provided for health care and other service providers through in-service workshops organized at hospitals and other health care and social service facilities. Ethnic-minority elders could be invited into such facilities to talk about aging in their countries of origin and to produce written materials that discuss the roles and values of elders in other cultures. Government information could be translated into the dominant languages of those living in the province. Formal courses could be provided for all service personnel, especially those in the medical professions and social work.

Cultural awareness: There must be a willingness to offer culturally sensitive health care and other services based on an understanding that the needs of ethnic elders may indeed be different than are those of other older persons.

Attitude changes: There must be attitude changes on the part of those who provide services to all multicultural clients, especially towards those who are older. This is because ethnic-minority elders represent a stigmatized group in our society but not necessarily within their own.

HEALTH CARE

No single topic is currently more contentious for all age groups in Canada than is that of health care, especially as regards hospital closures and the high cost of providing such care. From the perspective of older persons, access to affordable, competent, and local health care is crucial. Health is more than the absence of disease or injury; it is a multifaceted condition that includes physical well-being, mental competence, being socially accepted and supported for exactly who we are, and feeling good about ourselves and how we look and act in the world.

Browne (1998:19) differentiates between being in a good state of health and being "health functioning," which refers to

> one's ability to perform certain tasks to remain independent, such as bathing, eating, grooming, and toileting, as well as activities that focus on home management. Preserving health and health functioning are two primary concerns, particularly among older adults, since the ability to maintain an independent lifestyle is influenced by both.

Services such as flu shots, fitness classes, hearing and vision clinics, and foot and dental care all assist older people to stay well. Federally supported health promotion and prevention programs also help older people to remain active and to enjoy healthy aging.

As well as being aware of the difference between health and health functioning, it is important to differentiate between acute and chronic health conditions. The former are usually temporary (e.g., the result of injuries from accidents and minor infections), while the latter (which include hearing and vision loss, heart disease, arthritis, and hypertension) tend to be more long term. Most of those who live within institutions such as nursing homes suffer from chronic health conditions.

According to the 1996 Canada census, heart disease and cancer account for over half the deaths of Canadian seniors: "In 1996, 30% of all deaths of people aged 65 and over were attributed to heart disease and 26% were from cancer. Of the remaining deaths of seniors, 11% were from respiratory diseases, 9% were from strokes, while 24% were attributed to all other diseases and conditions combined" (Lindsay 1999:58).

This same report notes that one in four Canadian seniors has a long-term disability or handicap: "In 1996–97, 25% of all people aged 65 and over living at home had such a condition, compared with 20% of people aged 55 to 64 and less than 10% of those between the ages of 25 and 45" (62).

In terms of hospitalization, older persons make up the largest share of those who temporarily reside in such facilities. In 1996–97 there were, according to Lindsay, "three times as many hospital separations for every 100,000 people aged 65 and over as there were among people aged 45 to 65" (65). Seniors also tend to stay in hospital for longer periods of time than do younger people: "in 1996–97 the average hospital stay of people 65 and over was 17 days, compared with 9 days per visit for those ages 45 to 64, 7 days among people aged 35 to 44, and 6 days or less among those in age groups under age 35" (ibid.).

DEMENTIA

Dementia is amongst the most distressing and demanding of illnesses encountered in later life, not only for the person suffering from it, but also for their important ones. The prevalence of dementia increases sharply in old age, and women are twice as likely to suffer from it as are men (Lindsay 1999:63). A small percentage of seniors were reported to be suffering from Alzheimer's disease in the 1996 Canada census. In 1995, according to Lindsay, "2% of all people aged 65 and over suffered from this condition; that year, an estimated 82,000 seniors had this disease" (ibid.).

Most seniors with Alzheimer's or other forms of dementia live in a health-related institution such as a nursing home, an Alzheimer unit in a hospital, or other assisted-care facilities. Lindsay further notes that, "in 1995, 78% of all those aged 65 and over with this condition were in an institution. That year, 35% of all seniors living in these institutions had Alzheimer's disease or other dementia" (ibid.).

By the year 2031, the number of people with dementia in Canada is expected to triple from 252,000 (in 1991) to close to 800,000 (Lilley and Campbell 1999:31). There are presently no known cures for Alzheimer's disease, and there are many suspected causes, ranging from genetic background, chromosomal makeup, the destruction of neurons in the brain, to the aging process itself (Snowdon 2001:129). What does seem clear, though, is that many older persons may be diagnosed with this form of dementia as more progressive techniques are developed for measuring this disease.

CAREGIVER NEEDS

While conducting research into the respite care needs of those living in Lunenburg County, Nova Scotia, Jeanette spoke with many who were caring for elderly relatives or friends who were suffering from Alzheimer's disease and other forms of dementia (Auger 2000b). It was clear then that caregivers do not have adequate supports to assist them in dealing with their patients. As Lynn, a fifty-three-year-old caregiver who was caring for her seventy-seven-year-old mother, stated:

> Looking after Mum is a total nightmare. I have two kids still at home who need a lot of attention. I have a full-time job I am trying to hold down. Most of the time Mum doesn't have a clue about who any of us are. She spends an awful lot of time just sitting there crying and there is no one else to help us out with all of this. There is an Alzheimer's wing in the local nursing home but they have a two-year waiting list. It's just a total nightmare and most of the time I am at my wit's end.

Anne, who was caring for her father-in-law (who has Alzheimer's), also noted the lack of support for caregivers: "I would like to see more emotional support for caregivers. I would like caregivers to have some help so that they can learn how to deal with their role, maybe even some workshops on stress management so we don't take out our stress on our care receivers."

The majority of informal caregivers of the elderly are women. There is, in our culture, a general expectation that such care is "women's work" and that women are somehow "better suited" to this type of activity. These attitudes have an impact on government policies such as homecare and long-term care programs, which aim to keep older people in their own homes as long as possible. The result is that the government saves on health care costs by refusing to recognize the vital contributions of the pool of care providers that makes this possible. In the spring of 1998 forty-six female caregivers from rural Nova Scotia came together in four regional workshops to share and learn from their respective stories about care giving. This work was part of the Caregivers' Research Project, which was funded by the Maritime Centre of Excellence in Women's Health and which was undertaken by researchers at the Centre on Aging at Mount Saint Vincent University.

Most of these women worked as caregivers twenty-four hours a day, seven days a week, caring mainly for elderly parents, spouses, or partners, as well as disabled children and others. They unanimously agreed that their lives as care providers reflected ten realities:

1. Caregiving is invisible. We would like to have our contribution recognized by our families, our communities, and the health care system.
2. Caregiving is relentless. We need time off to care for our families and ourselves and to keep in touch with friends and communities.
3. Caregivers also need care.
4. Caregivers need information—about specific medical conditions and about the services available for ourselves and for those who receive our care.
5. Caregivers need the support of other caregivers.
6. Caregiving is complex. We would feel more confident about the care we provide if we had access to training.
7. Caregivers play a central role in home care. We would like more say in the home care plan.
8. Caregivers would like a say in policy and planning for home care.
9. Caring at home can be expensive. We would like to be reimbursed for the direct costs of caregiving.
10. Caregivers are concerned about financial security. (Source: Newsletter of Community Health Promotion Network Atlantic and the Maritime Centre of Excellence in Women's Health, Dalhousie University, Halifax, May 5, 2000, 4)

The opinions shared by these caregivers echo those expressed by all who were interviewed by and/or participated in the focus groups facilitated by Jeanette (Auger 1993).

A special feature entitled "Caregivers in Crisis: Silent Victims in a Silent System" appeared in the August 1999 edition of *Fifty Plus*. It focused upon the realities of life for the thousands of older women and men who provide care to their elderly important ones, primarily at home. Recounting actual stories in the everyday lives of caregivers and "putting a face on home care" (9), CARP suggested that, with bed closures in hospitals, with long waiting lists for nursing home and other assisted-living facility beds, there is more need for at-home caregivers to be recognized, supported, and compensated for their work as health care providers. Without these people, "the shift in healthcare across Canada from institutional care to home care is not possible" (9).

CARP makes several recommendations with regard to how to address the complex problems of care for the caregiver. These include, but are not limited to:

1. *Compensation*: Recognize the role of the caregiver; people who have left employment to care for family members should receive tax credit adjustments for employment insurance and for the Canada Pension Plan. Governments should encourage companies to develop caregiver leave programs for employees engaged in short- or long-term periods of caregiving. Governments should develop direct payment policies to compensate family caregivers for work done or for the management of caregiving.

2. *Standards*: Federal and provincial governments should develop national standards for informal caregivers with regard to working conditions and hours, safety, and so on. Community-based agencies should provide clear, understandable information to informal caregivers and care recipients alike.

3. *Sustaining the Caregiver*: Governments at all levels should develop, fund, and widely publicize an information network for informal caregivers that can be easily accessed through a twenty-four-hour, toll-free number, by fax, Web site, and e-mail. (Adapted from "CARP's Recommendations for Supporting the Informal Caregiver," CARP News, August 1999, 9).

These recommendations were similar to those proposed by the National Advisory Council on Aging in its 1995 publication entitled "The NACA Position on Determining Priorities in Health Care: The Senior's Perspective" (Government of Canada, Ottawa, February 7–9, 1995). So-called "health reform" is about shifting responsibility for care of the sick and infirm elderly onto communities and families. As Lilley and Campbell (1999:32) note: "Increasingly, frail elders are being cared for at home. Many need a range of health care services, including nursing care, and physical and occupational therapy. Institutional short-term 'respite' beds are needed to relieve family caregivers and for short stays when care at home is not feasible."

Eve, an eighty-six-year-old from a small town in rural Nova Scotia who recently moved to an assisted-living apartment, cannot get over the fact that she has to pay for everything. When she was living in her own apartment, homecare was paid for, as was blood collection and foot care. Now that she has moved into assisting living accommodations, not only does she pay more rent, but she also has to pay for laundry, housekeeping, blood collection, foot care, and nursing services. As she says: "I should have stayed in my apartment. Homecare came in and did everything and it was covered. I am spending all my money that I worked so hard to save. Why can't I get medical insurance coverage under these circumstances? I don't understand it. I feel like I am being robbed!" Eve has federal medical coverage with Sun Life. However, when you are residing in assisted-living housing, the government will not pay for the same medical expenses it would cover when you are living on your own. Not only do you have to pay more rent, but you also have to pay more medical expenses than ever before. Clearly, this system is very unjust.

Another case we heard about concerns Ed, a retired clergyman from a small university town. His wife had Alzheimer's disease, and, finally, the family could no longer look after her at home. She was in long-term care for two and a half years before she died. The clergyman's money was totally used up. He is ninety-three and still in fairly good health, but when he can no longer look after himself he will be at the mercy of the system:

> I didn't really plan for this and maybe I couldn't have anyway. We always thought we could look after her but things got so bad that we finally had to put her into long-term care. Not only was that so hard for me, but also the fact that all my savings are gone makes it even worse. I have always been independent and now I will be dependent on a system that seems to go up and down. Nothing feels secure. I feel really sad and depressed at this time.

We heard similar versions of this type of experience many times; always these opinions were expressed with a sense of frustration, anger, and helplessness. In the future, as governments continue to see homecare as an alternative to the rising costs of institutionalized services, and as the population of persons aged sixty-five and over increases, the challenge to improve homecare services for the elderly and their important ones will expand, as will public and community pressure on governments to recognize and support informal caregivers.

MENTAL HEALTH AND AGING

Although the literature emphasizes the general physical health status of Canadian elders, there is increased recognition of the need to attend to mental health issues as well. Mental health is, according to Birren and Renner (1980:5), not just about the absence of mental illness, it is also about one's "ability or capacity to deal with the issues of life in an effective, if not pleasurable or satisfying manner."

As well as dementia, mental health refers to such phenomena as depression and loneliness as well as to such diseases as Parkinson's and other organic brain disorders. According to Novak and Campbell

(2001:103), the Canada Health Survey conducted in 1981 found that, compared with those aged fifteen to sixty-four,

> people 65 and over had more than two and a half times the rate of self-reported mental disorders (12.3% of 65 and over, compared with 4.5 percent of people from 15 to 64), and that older women reported mental disorders at almost twice the rate of older men (15.4% of women 65 and over compared with 8.5% of men).

Enjoying a fulfilling and rewarding life is key to avoiding depression in any age, as is being socially and physically active, living in a supportive community, and having access to friends, family, and neighbours. Wigdor and Fletcher (1991:18) have noted that health is an important predictor of depression amongst the elderly:

> Health problems, and resulting limitations and problems, seem to play a major role in triggering depression in the elderly. Illness, in addition to its purely physical consequences, can influence the emergence of depression by interfering with the sources of self-actualization and self esteem, since illness limits activities and social relationships and reduces the individual's feelings of control and independence.

In conversations with social workers and other support staff who care for older clients with depression (normally those residing in institutions), it has been noted that very few psychotherapists choose to work with older clients. As a nurse practitioner working in a Halifax nursing home explained to us:

> I have many patients who are depressed and suffering from loneliness. They just feel isolated and alone and don't seem to have much to live for. I have tried to suggest to the administrator that we hold some sort of counselling sessions for them, either one-on-one or in groups, but therapists just don't want to be bothered with them. It seems that they have some kind of idea that it isn't worth doing therapy with old people because they just die.

In Jeanette's Sociology 2343 course at Acadia (Community Development with the Rural Elderly), students are required to visit older persons who live in nearby nursing homes. Overwhelmingly, these students return to class with stories of the depression and loneliness experienced by those living in such homes.

At the local nursing home, there is one activity coordinator for over sixty patients, most of whom are mobility impaired. This situation is common throughout similar institutions in the Maritimes. Due to a lack of funds, staff, volunteers, and family awareness, along with the inability of some older persons to ask for what they need, there are insufficient opportunities for institutionalized elders to participate in activities that would provide them with an active and meaningful social life. This being the case, they are given little chance to effectively deal with their loneliness and depression.

Wigdor and Fletcher (1991:27) conclude their discussion of the mental health status of older Canadians with the following comments— comments with which we are in complete agreement: "A number of seniors have more difficulties than the average in coping with depression, loneliness and grief. It is for these seniors that it is important to improve our prevention and intervention strategies, especially in making the services more available."

There have been very noticeable cutbacks in the entertainment and stimulation made available for many people in long-term care and assisted-living accommodations. Several years ago Diane was a regular visitor at a long-term care facility in the Annapolis Valley. At that time people were taken out on excursions, had daily physical activities, and attended many entertaining events. While church services continue, very little else is planned, especially in the assisting-living apartments. This lack of stimulation and events to "look forward to" is detrimental to the mental health of many seniors. Dottie, who is in her eighties, explains her perspective as follows:

> I get so tired of everyone going to church. There is nothing else to do so we all go. Some people think we are being so "holy," but really it is something to do. The music is good sometimes and that is positive. We feel so isolated. We would love to see young people come and talk to us, do projects with us, or listen to our stories. All we do is sit and talk, some play cards and go to church—eat and sleep. There is nothing to look forward to. The people who have no family around find it very lonely. I don't have any family. I have a few friends but it is very depressing some days!

In speaking with staff in nursing homes and other special care homes over the years, the comments we generally hear concern shortage of funds for specially trained activity staff as well as the high ratio of staff to patients, especially in dementia wards and other wards dealing with mental health problems. This is another example of the institutional, internalized ageism so prevalent in health care systems across this country (and many others).

SUICIDE AMONGST THE ELDERLY

Suicide is often an unfortunate consequence of depression, loneliness, anxiety, and grief. Even though, overall, seniors are less likely than are young people to commit suicide, in 1996 there were "14 suicides for every 100,000 people aged 65 and over, compared with 18 per 100,000 population among those aged 25 to 44 and 17 for every 100,000 people aged 45 to 64" (Lindsay 1999:61). Among seniors, men are much more likely than are women to be successful in suicide attempts, although more women try to take their own lives. In 1996 "there were 26 suicides for every 100,000 men aged 65 and over, compared with less than 5 for every 100,000 women in this age range" (ibid.).

In Chapter 3 we talked about ageism and its negative impact on the lives of older persons. Nowhere is this reality more evident than in the statistics on suicide, which show that a lack of respect and socio-medical supports can cause some individuals to give up on life. Stressors inherent in the aging process, such as a lack of self-respect and dignity, the loss of a partner or spouse, fear and anxiety concerning what the future may hold, all affect an individual's desire to live or not to live.

Programs aimed at assisting older adults to remain healthy and active (e.g. adult day programs that provide opportunities to socialize with others and to participate in exercise and fitness programs at all levels of competence and mobility) will help the present generation of elders to continue to enjoy good health. And with improvements in access, affordability, and cultural sensitivity, they will provide long-term health benefits for those who will become older in the future.

SPEAKING OF DEATH AND DYING

In Jeanette's death and dying course and her aging course, when students are asked, "Who do you think worries the most about death and dying?" they invariably say that the elderly do. They also say that they think "older people worry more about death" than younger people and that the old are "closer to death" than those in any other age group.

When, in Chapter 3, we spoke about ageism, we did not discuss the notion that one of the reasons for this attitude and the subsequent behaviour that arises from it has to do with a fear of death. As a culture, not only do we fear, perhaps even dread, aging, but we also associate the old with death; this connection between death and aging is one of the reasons our culture does not celebrate and look forward to growing older. As we grow older we do indeed become frailer, our bodies do decline in both height and stature, and we may, as Featherstone and Wernick (1995) suggest, represent to many the image of the "grim reaper." They point out that, for many, the aging body represents "decay, decrepitude, and death" (12).

Over the years we have both had a great deal of experience working with and for persons who are dying, and most of these individuals have been over the age of sixty-five. Whereas it would not be true to say that older persons are more comfortable talking about dying than are younger ones, or that older people are more ready to die than are younger people, it seems to be the case that many older persons have given a great deal of thought to their passing years and to the inevitability of death.

Eloise, who was a seventy-seven-year-old woman dying of lung cancer, spoke with Jeanette in an interview in March 2001. Here are her thoughts about death: "No, I wouldn't say that I am afraid. I would rather it not be happening because there are so many things I wanted to do with my life, but you have to accept your fate don't you? I thought I would be older when I died, but with this dreadful cancer what can you do?" Eloise's partner, Bill, who was in his early eighties, was ill with heart troubles. He was pleased that they had sought the assistance of a local palliative care program because it meant that "help would be there when I couldn't manage her at home any more." Not all provinces and territories in Canada have palliative care or hospice programs, which are of great assistance to the dying and their important ones.

We both work in the field of hospice and palliative care, which offers alternative approaches to care for the dying and their important ones.[4] For the past nine years we have been attempting to create a freestanding hospice, the first in Atlantic Canada, in our community. Throughout this community development initiative we have spoken with many older persons about their wishes and concerns regarding death and dying. Overall, the people we work with and for are not overly concerned with death itself, which they recognize as an inevitable part of life, but, rather, with the dying process. In particular, they want to ensure that they not die in pain or in a "strange place" attended to by people they do not know (which is the case for most who die in a hospital setting in North America).

McPherson (1998:366) notes that older adults "now understand more about the process of dying, they continue to express concerns about experiencing pain, losing self control and becoming a burden to others and to society." He recognizes that:

> Regardless of whether an individual dies in an institution or at home, an increasing number of older people have expressed a wish to experience a "good death" or to avoid a "bad exit"—for themselves, and for their survivors, especially a spouse. They do not want to be neglected or abandoned; yet they do not want to be a burden to others. Consequently, some older adults are planning how to die (through advance directives) and are making decisions to hasten and facilitate the process of dying. (ibid.)

Fred R. MacKinnon, director of the Nova Scotia Seniors' Secretariat, wrote an article in the *Seniors Advocate* (March 1992, 14-15) entitled "Living Wills and Other Issues Associated with Dying." He noted that he had received many calls about living wills, death and dying, and the quality of life of chronically ill and disabled seniors. He suggested that there were three main issues to be discussed:

> First, how and why has this subject matter become so relevant and significant in this time? Second, what does the system now provide which may help us cope with these problems? Third, what are the issues we have to face in planning long term care of seniors and what should we seniors be doing about confronting these issues? (14)

MacKinnon went on to discuss the fact that many seniors are living to be numbered among the very old and that many of them are chronically ill. He noted that, even though we now have medical technology to prolong life, "is it enough to just be kept alive?" He suggests that seniors crave the right to be independent and to make their own health care decisions:

> The ability to be one's own person, to do one's own thing, is the most priceless possession in life. The flowering of creativity and genius grows in the rich soil of independence. Most of us—not all by any means—gain independence by our late teens, but then, all too soon, old age begins to reverse the old familiar family relationships. Now our children begin to worry about us and in do doing, show the same concern for our comings and goings as

> we did for them in the early years. Eventually if we live to be very old, we become more and more dependent on others and that is not a pleasant experience to anticipate. (14)

MacKinnon suggests that seniors need to become more verbal in terms of expressing their needs to be involved and informed on matters concerning end-of-life choices. He also insists that "seniors' organizations should be studying the issues and finding out where we are and if legislation or community action is required, pressing vigorously to these ends" (ibid.).

In 1997, Canadian Pensioners Concerned, a national organization for older persons and their supporters, conducted a series of workshops in each province of Canada asking seniors what they saw as end-of-life issues. This program was called My Plans For Me. Jeanette was a member of the advisory panel and participated in one of the groups, held in Halifax in September 1997. Overall, seniors wanted to know more about living wills, medical directives, euthanasia policies, and the availability of palliative care, hospice services, and ethical wills. The three main objectives of the national workshops were: (1) to educate each other concerning advance directives; (2) to share ideas on personal directives—what the individual considers important to quality of life if, for whatever reason, she/he is unable to speak for her/himself; and (3) to give an example of, and to discuss, how to facilitate a workshop or discussion group on advance directives with a senior (or others) on a one-to-one basis (taken from material sent to Jeanette in preparation for the initial workshop, which took place in September 1996).

An advance directive, which can also take the form of a living will, is a document that a mentally competent individual prepares, or has prepared, stating what her or his wishes are regarding end-of-life decisions, such as consenting to or refusing medical treatment, choosing someone to represent her/his wishes in the event that she/he is not capable of making such decisions (i.e., the naming of a proxy), and so on.

In an article entitled "Death directives can save dignity, dollars, study says" (*Globe and Mail*, March 15, 2000, A2), Krista Ross reports on a study undertaken by Willie Molloy, a professor in the School of Medicine at McMaster University in Hamilton. In this study, the residents of six Ontario nursing homes were asked to "define what they considered a reversible and irreversible condition, and then to detail the exact kind of life-saving measures and even feeding, they would desire in both cases" (ibid.). The study, which is entitled Let Me Decide and which is also the name of Molloy's (1989) publication, provides a detailed account of the steps individuals can take to make clear their end-of-life requirements. It found that the vast majority of elders "wanted little medical intervention." Clearly, according to this study, when older persons are fully informed, educated, and aware of the options available to them in terms of prolonging their lives at any cost, they focus on the "quality" of life rather than the "quantity."

Jeanette, as past president of the Gerontology Association of Nova Scotia, saw a great deal of interest amongst seniors with regard to ethical wills—documents, videos, films, or audio-taped recordings in which people record their last wishes. Ethical wills focus not on property or possessions but, rather, on philosophies of life and the non-material things that people felt gave their lives meaning. The final document or recording is made available to family members and friends upon the individual's death. Older persons see the ethical will as a way of passing on their values and beliefs to their grandchildren in a legitimate, if not strictly legal, manner. The writer of the ethical will has the opportunity to reflect upon and to articulate her/his values and experiences; it enables her/him to affirm the past and to be positive about the future.

Novak and Campbell (2001) have noted that death occurs more often in old age today than it did in the past, and it also occurs more often in an institution. These trends will increase as the population ages. Given this, it will be crucial that we have more options available to us in terms of the settings in which we wish to die as well as in terms of being informed about our choices when facing end-of-life decisions.

In June 2001, Diane, in her capacity as a palliative care volunteer, had the opportunity to be present at the death of Gwen, a resident in a home for special needs people located in the Annapolis Valley. A newly constructed palliative care suite had recently been added, and specialized palliative care nurses were on duty twenty-four hours a day. Diane spent five hours with Gwen during the last day of her life.

Gwen was eighty-six years old and was suffering from Alzheimer's disease as well as recently diagnosed cancer. Diane and Gwen were given privacy, with hourly checks by nurses to make sure all was well. Diane, family members, and staff worked together to make sure a pain management plan was in effect. This enabled Gwen to have the easy and peaceful death she had requested. Gwen had made a living will while she was still living in Ontario; in it, she clearly stated her wishes that no heroic measures be used to keep her alive. Diane was able to pray, sing, and be "in silence" with Gwen in her final hours. Gwen had been a resident at the home for special care for six months, so she just needed to move "down the hall" to the palliative suite. Diane reflected upon this particular experience as follows:

> I couldn't have wanted a better death myself. Everything went as we had hoped and prayed for. She was given enough medication to keep her pain level down so she could peacefully listen to my singing and my prayers. She woke up once and looked at me with a smile. "You are here," she said. She then nestled down in the covers and went back to sleep. She died early the next morning, pain free.

This death exemplifies the philosophy of care for the terminally ill held by those who work with and for the dying (and their important ones) within palliative care and hospice programs.

While writing this book Jeanette had a friend die of lung cancer in a palliative care unit in a hospital in British Columbia. Joanne was fifty-three years of age, she had enjoyed a full and vibrant life, and chose, after much discussion with her partner (who agreed that she could not be cared for adequately at home), to move into a palliative care unit. Jeanette spoke with Joanne on a regular twice-weekly basis. Even though Joanne often had trouble breathing, even with a ventilator, she said, "Being in this palliative care wing is the best decision I ever made. They make me so comfortable here, I can't imagine why anybody would want to be dying anywhere else."

This experience stands in contrast to one that Jeanette had in early March 2001. A friend, John, who was seventy-six years old, was also dying of lung cancer. Even though he strongly expressed his wish to die at home, it became increasingly clear that his wife, who had recently undergone a hip replacement operation, could not manage his care. Because there was no hospice in their community, John spent many pain-filled days at home waiting for nurses to attend to him. His physician was reluctant to prescribe adequate pain medication in case he "became addicted to the morphine"; consequently, John spent his final days in needless pain. He was moved into the local hospital the day before he died—something he had dreaded.

There is a great need for more hospice and palliative care programs across Canada, in rural as well as in urban communities. Fortunately, this issue is well supported by seniors who are actively pressing governments, at all levels, to provide more options for the dying and their important ones. We are delighted to be part of this struggle.

NOTES

1. Jeanette A. Auger and Paula Chegwidden, "Women, Work and Retirement," unpublished document (funded by a grant from the Acadia University Faculty Association, 1995).
2. Copies of Con Desplanque's letters, March 29, 2001.
3. Creative Retirement Manitoba, 202-283 Portage Avenue, Winnipeg, Manitoba. R3B 2B5. Newsletter and Course Schedule, Winter 2001.
4. For a more detailed discussion and explanation of hospice and palliative care, see Auger (2000a), especially Chapter 6.

Chapter Five

Where Do We Go from Here?

We said at the beginning of this book that gerontologists need to include the experiences and voices of older persons within their work. We also noted that when Jeanette conducted research for a doctoral dissertation in 1983 seniors expressed concern that gerontologists were not interested in listening to, or documenting, their versions of reality. Because so little has changed with respect to the integrated involvement of older persons into the gerontological enterprise, we thought it relevant to include bits of that research in *From the Inside Looking Out*. At that time older persons made the following sorts of comments regarding what they identified as the issues:

> You should build a bridge between what the gerontologists do, their research and publications, by writing something about all this in their own language. Gerontologists could send things in to the seniors' papers. They could share instead of store their information. (Interview with then president of the Old Age Pensioners Association, November 1982)

Recognizing that, as scientists, gerontologists face restrictions upon their work from their employers and their clients, the above informant was aware of some of the hidden agendas that face the academic researcher. He also pointed out that what separates gerontologists from other scientists is their own claim to help the aged:

> Well, they get themselves into this mess all the time. They say that they want to do work for the old, to help them have fuller lives and to live longer and better, that sort of thing. They also say that they would like to help them to establish projects and to really use them in a sort of consultant way. So, of course, we expect them to write about things which we can understand. Other scientists don't even bother to say that they'll help their research subjects. They can work in their labs for years, blissfully studying whatever they want. They need not be responsible to the public, just their colleagues, their universities, and their funders. Not so the poor, well-meaning gerontologists who try

to convince us that their work is meaningful and understandable but not in any way where most older people can understand what they are doing or what they say.

Claiming that the old have trouble in "understanding" much of gerontology because of its "jargon," this informant also suggested that the research is seemingly irrelevant to them, that they have "trouble recognizing themselves in a lot of the research topics which the gerontologists get involved in."

In an article in the *Elder Statesman*, Rollo Boas (1982:9), a former president of the Old Age Pensioners' Association of British Columbia, with reference to a forthcoming conference on aging, likened himself and older people to "little mice" hiding in "the corner of the conference" listening to "what they are saying about us." He offers some explanations as to why the old have trouble relating to topics deemed relevant by researchers:

> These topics of concern for discussion and answers might surprise many of you readers. I know of some seniors who consider them "sloppy thinking and irrelevant" .... Could it be that many of us try to "push away" the reality of these matters with the hope that they might not happen to us? Could it be that the material, everyday matters of life are so difficult to face that issues such as these would swamp us? Could it be that we have never before seen such a list as the above, being important enough to become the basis of a full-scale conference? Could it be that we have given in to the effects of such matters as being inevitable to growing older? (9)

Boas questions the input of seniors into gerontological work, stressing that the old have trouble in recognizing that gerontological concerns can also be their concerns.

> You know, we are a generation used to denials. We have been denied work, a decent place to live if we cannot afford high rents and housing upkeep. We have been denied self respect and self worth. How can we believe that we are worthy of such interest from the experts in our society? We do not fight when the governments take away our Denticare programs or our Renters Tax Credit. We do not protest when experts talk about us as if we do not exist, in a language that we usually do not understand.

Like some of his peers, Boas foresaw the potential of an appropriate gerontology, reiterating that we "must retain a vision of how a good life for the old, and all society could look, helping create, support, and emphasize this good life through non-jargonistic gerontological knowledge."

Social scientists and laypersons alike frequently invoke the issue of creating a "good life" for members of "society." For social scientists, such notions become problematic due to competing definitions of what constitutes "good" and who constitutes "society." Positing a reality from competing perspectives becomes an ethical issue, especially for those involved in fieldwork. As Whittaker (1981:437) has pointed out: "Despite the best intentions of anthropologists, it is often difficult for the people studied to see the result as beneficial for anyone but the researcher or the researcher's culture."

In his column in *Pioneer News,* the late Chuck Bayley (1981:12) reiterated the notion that much of gerontological research is jargonistic: "Most articles of the thousands being published are for professionals and academics. They are about us, but too many with jargon and intricate mathematics, for us to understand." Thus, a more appropriate gerontology would produce knowledge not only about the old, but also for the old. Boas did not play the old against gerontologists but, rather, suggested that the latter take more responsibility for "what they do" because "we older people are about as slow as the politicians, professionals, and bureaucrats in being with the times. We must watch them carefully and have them respond to our needs." This seniors advocate suggested that the old and young should form a conspiracy whereby they worked together to create social change. In this way, he echoes the opinions of the late Maggie Kuhn (1978b:78):

> Let's not pit ourselves against the young. We don't want to be adversaries. And you young people—together we will conspire. We need radical social change, a new agenda. Such an agenda would include age-integrated housing, an end to mandatory retirement. Together we can devise holistic health centers—to challenge and change, to point the way to large institutional change.

Kuhn suggests that young and old could work together to create a new kind of societal awareness of aging—an awareness that would not only incorporate the experiences and resources of the old, but that would also recognize them as "critics" of the type of social systems that now rule and govern our lives:

> We the elders, are also social critics .... Out of our own
> remembrances of the past can come some very solid social
> criticism of the present that leads us into the future and a new
> age .... We the elders have an opportunity to be forthright and
> radical in our social views! I think of old people as educators of
> the young, by our example and by our reaching out and sharing
> what we know. The experience and skills of old people should
> be valued and utilized. (5)

Although many older people agree with Maggie Kuhn's philosophy, and
many try to "share" what they know, their "experiences and skills" are
not always "valued" or "utilized." Chuck Bayley alluded to this experience:

> After I did a presentation to a three-day workshop at Simon
> Fraser University, at their wrap-up dinner, the president of the
> Canadian Association on Gerontology said to me, "perhaps the
> gerontologists and seniors might work together on common
> interests. Later, I dropped her a note and asked for suggestions
> as to how. She wrote back suggesting contact with B.C. ger-
> ontologists. They wrote back suggesting others .... Lip service
> is what we call it. (Personal communication, November 18,
> 1982)

Bayley not only tried to share his skills with gerontologists at the national
level, but also at the provincial level: "The president of the Gerontology
Association of B.C. said that she was thinking of 'Goals for the 80s' for
their next conference. I sent her ten alternatives. I have never had a word
back." When questioned about these ten alternatives, "the president of
the gerontology association replied that they were good ideas but that
they were not specific to the needs of professionals in the field."

As part of her doctoral research Jeanette organized a discussion
among researchers and practitioners regarding what would constitute an
appropriate gerontology. A participant suggested that the question be
broken into two parts, one of which would address theoretical concerns,
the other of which would address practical ones. Another subdivision
was also suggested: "Let's also break it up into what older people can do
and what gerontologists can do." The responses to these questions reflect
the prevalent ideology and membership categorization devices pertaining to "gerontologists" and "the old." Here is how the model for an
appropriate gerontology (AG) was described by the older persons who

participated in this focus group, which took place in Vancouver, British Columbia, in the spring of 1983.

THEORETICAL CONCERNS

First an AG would recognize the potential and power of older people as informants and providers of information on the aging process in terms of issues and topics that they deem to be relevant to their lives. This particular viewpoint was agreed upon by all and, as has already been shown, was invoked as an important issue by many older persons.

Second, an AG would recognize, document, and highlight the rural and urban differences in growing old. It would also recognize, through its research endeavours, the impact of the ethnic elderly on the Canadian "mosaic." George, a seventy-nine-year-old group member, was quick to point out the vast differences between the needs of older persons in rural as opposed to urban areas—differences agreed upon by many of the national delegates at the first meeting of the National Advisory Council on Aging: "It's all very well to do research on the city folks. You're very lucky in the urban areas. For us in the country, it is very difficult to supply services. You can never have your pick of facilities for meetings and such. We have to even get on a waiting list to use the fire hall." The ethnic-minority elderly are only recently beginning to emerge as viable research interests to gerontologists. In British Columbia this group of persons constitute 34 percent of the total population of those aged sixty-five and over (Census of Canada 1971).

Third, an AG would recognize and document the vast differences between growing old as male and growing old as female. One of the group members pointed out that it is important to recognize that we are speaking about:

> males and females from another era and that those rigid roles could change so that it would be a bit better for future older people. One of the reasons why 73 percent of women aged sixty and over live below the poverty line is because their husbands didn't take care to leave them adequately provided for, and they didn't know how to talk about this sort of thing. I know this won't happen to my daughter.

Fourth, when collecting data, an AG would recognize that what the elderly say and how they say it is a gift to be shared, a privilege that they grant to the researcher, not vice versa. This view was frequently expressed by seniors and was eloquently put by the then president of the

Old Age Pensioners' Association of British Columbia:

> There must be more personal contact and sincere dialogue between older persons and the researchers .... For the student in gerontology, this means acknowledging that their ability to look objectively at the lives of older people and collate what they observe is only a small half of that which must come from the older people themselves .... To do this the student needs to learn to take the position of one who is receiving a precious gift.

Fifth, an AG would question basic assumptions regarding why things work as they do rather than merely accepting them as givens. In this regard, topics like retirement, age stereotyping and discrimination, and types of services available to the old would be treated as social constructions to be explained rather than as "facts" to be accepted. When older people speak about retirement, they often talk about how loss of work has affected their lives. Perhaps, as gerontologists, we could ask questions like "What work does work do in our society?" This would enable researchers to look at social processes and life as ongoing accomplishments rather than as fixed phenomena. Asking questions in different ways would be a way of discovering new tools for looking at the lives of the old, and it would help us to use the most appropriate methods for obtaining information.

PRACTICAL CONCERNS

First, an AG would utilize older people as a resource with regard to constructing research topics and data. This "utilization" would take the form of seeking the help of the elderly in making gerontological research more "visible" and relevant to the needs of the old.

Second, an AG would work with the old and offer whatever assistance necessary to train them to be advocates in areas that affect their lives. In this way, the gerontologist–researcher would take an "action" stand similar to the one already taken by many anthropologists and sociologists.

Third, AG practitioners would take research-funding applications to the old and ask for their input. If this were done, then the research undertaken by gerontologists would have more meaning to older persons and the communities in which they live. As one group member said:

> A lot of money from grants and that go to people because they

show that the findings will benefit the community. Some of the things done in the West End [of Vancouver] certainly don't benefit the seniors. But they don't come to us. They go to the community centre director and he doesn't know much about seniors or about research. They could come to us and we on the seniors committee would love to give them feedback.

This process would ensure an interactive relationship between the researcher and the elderly with regard to research topic, methods, and application of research findings.

Fourth, an AG would encourage the old to liaise with health care services and transportation, housing, and social service planners in order to make clear their perspective on these potentially life-enhancing programs. In 1983 Vancouver, there was a trend towards involving older persons in these very service-oriented decision-making processes. Such involvement could continue and increase.

Fifth, an AG would support seniors organizations and services by working closely with them and by acknowledging their work at conferences, meetings, and other places where gerontologists gather to discuss the old. This strategy was invoked in recognition of the fact that grassroots groups of seniors work on behalf of their members and provide gerontologists with a great deal of information about the old.

POSSIBLE CONTRIBUTIONS OF THE AGED

First, the aged could be critical of the work of gerontologists and let us know when we don't understand what they're saying. As one person involved in the 1983 discussions said, it would be "better" to criticize gerontological research than to "bitch" about it. Another said that the old "should organize, not agonize" over how gerontologists construct the "reality" of old age.

Second, the aged have learned much in their lives and could be very useful to those who are trying to learn. For example, according to one senior:

> We must find some way of incorporating our skills into society. I used to be a teacher and I have offered to teach for free to four schools. Each time I was rejected. I have a friend who is a retired psychologist, he has offered to counsel people for free. Each time he has been rejected. We need to recognize the worth of seniors in our society. We need to mobilize them and activate them. We also need to be supportive of each other.

Another suggested that older people are not supportive of one another, perhaps due to what is referred to as "tenderness of thoughts" (i.e., not wanting to speak out in case one is seen as complaining and, hence, rendered vulnerable to being emotionally threatened):

> I do understand your difficulty in getting older persons to "level" with you. It is my conviction that they seldom level with their peers. There is but little meaningful dialogue amongst seniors. I do not know why this is so. It could be the "tenderness of thoughts" .... We older people sit in a secure place in life ... that is, within ourselves. We have years of living behind us .... When we are approached by younger persons, especially those zeroing in into our age level, we measure their sincerity and their teachability by their willingness to listen or to receive and then give .... Is this too much to ask of searchers and researchers? I think not.

Other seniors, reiterating the notion that an AG should recognize that they can offer a great deal to society and still enjoy their lives, said, in response to questions posed to *Vancouver Sun* readers in June 1982:

1. Seniors should help themselves as much as possible. I'm 81, dance three times a week, keep in shape and enjoy myself.
2. Older people can only speak for themselves.
3. Seniors do best, doing for themselves. When aid is needed, it should be provided. I am 79 and do everything for myself and enjoy life.
4. Older people should be expected to do as much as they can. The essential thing is they are made aware of what they can do. Opportunity, and knowledge of opportunity, places the onus where it belongs.

All these persons share the idea that they can continue to contribute to society and that gerontologists should recognize this.

Third, the aged, even if they do not wish to join them, could support their age-mates in their efforts to improve their lives. Many older people resist age-typing on the basis of expectations. They also tend to reject what they see as "stereotypical" behaviours: "I don't really think that we support one another nearly enough. We are scared of running around in old tennis shoes, and pattering with our friends. But if that's what some old people want to do, why not support them in it? It's their life, after all." In other words, older people could be more tolerant and supportive of others' rights to act as they choose.

Fourth, the aged could take credit for what they know and for what they can do as well as being able to ask for help when they need it. As one of the group mentioned, many older people are "afraid to ask for help because of being seen as a 'burden' especially to friends and family." However, as another said:

> I don't think that we should think of services as hand-outs, we helped pay for them and if we need them, we are entitled to receive them. We are used to thinking only that we might be burdens, but we also can contribute if they would let us. We must make older people realize that they can do both of these things if and when they have to.

As this informant says, the old are "entitled" to any social service benefits that they need, and an AG would try to help them recognize this fact.

POSSIBLE CONTRIBUTIONS OF GERONTOLOGISTS

Gerontologists could (1) recognize that they will be "old one day too" and think about how they would respond to some younger people prying into their lives; (2) learn to speak and write about their research in ways that are easy to understand; (3) be less paternalistic and condescending to the old; (4) leave their ivory towers once in a while and come and enjoy life amongst the old instead of only coming to see them for research purposes; (5) look as if they care about the old and listen to them rather than just writing down what they say; and (6) send those they study copies of their findings. The president of the Old Age Pensioners' Association of British Columbia echoed some of the aforementioned points:

> There are two things which must be reconsidered about all interviews with older people. One: Seldom is there the courtesy on the part of the researcher to make a return visit, or a letter sharing the "findings" of such an effort. At this point the older person becomes a used thing! Two: The written record of such interviews is usually in words and terms familiar only to the scientific world. To the older person that is like writing in a foreign language. This is almost another way of saying "the reactions and understanding of the older person is of no conse-quence." All that matters is the world of social science that can give acknowledgment and even praise.

This informant reminds those who conduct interviews that they must be faithful to the information entrusted to them and that they must share their findings and written work with the old so that they do not feel like "used persons."

It is important to recognize the coping behaviours of the old. Maggie Kuhn (1978a:3) clearly makes this point: "Older persons have demonstrated their ability to cope. They have dealt with the setbacks and tragedies of life, interacting with others in the process." An appropriate gerontology would recognize the coping behaviours of the old, would reinforce and support these behaviours, and would not see all older persons as victims.

These ideas came together to form potential terms of reference for an appropriate gerontology after one four-hour session that was conducted on June 12, 1983. In some ways, what was said reproduces the world of gerontology as it now exists. However, the members of the group that put these notions forward have been thinking about and reflecting upon how to improve gerontology for many years. They want to draw up potential plans for action—plans that would make gerontology a more reflexive, meaningful discipline, more useful to the old as well as to others.

On November 3, 1978, Monique Begin (1978), then minister of health and welfare, made the following comments to the Canadian Association on Gerontology in Edmonton: "I appeal to all Canadians and especially people working in the field of gerontology to work together in order to solve the challenge we are facing so that Canada will be a better place to live, not only for the old, but for all Canadians." In January 2001, Jeanette revisited some of her earlier informants to see whether, some eighteen years later, anything had changed. Overall, their reactions were that "nothing much had changed." As one seniors advocate, now in his late eighties, suggested:

> Well it seemed at the time that our message was getting across, over the years though I see more and more money going into research and less into services which help the old. I had these great plans and dreams that we would get through to the researchers and they would come to us for input. It never happened and it isn't likely to now.

When we asked our Nova Scotia focus groups and our interviewees how they thought that the old and gerontologists could work together they provided a range of responses, some of which we have already discussed. It is not only older persons who are committed to restructuring the ways in which old age is produced, it is also some of those who work with and for them. For example, Bryan S. Green (1993) argues that gerontology reifies the old and the problems associated with them. He believes that this discipline should "echo the struggle ... of critical and humanistic practitioners to rescue individual elderly people from the objectifying, scientizing, bureaucratizing hold of 'the elderly' .... It is in this context that questions of discourse such as what is Gerontology? need to be asked" (202). His argument is similar to Maggie Kuhn's, which points out that, by reifying the concept of "the old," gerontology creates an "us" and "them" scenario that tends to further alienate older persons from mainstream culture and activities.

Kathleen Woodward (1991:193), notes that "gerontophobia," or fear of the old, hinders our ability to see aging people other than as stereotypically frail, weak, sick, and close to death: "Certainly the profound gerontophobia in our culture should be extirpated, and one of the ways to begin this process is to examine critically our representation of aging and to work to produce new ones." If, as we have argued consistently throughout this book, gerontologists are in the business of creating science and knowledge about the elderly and old age, then it is within their purview to ensure that the images that they create, maintain, and present to the lay and academic communities fully represent the entire spectrum of how people age.

Featherstone and Hepworth (1995:31) claim that social gerontologists can insist upon a "radical deconstruction and displacement of negative images of aging and the elaboration of an alternative positive imagery." They argue further that gerontologists, as cultural producers of knowledge and values about aging, could accomplish this goal by "establish[ing] a new discourse of later life through the deconstruction of the long held associations between old age and illness, disability, disengagement and decline" (31).

As part of a panel on the practical applications of gerontology to the community, which was held in one of Jeanette's sociology of aging courses in the fall of 2000, an eighty-four-year-old seniors advocate named Bill suggested the following: "Well, you young people who study us, could come to us more often and ask what we think are important issues, rather than deciding ahead of time what those issues might be and then just getting our feedback on them. Why do you always come to us only after *you* have decided what *we* need?" (emphasis in original). In the same session, Violet, a locally well known "mover and shaker," made the following comments regarding how older persons and gerontologists could work together:

> Well, you could start out to recognizing that we have a lot to offer. We are not sitting around on our duffs waiting for gerontologists to do something for us. We are out there trying to make things happen while you sit at your cozy computers and learn about us. Any changes, which are made by governments and lawmakers, are done for you to benefit from too. This isn't just about what we can get out of it as seniors, but any work we do together benefits you and your grandchildren too.

Violet, and others on this panel of six elders, were very outspoken in their belief that, if long-lasting beneficial changes are going to be made for both the present and future generations of older people, then the elderly need to work closely with gerontologists and others who study the old.

Lucy is an eighty-two-year-old AIDS/HIV activist whose husband died of AIDS after he had been accidentally injected with tainted blood products. She is very outspoken on many issues that affect the lives of older people, and, when asked what gerontologist could do to work together, she responded as follows:

> First you could stop treating us as though we were children, we aren't deaf, but some of us are hard of hearing. We aren't stupid, we've been around. Second, you could ask us what we need, instead of telling us, and anybody else who'll listen, what you think we need. How the hell do you know, are you us, are you even old? Third, we appreciate what you try to do for us, but don't do it without involving us, I don't need you to speak for me, and I need you to do the research, find the information and then give it to me so that I can speak for myself. I need you to be my advocate, not my voice.

The general consensus among the seniors with whom we have spoken is that gerontologists should use their academic and policy expertise to conduct research and to discover information about growing older; they should then pass this information along to older people to use as they see fit.

CHALLENGES OF AN AGING POPULATION

During our recent research it has become evident that we, as a society, are facing a huge challenge as we move into the twenty-first century. Ken Dychtwald (1999) maintains that the challenges will be many as the aging population grows. He notes that the United Nations experts predict that, by the year 2050, there will be approximately two billion people in the world who will be aged sixty years and older. This number matches the combined population of the North Americas, Europe, and India. According to the current United Nations Population Division, one in ten persons living is aged sixty or over. In 1999, Dychtwald pointed out that "those eighty and over constitute 11% of the world's 60+ population and that by 2050, 16% of the older population will be more than 80 years old" (4).

Are we ready to face the challenges that these increases in the aging population will produce? How will it be possible to help this population age successfully? Who should assist the current elderly in their quest for successful aging? What form should that assistance take? These are questions that we believe to be both timely and important.

Lassey and Lassey (2001) examine the quality of life for the elderly internationally. They suggest that the priorities ought to be:

> Freedom and choice should be optimized—older individuals ought to have substantial control over their lifestyle in later life.

> Older individuals should receive ongoing informal support in the context of family and community, whenever possible.

> Every older person should have ready access to health care, mental health care and long-term health care at modest personal cost.

> Older individuals and couples should have good housing that fits their needs—in a pleasant community setting with required services close at hand.

> Disabled older individuals unable to manage in a private home should have access to residence in supportive homelike environments as close to family and friends as possible.

> Basic income supports should be universally available and adequate to meet primary needs and insure a good quality of life.

> Lifestyle choices should allow older individuals to continue working if they wish, remain active in community and society, enjoy retirement and leisure, and achieve their potential for a high-quality later life. (450)

Difficulties arise when attempting to prioritize various needs with a limited amount of funding. Lassey and Lassey warn that committing too many resources to the needs of the elderly might be detrimental to other members of society. The challenge then becomes how to balance everyone's needs. These authors ask the following basic questions:

> How much should society tax itself to publicly subsidize programs for older people?
>
> Is there a danger that the growing commitment of federal resources to programs for the aged will crowd out other fundamental needs, such as education for young people, managing natural resources, research, and other public priorities?
>
> Should means testing be used to give greater benefits to older people with lower incomes and greater need, while requiring those with resources to pay more of their own way?
>
> Should the age of eligibility for income support and other benefits be raised as the health and functioning of the older population improves? (451)

These are crucial questions, and Lassey and Lassey present them in the hope of stimulating dialogue and thought rather than in the hope of obtaining quick and easy answers. While individual choice and social support were high on the priority list of the vast majority of the members of our focus groups/questionnaire respondents, health care, long-term care, income, and education seemed to be the most pressing concerns.

MAINTAINING GOOD HEALTH

Lassey and Lassey (2001:453) argue that private enterprise has a role to play in preventing disease, maintaining good health, and caring for individuals who do become ill. People need to be encouraged to maintain good nutrition, exercise habits, and social activities. One of society's goals should be to cut down on the numbers of chronically ill, and being educated about good health practices would enable people to live healthier lives than is now the case. Lassey and Lassey suggest that health care education should be available to all but that its funding should be both private and public. The debate concerning who should finance health care is going on in many countries besides Canada. While the prevailing pattern is for governments to play a large role in the funding of services, as the population ages and its needs become greater, it may be necessary to look at other possibilities. However, what should happen with regard to the care of the lower-income person is clear. It is obvious that private enterprise is not remotely interested in those who cannot pay; therefore, it is essential that the government ensure guaranteed health care for all.

Mental health care is also a priority. According to Lassey and Lassey, the most common disorders—depression and dementia—are only partially related to heredity (454). The afflicted individual and her/his family members may not have the expertise to deal with these difficulties. Well trained mental health professionals can be very helpful with regard to early diagnoses, counselling, and (where advisable) the dispensing of prescription drugs. Costs can be high, but the government must ensure that these services are universally available. We have noted that community services are preferable to institutional services, and, indeed, community mental health clinics would help people by, among other things, encouraging them to stay in familiar surroundings. We know that many physical health problems have a mental origin and can be aggravated when the latter is not taken into account. A greater investment in diagnosis and treatment of mental disorders could lower the costs of physical care (Lassey and Lassey 2000:455).

Many of the focus group participants emphasized the importance of the state of their health. Their worst fear was having to go into long-term care. Cost and loss of independence were the two major fears surrounding having to enter an institution. How can we humanize nursing homes and long-term care institutions? We have seen that there are many lonely, depressed, and grieving people within the walls of these facilities. We must find the funding to encourage psychologists, social workers, and recreation program directors to concentrate on older persons and their mental well-being. As we have noted earlier, we are never too old to learn new things, and social contact and mental stimulation can greatly improve one's attitude towards life, even in a long-term care facility. Providing sufficient staff, so that residents can "do for themselves" as much as possible, is one way of encouraging independence. When staff members do not have to "hurry" residents, then they can do many things for themselves (e.g., dressing, dusting, picking up, etc.). It just takes them longer than it used to. Providing a variety of activities that are relevant to the residents' experiences and diverse interests would be a good way to keep people busy and interacting with others.

In our research we have also noted that we need to provide opportunities for older persons to practise their sexuality and to experience intimacy in whatever form they so choose. In one private retirement home it was quite common to see an elderly silver-haired man arrive and quickly disappear into his woman friend's private quarters. While this activity provided the other residents with a chuckle and much to talk about, it also gave the couple the ability to be alone together and to share intimate moments. No doubt some of the other residents were envious. In long-term care facilities such opportunities for intimacy are few and far between. It seems to us that there should be "visiting quarters" that people could book in advance and so have some quality time together. Each facility and each resident will have different circumstances, needs, and abilities. However, it is important to provide some form of opportunity for people to be intimate with one another.

Many institutions have organized "pet therapy" sessions as a means of enabling residents to have their own, or visiting, pets provide them with comfort and love. As well, some nursing homes encourage young people to assist as volunteers in a variety of activities. As has been mentioned, every year, in two of Jeanette's classes, students are required to volunteer, for credit, in a local nursing home. Generally, at the beginning of term students are anxious and concerned about visiting with older people; at the end of term, friendships have been forged, a greater awareness of nursing-home life and the needs of older people within these facilities has been gained, and students usually feel that their nursing-home experience ranks amongst the best they have had in their academic careers. Working together is not a mysterious or complex process; learning from each other is natural, it merely takes some organization and development.

As was stated in Chapter 4, rules, regulations, and fixed pensions can be detrimental to older persons receiving the care they need without going bankrupt. The members of our focus groups expressed the desire to pay their own way (within reason) and to stay in their own homes for as long as possible. Improved homecare and community-based services are clearly advisable. Here again both for-profit and non-profit enterprises should play a role in providing this service, with governments helping through sponsoring public insurance programs or offering direct payment. The idea of decentralizing the management of such health care programs has been gaining support even in Canada. It would, of course, be necessary to have a regulatory system that would ensure high-quality service. As the need for more long-term facilities grows, the financial burden will increase, and older people will not have the resources to meet it. Smaller families, fixed pensions, and the like will increase the pressure on governments to provide funds for care.

According to Lassey and Lassey (2001) some form of public insurance program—such as those in Germany, Sweden, and the Netherlands—might be the best option. Payroll taxes would be used to raise the needed revenue, and all individuals with insufficient resources would be eligible to receive a subsidy. When possible, room and food costs would be paid from pension income (456).

Some countries guarantee an adequate basic income to all, regardless of their employment status. This is advantageous to many older women who have not worked for high wages and who do not have an adequate pension. Countries like the United States, Japan, and the United Kingdom still have a way to go here. While in Canada the situation is somewhat better, the funds available are not adequate now and certainly will not be adequate in the future. As Lassey and Lassey indicate, the government will have to play a role in establishing an adequate minimum income for all. They go on to point out that the World Bank has recommended

> that the pay-as-you-go social security systems be replaced in part by mandatory and privately managed savings arrangements. At retirement the money accumulated would go to each retiree based on their contribution. This approach is quite similar to many private pension schemes already in existence, such as the Teachers Retirement and Annuity Association and College Retirement Equities Fund for educators, the largest single private retirement fund in the world. The United Kingdom, The Netherlands, and Sweden have adopted variations of this approach, and similar options are under consideration in the United States. (458-59)

Nicole Owen (2001:8), a long-term care specialist, lends her support to the concept of long-term care insurance: "Long term care insurance is one way of ensuring access to adequate care in the face of debilitating illness. This insurance provides funds to cover a range of nursing and social services in the home, community or long term care facility for people who need ongoing assistance." She goes on to explain that, "when we are in good health, we often take for granted some of the simplest things that make or break our quality of life—being able to bathe, dress or eat for example. Yet when faced with a serious illness, these are the things that help us maintain our dignity" (ibid.). As our research has shown, and as Owen suggests, when adequate finances are not available for these services the burden often falls onto families. While we know that insurance cannot replace good health, it can help to provide peace of mind and to ease the financial strain on maintaining quality of life.

Valerie White (2000), director of the Nova Scotia Seniors' Secretariat, reiterates the point that there are direct linkages between well-being and having adequate income to obtain the necessary help to remain independent for as long as possible. White goes on to say that it is most important for policy makers and the health care system to note the estimated dependence-free life expectancy of seniors aged eighty-five and over. This age group, as our research has shown, is the largest growing segment of our population. Many of these people will suffer poor health, and it is imperative that we help them maintain their autonomy (which, aside from being ethical, is also the most effective way of dealing with the dual challenges of an aging population and funding constraints on health services). White goes on to suggest that "the healthy habits practiced over a lifetime will contribute to well-being, independence and longevity" (5).

It is imperative that governments attempt to increase the cost-effectiveness of all programs. While the trend has been to add co-payments, user fees, and so on, this could become a burden on those in middle- and lower-income brackets. Lassey and Lassey (2001:458) suggest two solutions:

1. Increasing basic pension incomes sufficiently to cover the co-payment, deductible and direct costs of health care, or
2. subsidizing these costs as part of the health and long-term care insurance package.

It appears that the funding of long-term health care is a major issue for future generations not only in Canada, but also in the world.

Another funding issue concerns the lack of medical coverage for alternative medicine. Many Canadians are turning to alternative medicine as they search for good health and longer life. Many people have found such alternatives as massage therapy, homeopathy, natural medicine, and acupuncture to be very helpful. With regard to mental health issues, therapies such as psychosynthesis are helping people to maintain a healthy sense of self and well-being. Government and private insurance plans do not cover many of these therapies, and this is a major problem in our system. Many in the caring fields agree that traditional and alternative methods of caring for people need to be combined. Holistic treatment is the method of the future, and it is imperative that funding be made available to proven alternative forms of healing.

Maintaining a satisfying lifestyle is a priority for most people, regardless of age. People value family and friendships, and they want regular interaction with their important ones. Without these close relationships one's quality of life can diminish. A satisfying community setting is very important to one's quality of life. Ready access to familiar services is crucial for daily needs as well as for crisis situations. Recreation and entertainment are also crucial. With cuts in federal and provincial funding, we have seen the decay of recreation and entertainment in our long-term care and assisted-living facilities. It is now up to the residents to provide their own entertainment. Although some residents are capable of doing this, in many cases it is essential that staff members take the initiative.

Lassey and Lassey (2001:459-62) offer a list of what they believe to be the major issues that must be addressed if we are to improve the quality of later life:

1. Increasing the Efficiency and Quality of Care Systems
2. Geriatric Assessment and Care Management
3. Overcoming the Disadvantages of Older Women
4. Improving Care and Treatment of Dementia
5. Case or Care Management
6. Use of Means-Testing
7. Optimizing Independence
8. Limited "Unnecessary Care"
9. Limiting Transfers to Hospitals
10. Wider Use of Hospice
11. Insurance Reforms
12. Assurance of Intergenerational Equity.

In discussing the whole issue of well-being and successful aging, it is important to find ways to use the wisdom and expertise of the newly retired person. Many retired persons have assisted in literacy training, mentorship, and health care volunteering.

An article by Fried et al., published in Doyle (1997), caught our attention. They contend that our social vision of aging is twofold: "either we fear a decrepitude, dependency and relegation to a rocking chair or at the other extreme, idealized images of limitless recreational time in a retirement community, often segregated from other age groups" (143). We have talked a great deal about "growth" in our older years, both in our focus groups and in our literature review. Fried et al. remind us of the final stage of Erikson's (1982) stages of development—integration and generativity. They contend that it may be that successful aging is related to the opportunity to accomplish the adult development tasks of late life: integration and generativity. Defining and ensuring one's legacy is a core part of this task. According to Erikson, this is essential to psychological well-being in late life and, thus, to successful aging. It also appears that meeting these developmental needs in some circumstances may also confer health and functional benefits. (144)

As we reflect upon our lives we find that we often still wish to give back to the community/society in which we live. Fried et al. suggest that, within the context of education, a large number of retired persons could make a vast imprint on the lives of younger people. We know that funding for education, and many extracurricular activities, is being cut back. What would happen if seniors could share their expertise in the country's schoolrooms? Here is a chance to be productive and to make an investment in the country's youth. We know that older persons have expressed the need to keep busy, to live active lives, and to contribute to society. They have also expressed the need to reflect upon and to integrate their lives as they enter the last phase.

Fried et al. suggest that older adults could be investing in the development of a well educated workforce—one essential to the stability of such entitlement programs as Social Security (the Canadian equivalent is the Canada Pension Plan) and Medicare. If a large number of older people were to serve in the schools, then this would result in the establishment of a new image of older persons, their opportunities, and their roles. If such programs were developed based on the needs of the children in each school and were matched with the expertise of available older persons, then this could result in a broader educational base at no greater cost. This type of a program, if it were to be encouraged at the national level, could revolutionize the education system and create a new vision of aging. Fried et al. go on to explain that this type of mentorship and nurturing would not displace paid workers but, rather, would enhance their efforts and create "a new synergistic, intergenerational social contract of the future" (145). Further: "This contract is one in which the older generation are looked to, after retirement, to leave their legacy through strengthening the abilities of the young generation. Such cultural generativity is developmentally appropriate for those who have completed their own child-rearing responsibilities" (145).

In discussing successful aging, we have noted the need to express and practise various forms of spirituality. As McFadden (1996:171) suggests, given the "importance of religion for many older adults and the ways spirituality motivates people to seek meaning, it is now reasonable to suggest that religion and spirituality variables be included in future studies of aging." She goes on to say that,

> although aspects of religiosity will continue to appear as independent variables in research on differential outcomes in older people's lives, research should also attend to religious and spiritual orientations and experiences as dependent variables, particularly in studies of influences on development. In addition, there is a continuing need for well-designed qualitative studies of religion, spirituality and aging. These approaches can reveal the stories behind the numbers in quantitative research. (171)

According to McFadden, any future research needs to look at both organized and non-organized religious behaviours (172). Our investigations support this. As we discussed in Chapter 4, residents in long-term care and assisted living facilities who wish to attend organized services but cannot do so feel alienated. Their needs are not being met. Therefore it would be appropriate for any future gerontological studies to look at the religious/spiritual practices of older persons and their connection to successful aging.

Both those in the focus groups and those who responded to the questionnaires had suggestions regarding what constitutes successful aging. Chris, who is from a small town and is a busy, outgoing older woman in her eighties, described her perception of successful aging:

> I think we have to keep busy and active. I am not overly concerned that I am not going to live forever. I do not expect others to make a life for me—I believe in doing things for yourself, if possible. Older people need to become less apathetic, band together and help themselves. Perhaps joining CARP would be helpful. They need to work together at a local level and find ways to be heard. I am involved in the Retired Teachers Association (meetings with speakers on relevant topics, dinners, trips), Stellarite Seniors Club (presently secretary and working towards getting ramp access to the club room), Ladies Hospital Auxiliary, Sharon St. John Hand Quilters, YMCA/YWCA, Blood Services, United Church and sometimes as a volunteer at the Museum.

When asked who should be involved in finding solutions, this is what she had to say:

> There should be a team effort by the young and the old. In this
> area, there seems to be a problem in getting the younger retirees
> actively interested in this subject. Everyone seems so busy with
> personal interests. We need more people involved in decision
> making. Many older persons have "run out of steam." Many do
> not drive a car and those that do often cannot drive at night or
> during the winter. Past participation in such endeavours has not
> had positive results. Some feel that the "government should do
> it all!" Physical infirmities have limited their mobility. Many feel
> their opinions are not considered valid by young people, and,
> on the other hand, many have not kept up with the times and
> changing conditions. Some are apathetic: it is too easy to just
> "go with the flow."

She continued: "Older persons must be willing to respond to a request
for information. I would be interested to know just how many responses
you had to your request in the *Senior Citizens' Secretariat Newsletter*!"

The above participant mentioned the Canadian Association for
Retired Persons, and we came across an article in a special report entitled
"CARP's National Forum on the Environment," dated February 2001.

> CARP's environmental forum, the first of its kind to represent
> the views and highlight the perspective of 50-plus Canadians,
> sought to demonstrate the meaningful role this generation can
> play in improving the environment. Keynote speaker, scientist
> David Suzuki, suggested "seniors can act as environmental
> record keepers, teaching young generations how the lakes, the
> land and the air used to be before the blight of pollution set in."
> (Muggeridge 2001:8)

Thomas Benjamin of Environmental Alliance for Senior Involvement
(EASI), a coalition of environmental, aging, and volunteer organizations
hoping to promote opportunities for older adults to play an active role in
protecting and improving the environment, said: "The majority of retirees
are healthy, active and are often open to doing something meaningful
with their time" (Benjamin, cited in Muggeridge 2001). He also noted
that "they have skills, experience and knowledge to share, making them
perfect 'stewards of the environment.'" Since many of the activities these
volunteers do take place in their own communities, they can actually see
the results of their own endeavours.

Ruth Grier, former Ontario Health and Environment minister,

spoke about the influential political role seniors can play. She believed that organizing seniors to become involved in the environmental issue could "reenergize public debate": "If older Canadians clearly demonstrate the link between the ailing environment and poor health, governments of all levels will be alerted to the need for action" (8). Kelly McGee, an aspiring marine ecologist, stated: "Young people need mentors, not critics and by working with you, 50-plus Canadians can use their voices, expertise and background to inspire us to action" (ibid.).

AGE POWER: REFLECTIONS ON THE THIRD AGE

Ken Dychtwald (1999) claims that, as the population of persons aged sixty-five and over increases, and as birth rates decrease, the world will soon experience what he calls "age power"—a time when the old will have increased influence in politics, finances, and socio-cultural values in general. He further suggests that the world is about to experience an "age wave" that will cause a rapid shift of awareness and understanding with regard to the contributions and value of the older generation.

> Rebounding from a temporary period of poverty, powerlessness, and social isolation, today's elders have grown in numbers, have become powerful and influential, and have managed to become more financially secure than any group in our nation's history. They are extraordinarily well connected, vote in higher concentrations than any age group, and have AARP (American Association of Retired Persons)—the country's largest special interest group—to lobby for their interests. America is becoming a gerontocracy. (29)

For Canadian seniors, CARP would provide this important and necessary advocacy.

Betsy, an eighty-three-year-old from a small university town, also alluded to the power of the old:

> Well, we need to get it together. I have been active in social change movements all my life, especially working for peace. If we put our minds together we could show other age groups a thing or two. We have accomplished so much in our lifetime that younger people have no idea about. It's time we told them that what they have now is because we helped them get it.

Betsy is aware of the contributions that older persons have made to the quality of life that all of us currently enjoy, and she is committed to continuing her work for social change. Dot, a respondent from a small Gulf Island in British Columbia, is also aware of the need for older people to feel that they can make a difference:

> It is important that people feel that they can make a difference—that what they *do* makes a difference. Too many people, elders especially, most often women, have never thought about that. So—a question: In what area of your life do you feel that your decisions/actions have made a difference in your family and community? How can you apply that knowledge to your present situation? These are questions we all need to reflect on and take ownership of. I'm trying to get that sense that if I lead, others will follow and I do have something to offer. (Emphasis in original)

We have suggested that gerontology tends to focus on the negative aspects of growing older and that its practitioners need also to concentrate on the positive aspects of the third, post-retirement, age. Tallis (1999:230) agrees with us:

> The debate on the implications of the ageing population is highly negative. Gloomy about the present and doomy about the future. Negative factors include mounting pressures on the health services and an unequal balance between the numbers of producers and later-life dependents. But I want to argue for an alternative and more optimistic vision of the future. While ageing may remind us of physical limits to existence, it also provides the opportunity for a new kind of life beyond the traditional, largely unchosen narratives of ambition, development and personal advancements, and the biological imperatives of survival, reproduction and child rearing.

What Tallis and many others argue for is a new vision of aging—one that is positive and challenging and full of hope for the life to be. Jeanette conducts pre-retirement workshops for individuals who work with a division of Parks Canada, and, at one such event, one of the participants, who was soon to retire (after thirty-eight years in the federal public service), said:

We have to have a vision of a future which is brighter than the past. Yes I am concerned about how my life will be in retirement; yes I am anxious about my health and whether or not I shall have enough money. Yes I am worried that I will be under my wife's feet all the time and we will get on each other's nerves. But I have to choose how I want my life to be in my golden years and I choose to make them the best they can be. (participant in pre-retirement seminar, September 23, 1998, Halifax, Nova Scotia)

Gilleard and Higgs (2000:39) have a similar take on the post-retirement years:

> Older people can create their own structures around lives more free than they ever had while they were solely workers. Not only is such agency required as a means of improving the social and personal well being of retired people; it is also expected as the principal means of improving physical health in later life.

All stages of life include challenges, joys, and difficulties. For certain reasons (e.g., the desire to "help" the aged, the fact that most funding sources want researchers to study "problems" rather than "solutions") gerontologists have tended to "catastrophize" the aging experience. If more research attempted to recount successful experiences of aging, then perhaps growing older would be seen as a time of celebration and joy rather than as a time of pain and dread.

About five years ago a seventy-six-year-old student of Jeanette sent her a poem. Unfortunately, we could not track down the publication information, but we have chosen to conclude this book with it because it represents the face of the new aged. It is by Mildred Nutz (N.d.), and it is called "Grandma":

> The old rocking chair is empty today.
> Grandma is no longer in it.
> She's driving her car to the office or shop,
> And buzzing around every minute.
> No one shoves Grandma back on the shelf,
> She is versatile, forceful and dynamic,
> That is not a pie in the oven, my dear,
> Now her baking day is ceramic!
> You won't see her trundling off to bed early

From the place by the warm chimney nook,
Her typewriter clatters all through the night
Cause Grandma is writing a book.
She never takes a backward glance
To show her steady advancing;
She won't tend the babies for you anymore
Because Grandma has taken up dancing.
She is not content with crumbs of old thought
Or with meager or second-hand knowledge.
Don't bring your mending to do,
For Grandma is going to college.

Select Bibliography

Achenbaum, W.A, L. Jakobi, and R. Kastenbaum. 1993. *Crossing Frontiers: Gerontology Emerges as a Science*. New York: Cambridge University Press.

Albom, Mitch. 1997. *Tuesdays with Morrie*. New York: Doubleday.

Alexander, J. (ed.). 1986. *Women and Aging: An Anthology by Women*. Corvallis, OR: Calyx.

Atchley, Robert. C. 1976. *The Sociology of Retirement*. New York: Schenkman.

———. 1980. *The Social Forces in Later Life* (rev. ed.). Belmont, CA: Wadsworth.

———. 1982. "Retirement: Leaving the World of Work." *Annals of the American Academy of Political and Social Sciences* 464:120–31.

Atkinson, Suzanne. 1997. "Caregiver Perceptions of Stress and Burden: The Role of the Relationship in the Assessment Process." MA thesis, Acadia University, Wolfville, Nova Scotia.

Auger, Jeanette A. 1983a. "Gerontological Knowledge and Its Role in the Social Production of Agedness." PhD diss., University of British Columbia.

———. 1983b. "The Lives of Older Women from a Cross-Cultural Perspective." *Kinesis*, September, 9–11.

———. 1989. "Meeting the Needs of Ethnic Older Adults: Barriers to Accessing Health Services in Nova Scotia." Canadian Council on Multicultural Health Care Bulletin 6(2):17.

———. 1992. "Living in the Margins: Lesbians and Aging." *Canadian Women's Studies* 2(Winter):80–84.

———. 1993. "Ethnic Seniors: Accessing Health Services." In *Multicultural Health in Canada*, ed. Ralph Masi, Lynette Mensah and Keith McLeod, 155–67. Toronto: Mosaic.

———. 2000a. *Social Perspectives on Death and Dying*. Halifax: Fernwood.

———. 2000b. *The Respite Needs of Caregivers Living in Lunenburg County, Nova Scotia*. Lunenburg, NS: Victorian Order of Nurses.

Auger, Jeanette, and Gray Kyles. 1982–83. "Aging in Other Cultures: Conversations with Vancouver's Ethnic Elderly." A series of ten monthly articles appearing in *Elder Statesman* (Vancouver).

Bailey, Joe. 1975. *Social Theory for Planning*. London: Routledge, Kegan Paul.

Barron, Milton. L. 1959. "Minority Group Characteristics of the Aged in American Society." *Journal of Gerontology* 4:467–81.

Baum, Daniel. J. 1974. *The Final Plateau: The Betrayal of Our Older Citizens*. Toronto: Burns and McEachern.

———. 1977. *Warehouses for Death: The Nursing Home Industry*. Toronto: Burns and McEachern.

Bayley, Chuck. 1981. "Seniors Scene." *Elder Statesman* (Vancouver), October/November, 6–12.

Beaujot, R. 1991. *Population Change in Canada: The Challenge of Policy Adaptation*. Toronto: McClelland and Stewart.

Begin, Monique. 1978. "Aging Canadians: Working Together." Keynote address presented at the annual meetings of the Canadian Association on Gerontology, Edmonton, Alberta, November 3–5.

Bengston, Vern L., and K. Warner Schaie (eds). 1999. *Handbook of Theories of Aging.* New York: Springer.

Berger, Peter. 1963. *Invitation to Sociology: A Humanistic Perspective.* New York: Anchor.

Bianchi, E. 1994. *Elder Wisdom: Crafting Your Own Elderhood.* New York: Crossroads.

Birren, James. E. (ed.) 1959. *Handbook of Aging and the Individual.* Chicago: University of Chicago Press.

Birren, J.E., and V.J. Renner. 1980. "Concepts and Issues of Mental Health and Aging." In *Handbook of Mental Health and Aging,* ed. J.E. Birren and R.B. Sloane, 5. Englewood Cliffs, NJ: Prentice-Hall.

Birren J.E., and K. Warner Schnaie (eds). 1980. *Handbook of the Psychology Aging.* San Diego, CA: Academic Press.

Birren J.E., and R.B. Sloane (eds). 1980. *Handbook of Mental Health and Aging.* Englewood Cliffs, NJ: Prentice-Hall.

Bjerg Moller, Jonathan. 2001. "Porn calms Danish seniors, staff says." *Globe and Mail* (Toronto), September 5, A1 and A8.

Bloom, Martin. 1977. "Alternatives to Morale Scales." In *Measuring Morale: A Guide to Effective Assessment,* ed. Corrine Nydegger, 23–29. Washington DC: Gerontological Society.

Blythe, Ronald. 1979. *The View in Winter.* New York and London: Harcourt, Brace Jovanovich.

Boas, Rollo. 1982. "Conference on Aging." *Elder Statesman* (Vancouver) 9.

Bowling, Ann. 1993. "The Concepts of Successful and Positive Ageing." *Family Practice* 10(4):449–53.

Bromley, D.B. 1966. *The Psychology of Human Ageing.* Middlesex: Penguin.

Browne, Colette. V. 1998. *Women, Feminism and Aging.* New York: Springer.

Burgess, R.W., R.S. Cavan, R.J. Havighurst and H. Goldhamer. 1949. *Personal Adjustment in Old Age.* Chicago: Science Research Association.

Butler, Robert. 1969. "Age-ism Another Form of Bigotry." *The Gerontologist* 9:243–246.

Canada Mortgage and Housing Corporation. 1991. *Today's Senior's, Tomorrow's Housing.* Conference Proceedings, May 15–17, 1990, Charlottetown, Prince Edward Island.

Canadian Association of Retired Persons (CARP). 2001. "Declaring War on Ageism." *Fifty Plus,* 42-43.

Canadian Council on Social Development. 1998. "Social Spending across the Life Course: Summary Report." World Wide Web: www.ccsd.ca/pubs.hc/spend/htm

Carp, Frances. 1969. "Senility or Garden Variety Maladjustment?" *Journal of Gerontology* 24(2):203–08.

———. 1977. "Morale: What Questions Are We Asking of Whom?" In *Measuring Morale: A Guide to Effective Assessment,* ed. Corinne Nydegger, 15–22. Washington, DC: Gerontological Society.

Census of Canada. 1971. Vol 1 (1–11). Ottawa, Queen's Printer.

Chui, T. 1996. "Canada's Population: Charting into the 21st Century." *Canadian Social Trends* 42(Autumn):3–7.

Cohen, Leah. 1984. *Small Expectations: Society's Betrayal of Older Women.* Toronto: McLelland and Stewart.

Cole, Thomas. R., andrew, W. Achenbaum, Patricia L. Jakobi and Robert Kastenbaum (eds.). 1993. *Voices and Visions of Aging: Toward a Critical Gerontology.* New York: Springer.

Comfort, Alex. 1976. *A Good Age.* New York: Crown.

Cooley, C.H. 1972. "The Looking Glass Self." In *Symbolic Interaction*, ed. J. Manis and A. Meltzer, 231–33. Boston: Allyn and Bacon.

Cowgill, D.O., and L.D. Holmes (eds.). 1972. *Aging and Modernization.* New York: Appleton-Century-Crofts.

Cox, Harold. G. 2001. *Later Life: The Realities of Aging. New Jersey: Prentice-Hall.*

Cumming, Elaine, and W.E. Henry. 1961. *Growing Old: The Process of Disengagement.* New York: Basic.

Curtin, Sharon. 1972. *Nobody Ever Died of Old Age.* Boston: Little, Brown.

de Beauvoir, Simone. 1977. *Old Age.* Middlesex: Penguin.

Donovan, J. 1996. *Feminist Theory: The Intellectual Traditions of American Feminism.* New York: Continuum.

Dowd, James J. 1975. "Aging as Exchange: Preface to Theory." *Journal of Gerontology* 30 (4):584–694.

———. 1980. "Exchange Rates and Old People." *Journal of Gerontology* 35(4):596–602.

Doyle, Kathleen. (ed.). 1997. *Perspectives: Aging.* St. Paul, MN: Courtwise.

Dychtwald, Ken. 1999. *Age Power: How The 21st Century Will Be Ruled By The New Old.* New York: Tarcher/Putnam.

Ekerdt, David. 1998. "Disciplining Old Age: The Formulation of Gerontologic Knowledge. A Review." *Contemporary Gerontology* 5(2):44–45.

Elder, Gladys. 1977. *The Alienated: Growing Old Today.* London: Writers and Readers Publishing Cooperative.

Erikson, Arthur. 1982. *The Life Cycle Completed.* New York: W.W. Norton.

Estes, Carroll. 1979. *The Aging Enterprise.* San Francisco: Jossey-Bass.

———. 1978. "Political Gerontology." *Transaction*, July/August, 43–39.

Featherstone, Mike, and Mike Hepworth. 1995. "Images of Positive Aging: A Case Study of Retirement Choice Magazine." In *Images of Aging: Cultural Representations of Later Life*, ed. Mike Featherstone and andrew Wernick, 29–47. London: Routledge.

Featherstone, Mike, and andrew Wernick 1995. *Images of Aging: Cultural Representations of Later Life.* London: Routledge

Foss, Krista. 2000. "Death directives can save dignity, dollars, study says." *Globe and Mail,* Wednesday, March 15, A2.

Frankl, Victor. 1959. *Man's Search for Meaning.* Boston: Beacon.

Frideres, J. 1994. "The Future of Our Past: Native Elderly in Canadian Society." National Advisory Council on Aging, special edition, Aboriginal seniors issues, 17–37, catalogue No. H71-2/1-15.1994E, Ottawa: Minister of Supply and

Services.

Fried, Linda P., Marc Freedman, Thomas, E. Endres and Barbara Wasik. 1997. "Building Communities that Promote Successful Aging." In *Perspectives: Aging*, ed. Kathleen Doyle, 27–43. St. Paul, MN: Courtwise.

Fry, Christine L., Jeanette Dickerson-Putnam, Patricia Draper, Charlotte Ikels, Jennie Keith, Anthony Glascock and Henry Harpending. 1997. "Culture and the Meaning of a Good Old Age." In *The Cultural Context of Aging: Worldwide Perspectives* (2nd ed.), ed. Jay Sokolovsky, 99–123. Westport, CT: Bergin and Garvey.

Garner, Dianne. J. 1999. "Feminism and Feminist Gerontology." *Journal of Women and Aging* 11(2–3):3–12.

Gee, Ellen, and Meredith. M. Kimball. 1987. *Women and Aging*. Toronto: Butterworths.

Gee, Ellen, and Gloria Gutman (eds.). 2000. *The Overselling of Population Aging*. Don Mills, ON: Oxford University Press.

Geertz, Clifford. 1973. *The Interpretation of Cultures*. New York: Basic.

Gilleard, Christopher, and Paul Higgs. 2000. *Cultures of Ageing: Self, Citizen and the Body*. Essex, UK: Pearson Educational Limited.

Glendenning, Frank. 1992. "Educational Gerontology and Gerogogy: A Critical Perspective." *Gerontology and Geriatrics Education* 13(1–2):5–21

Gold, Yhetta. 1980. "Ethnic and Cultural Aspects of Aging." Paper presented at the Ninth Annual Scientific and Educational Meetings of the Canadian Association on Gerontology, Saskatoon, September 5–6.

Green, Bryan. S. 1993. *Gerontology and the Social Construction of Old Age: A Study in Discourse Analysis*. New York: Aldine De Gruyter.

Grumbach, Doris. 1971. *Coming into the End Zone*. New York: W.W. Norton.

Gubrium, Jaber. F. 1973. *The Myth of the Golden Years*. Springfield, IL: Charles C. Thomas.

———. 1975. *Living and Dying in Murray Manor*. New York: St. Martin's Press.

———. 1990. "Who Theorizes Age?" *Ageing and Society* 10:131–49.

———. 1993. *Speaking of Life: Horizons of Meaning for Nursing Home Residents*. New York: De Gruyter.

Gubrium, Jaber F., and James A. Holstein. 2000. *Aging and Everyday Life*. Springfield, MA: Blackwell.

Gullette, Margaret Morganroth. 1997. *Declining To Decline: Cultural Combat and the Politics of the Midlife*. Charlottesville: University of Virginia Press.

Hamilton, Richard. 1975. *Restraining Myths: Critical Studies of U.S. Social Structure and Politics*. New York: John Wiley and Sons.

Havighurst, Robert J., and Ruth Albrecht. 1953. *Older People*. New York: Longmans Green.

Healey, S. 1986. "Growing to Be an Old Woman: Aging and Ageism." In *Women and Aging: An Anthology by Women*, ed. J. Alexander., 58–62. Corvallis, OR: Calyx.

Health Canada. 1993. *Canada's Health Promotion Survey: Technical Report*. Ottawa.

———. 2001. Seniors Guide to Federal Programs and Services. Ottawa: Minister of Public Works and Government Services Canada.

Heilbrun, Carolyn G. 1997. *The Last Gift of Time*. New York: Ballantine.

Henderson, George, and Martha Primeaux. 1981. *Transcultural Health Care*. New York: Addison-Wesley.

Hendricks, Jon, and C. Davis. 1977. *Aging in Mass Society: Myths and Problems*. Cambridge, MA: Winthrop.

Hochschild, Arlie. 1978. *The Unexpected Community*. Berkeley, CA: University of California Press.

Hogarth, John, et al. 1979. *Background Paper on Mandatory Retirement*. Vancouver: Faculty of Law, University of British Columbia.

Holstein, Martha. 1998. "Opening New Spaces: Aging and the Millennium." *Journal of Aging and Social Policy* 10(1):1–11.

hooks, b. 1984. *Feminist Theory: From Margin to Center*. Boston: South End.

Illich, Ivan. 1977. *Disabling Professions*. Toronto: Burns and McEachern.

Jacobs, Jerry. 1974. *Fun City: An Ethnographic Study of a Retirement Community*. New York: Holt, Rinehart.

Jagger, Alison M., and Paula S. Rothenberg. 1984. *Feminist Frameworks: Alternative Theoretical Accounts of the Relations between Women and Men* (3rd ed.). New York: McGraw-Hill.

Jenike, Robb, B. 1997. "Learning to Volunteer: Women's Support Networks for the Care of the Elderly in Urban Japan." Paper presented at the 94th Annual Meeting of the American Anthropological Association, November 18, 1997.

Jerome, John. 2000. *On Turning Sixty-Five*. New York: Random House.

Jessome, Jeannine, and Clare Parks. 2000. "Everyday Technology and Older Persons: Friends or Foe?" In *Newsletter of the Centre on Aging*, Mount Saint Vincent University, Halifax, Nova Scotia, 4.

Joe, Rita. 1969. *Song of Rita Joe: Autobiography of a Mi'kmaq Poet*. Charlottetown: Ragweed.

———. 1988. *Song of Eskasoni: More Poems by Rita Joe*. Charlottetown: Ragweed.

Jones, Maxwell. 1988. *Growing Old: The Ultimate Freedom*. New York: Human Sciences Press.

Kaiser, M., and S. Chawla. 1994. "Caregivers and Care Recipients: The Elderly in Developing Countries." *Ageing International* 11:42–49.

Katz, Stephen. 1996. *Disciplining Old Age: The Formation of Gerontological Knowledge*. Charlottesville: University Press of Virginia.

Kuhn, Maggie. 1978a. "An Open Letter." *Gerontologist* 18(5):423–27.

———. 1978b. "New Life for the Elderly: Liberation from Ageism.' In *The New Old*, ed. R. Gross and B. Gross, 78–109. New York: Anchor.

Lassey William R., and Marie L. Lassey. 2001. *Quality of Life for Older People: An International Perspective*. New Jersey: Prentice-Hall.

Lazerfield, Paul. W.H. Sewell, and Harold Wilensky. 1967. *The Uses of Sociology*. New York: Basic.

Lemon, O.W, Vern Bengston, and J.A. Peterson. 1972. "An Exploration of Activity Theory of Aging: Activity Types and Life Satisfaction among In-Movers to a Retirement Community." *Journal of Gerontology* 27(17):512–22.

Lerner, Max. 1939. *Ideas Are Weapons: The History and Uses of Ideas*. New York: Viking.

Lilley, Susan, and Joan M. Campbell. 1999. *Shifting Sands: The Changing Shape of Atlantic Canada*. Halifax: Health Canada, Atlantic Regional Office.

Lindsay, C. 1999. *A Portrait of Seniors in Canada* (3rd ed.). Cat. no. 89-519-XPE, Ottawa: Statistics Canada.

Macdonald, Barbara, with Cynthia Rich. 1983. Look Me in the Eye. San Francisco, CA: Spinsters Ink.

MacKinnon, Fred. R. 1992. "Living Wills and Other Issues Associated with Dying." Senior's Advocate (Waverley, NS), 14–15.

Manis, J., and A. Meltzer (eds.). 1972. *Symbolic Interaction*. Boston: Allyn and Bacon.

Marshall, Doris. 1987. *Silver Threads: Reflections on Growing Older*. Toronto, ON: Between the Lines.

Marshall, Victor. 1980. *Aging in Canada: Social Perspectives*. Don Mills, ON: Fitzhenry and Whiteside.

———. 1996. "The State of Theory in Aging and the Social Sciences." In *Handbook of Aging and the Social Sciences* (4th ed.), ed. Robert H. Binstock and Linda K. George, 12–30. San Diego: Academic Press.

Marshall, Victor, and Joseph Tindale. 1978–79. "Notes for a Radical Gerontology.' *International Journal of Aging and Human Development* 9(2):163–69.

Martin-Matthews, Anne. 2000. "Canadian Research on Aging: Two Decades of Growth, Time of Change" *Canadian Journal of Aging* 19(4):i–xv.

Marx, Karl. 1918. *A Contribution to the Critique of Political Economy*. Trans. N.I. Stone. Chicago: Charles H. Kerr.

Matthews, Sarah. 1979. *The Social World of Old Women: Management of Self-identity*. Berkeley, CA: Sage.

McDaniel, Susan. A. 1986. *Canada's Aging Population*. Toronto: Butterworths.

McFadden, Susan. 1996. "Religion, Spirituality, and Aging." In *The Handbook of the Psychology of Aging,* ed. James E. Birren and K. Warner Schnaie, 162–77. San Diego, CA: Academic Press.

McPherson, Barry. D. 1998. *Aging as a Social Process: An Introduction to Individual and Population Aging* (3rd ed.). Toronto: Harcourt Brace.

Mead, George Herbert. 1934. *Mind, Self, and Society: From the Standpoint of a Social Behaviorist*. Chicago: University of Chicago Press.

Minister of Industry, Science, and Technology. 1994. *Canada Year Book*. Ottawa: Statistics Canada, Health Statistics Division. On-line at www.statcan.ca/census9.start.html/english/pgeth/

Moberg, D.I., and P.M. Brusek 1978. "Spiritual Well-Being: A Neglected Subject in Quality of Life Research." *Social Indicators Research* 5:303–23.

Molloy, William, and Virginia Mepham. 1989. *Let Me Decide: The Health Care Directive that Speaks for You When You Can't*. Toronto: Penguin.

Moody, Harry. 1994. *Aging: Concepts and Controversies*. Thousand Parks, CA: Pine Forge.

Moore, E. 1995. "Aboriginal Women in Canada." In *Women in Canada: A Statistical Report* (3rd ed.), Statistics Canada, 147–62. Ottawa: Minister of Supply and Services.

Muggeridge, Peter. 2001. *CARP Special Report: National Forum on the Envirnment*.

Ottawa: Canadian Association of Retired Persons.

Noggle, Ann. 1986. "Youthenasia: A Photo Journal." In *Women and Aging: An Anthology by Women,* ed., J. Alexander, 37–49. Corvallis, OR: Calyx.

Novak, Mark. 1980. "The Professional in the Field of Aging." Paper written for Department of Sociology, University of Winnipeg.

————. 1997. *Aging and Society: A Canadian Perspective* (3rd ed.). Toronto: Nelson.

Novak, Mark, and Lori Campbell. 2001. *Aging and Society: A Canadian Perspective* (4th ed.). Toronto: Nelson.

Nusberg, Charlotte (ed.). 1981. *Self Determination and the Elderly.* Washington, DC: International Federation on Ageing.

Nutz. Mildred. N.d. "Grandma." N.p.

Nydegger, Corinne (ed.). 1977. *Measuring Morale: A Guide to Effective Assessment.* Washington, DC: The Gerontological Society.

Oliver, David B., and Jocelyn Eckerman. 1979. "Tracing the Historical Growth of Gerontology as a Discipline." Paper presented at the Gerontological Society annual meetings, Washington.

Ovenell-Cart. Julie. 2000. "Older and Wiser: What Is 'Old' Really?" *Canadian Living,* June, 71–76.

Owen, Nicole. 2001. "Long-term Care: Planning for the Unexpected." *Seniors' Advocate* 17(6):8.

Palmore, Erdman, and G.L. Maddox. 1977. "Sociological Aspects of Aging." In *Behaviour and Adaptation in Later Life,* ed. E.W. Buisse and E. Pfeiffer, 47–59. Boston: Little Brown.

Paul, Irene. 1976. *Everybody's Studying Us: The Ironies of Aging in the Pepsi Generation.* San Francisco: Volcano.

Philibert, Michel. 1965. "The Emergence of Social Gerontology." *Journal of Social Issues* 21(4):4–12.

————. 1974. "The Phenomenological Approach to Images of Aging." *Soundings: An Interdisciplinary Journal* 57:303–22.

————. 1977a. "A Philosophy of Aging for the 21st Century." Talk given at the University of British Columbia, November 14th.

————. 1977b. "Reflections on the Teaching of Gerontology." In *Canadian Gerontology Collection 1, Selected Papers,* ed. Blossom L. Wigdor, 24–31. Ottawa: National Advisory Council on Aging.

Powell, Brian J., and James K. Martin. 1978. "Economic Implications of an Aging Society in Canada." Paper presented at the National Symposium on Aging, Ottawa.

Quadagno, Jill. 1999. *Aging and the Life Course: An Introduction to Social Gerontology.* Boston: McGraw-Hill.

Rabinowitz, Dorothy, and Yadida Neilsen. 1971. *Home Life: A Story of Old Age.* New York: Macmillan.

Ray, Ruth. E. 1999. "Researching to Transgress: The Need for Critical Feminism in Gerontology." *Journal of Women and Aging* 11(2–3):171–84.

Reinharz, Shulamit. 1986. "Friends or Foes: Gerontological and Feminist Theory." In *Radical Voices: A Decade of Feminist Resistance,* ed. Renate D. Klein and Doborah

Lynn Steinberg, 222–41. New York: The Athene Series, Pergammon.

Riley, Matilda W., Marilyn Johnson and Anne Foner. 1972. *Aging and Society*. Vol. 3: A Sociology of Age Stratification. New York: Sage Foundation.

Robb Jenike, Brenda. 1997. "Gender and Duty in Japan's Aged Society: The Experiences of Family Caregivers." In *The Cultural Context of Aging: Worldwide Perspectives,* ed. Jay Sokolovsky, 219–38. Westport, CT: Bergin and Garvey.

Rose, A.M., and W.A. Peterson. 1965. *Older People and Their Social World*. Philadelphia: F.A. Davis.

Rosow, Irving. 1977. "Morale, Concept and Measurement." In *Measuring Morale: A Guide to Effective Assessment,* ed. Corinne Nydegger, 39–45. Washington, DC: The Gerontological Society.

Rubenstein. R.L. 1994. "Generativity as Pragmatic Spirituality." In *Aging and the Religious Dimension,* ed. L.E. Thomas and S.A. Eisenhandler, 169–81. Westport, CT: Bergin and Garvey.

Sarton, May. 1978. Collected Poems, 1930–1973. New York: W.W. Norton.

———. 1984. *At Seventy: A Journal*. New York: W.W. Norton.

Schlesinger, Benjamin. 1983. "Institutional Life: The Canadian Experience." In *Sexuality in the Later Years: Roles and Behavior,* ed. Ruth B. Weg, 259–69. New York: Academic Press.

Schaie, K.W. "Translations in Gernontology: From Lab to Life. *American Psychologist* 29: 802–07.

Schutz, Alfred. 1973. *Collected Papers. Vol. 1: The Problem of Social Reality*. The Hague: Martinus Nijhoff.

Scott, Robert A. 1969. *The Making of Blind Men: A Study of Adult Socialization*. New York: Sage Foundation.

Scott-Maxwell, Florida. 1968. *The Measure of My Days*. New York: Alfred Knopf.

Seskin, Jane. 1980. *More than Mere Survival: A Woman's Guide to Aging*. New York. Newsweek Books.

Shack, Sybil. 1984. "The Best Is Yet to Be? Challenging the Myths about Aging." *Aging/le 3eme* 5(3):1084.

Smith, Dorothy. 1975. "An Analysis of Ideological Structures and How Women are Excluded: Considerations for Academic Women." *Canadian Review of Sociology and Anthropology* 12(4):9–15.

Snowdon, David. 2001. *Aging with Grace: What the Nun Study Teaches Us about Leading Longer, Healthier and More Meaningful Lives*. New York: Bantam.

Sokolovsky, Jay. (ed.). 1997. *The Cultural Context of Aging: Worldwide Perspectives*. Westport, CT: Bergin and Garvey.

Sontag, Susan. 1973. "The Double Standard of Aging." *Saturday Review,* 23 September, 29–38.

Statistics Canada. 1995. *Women In Canada: A Statistical Report* (3rd ed.). Ottawa: Minister of Supply and Services.

———. 1997. *Vital Statistics, Vol 111, Births and Deaths 1975–1977*. Ottawa, Health Division, Minister of Supply and Services.

———. 1998. *Canada Year Book*. Cat. No. 11-412E, Ottawa, Ministry of Industry Statistics.

———. 1999a. *Canada Year Book*. Cat. No. 11-404E. Ottawa, Ministry of Industry, Science and Technology.

———. 1999b. *A Portrait of Seniors in Canada* (3rd ed.). Ottawa: Lindsay, Colin.

———. 2000a. www.statcan.ca/English/Pgdb/People/Health/health38.htm

———. 2000b. www.statcan.ca/english/ads/82-003-XIB/summary1.htm

———. 2001. www.statcan.ca/english/Pgdb/People/Population/demo10a.htm

Streib, Gordon. 1965. "Are the Aged a Minority Group?" In *Applied Sociology*, ed. H. Gouldner and S.M. Miller, 311–24. New York: Free Press.

Streib, Gordon, and Harold. L. Orbach. 1967. "The Development of Social Gerontology and the Sociology of Aging." In *The Uses of Sociology*, ed. Paul Lazerfield, W.H. Sewell and Harold Wilnesky, 612–40. New York: Basic.

Tallis, R. 1999. "Old Faces, New Lives." *The Times Higher* (Winnipeg), July 9, 23.

Thomas, L.E., and S.A. Eisenhandler (eds.). 1994. *Aging and the Religious Dimension*. Westport, CT: Bergin and Garvey.

Thorne, Ruth Raymond. 1992. *Women and Aging: A Report on the Rest of Our Lives*. Binghampton, NY: Harrington Park.

Torres, Sandra. 1999. "A Culturally Relevant Theoretical Framework for the Study of Successful Ageing." *Aging and Society* 19:33–51.

Troll, Lillian E., Joan Israel, and Kenneth Israel. 1977. *Looking Ahead: A Woman's Guide to Growing Old*. Englewood Cliffs, NJ: Prentice Hall.

Tulle-Winton, Emmanuelle. 1999. "Growing Old and Resistance: Towards a New Cultural Economy of Old Age." *Aging and Society* 19:281–99.

Tullock. John. 1995. "From Grim Reaper to Cheery Condom: Images of Aging and Death in Australian AISA Education Campaigns." In *Images of Aging: Cultural Representations of Later Life*, ed. Mike Featherstone and Andrew Wernick, 263–79. London: Routledge.

United Nations. 1991. *Bulletin on Aging* 5(2).

United States Census Bureau. 2000. *International Data Base*. Online at www.census.gov

Weg, Ruth. B. (ed). 1983. *Sexuality in the Later Years: Roles and Behavior*. New York: Academic Press.

Weininger, Ben, and Eva L. Menkin. 1978. *Aging Is a Lifelong Affair*. Los Angeles, CA: Guild of Tutors Press.

Weisskopf, V.F. 1977. "The Frontiers and Limits of Science." *American Scientist* 65:273–74.

White, Valerie. 2000. "Well-being and Life Expectancy." *Seniors' Advocate* 17(5):5.

Whittaker, Elvi. 1981. "Anthropological Ethics, Fieldwork and Epistemological Disjunctures." *Philosophy of the Social Sciences* 11:437–51.

Wigdor, Blossom, and Susan Fletcher. 1991. *Mental Health and Aging*. Ottawa: The National Advisory Council on Aging.

Woodward, K. 1991. *Aging and its Discontents: Freud and Other Fictions*. Bloomington, IN: Indiana University Press.

Znaniecki, Florian. 1975. *The Social Role of the Man of Knowledge*. New York: Octagon.

Zych, Adam. 1992. "The Development and Main Ideas of the Pedagogy of Aging and Old Age." *Gerontology and Geriatrics Education* 13(1–2):23–43.

Index